Justice and Equality in Education

**Books are to be returned on or before
the last date below.**

LIBREX–

WITHDRÁWN

Also available from Continuum

Philosophy of Education, Richard Pring

Analysing Underachievement in Schools, Emma Smith

Education and the Community, Dianne Gereluk

Justice and Equality in Education

A Capability Perspective on Disability and Special Educational Needs

Lorella Terzi

continuum

Continuum International Publishing Group
The Tower Building, 11 York Road, London SE1 7NX
80 Maiden Lane, Suite 704, New York NY 10038

www.continuumbooks.com

© Lorella Terzi 2008
This edition published 2010

British Library Cataloguing-in-Publication Data
A catalogue record for this book is available from the British Library.

ISBN: 978-0-8264-9710-9 (hardcover)
978-1-4411-0831-9 (paperback)

Library of Congress Cataloging-in-Publication Data
A catalog record for this book is available from the Library of Congress.

Typeset by Kenneth Burnley, Wirral, Cheshire
Printed in Great Britain by the MPG Books Group, Bodmin and King's Lynn

Contents

Acknowledgements

I began working on the ideas developed in this book in 2001, when the struggle for egalitarian causes had nearly disappeared from political debates, and was suffering critical setbacks in education, too. Harry Brighouse first suggested that I direct my concern for justice to the case of educational equality for children with disabilities and special educational needs, and always more than generously gave of his suggestions, critical insights, and unfailing support in supervising my work. This book is not that work, but its ideas are. My first and considerable debt of gratitude is therefore to Harry, for this book would not have been written without his inspiring guidance. While I remain solely responsible for my mistakes, I certainly have been extremely privileged. Warm thanks are due to Terence McLaughlin, who always provided wise advice and sustained encouragement. His sudden death in 2006 meant the loss of his invaluable comments. I then owe thanks to many other scholars, colleagues and friends, who engaged in discussions of my ideas and supplied extremely helpful comments in different forms and contexts. David Archard provided prompt and vital advice at critical points, thus averting possible pitfalls: my sincere thanks to him. I am extremely grateful to Alan Cribb for organizing ideal conditions during my fellowship at the Centre for Public Policy Research at King's College London, while completing this book. Special thanks are due to the colleagues at the centre, Alan Cribb, Louise Archer, Peter Duncan, Sharon Gewirtz, Meg Maguire, Anwar Tlili, Chris Winch and Gerald Lum, for their robust and insightful comments, and for their warm hospitality. I have also benefited a great deal from sharing ideas with scholars of the Human Development and Capability Association, and its Education Thematic Group. Thanks are due to Melanie Walker and Elaine Unterhalter, for their kind support, to David Bridges, Sèverine Deneulin, Mozaffar Qizilbash, Ingrid Robeyns, Rosie Vaughan and Michael Watts.

Several sections of this book, at different stages of development, were presented at conferences, seminars and workshops. I received helpful comments from audiences at Stanford University, the University of Pavia, Italy, the Institute of Education, London, the Accessibility Research Group at the Department for Civil and Environmental Engineering at University College London, the Centre for Public Policy Research at King's College London, The University of Bielefeld, Germany, Teachers College at Columbia University, and the University of Illinois at Urbana-Champaign. I am also extremely grateful for the insights and suggestions received from Len Barton, Kimberley Brownlee, Dan Brock, Eamonn Callan, Adam Cureton, Randall Curren, Walter Feinberg, Leslie Francis, John Baker, Ron Best, Guy Kahane, Meira Levinson, Ingrid Lunt, Mary Mahowald, Brahm Norwich, Jonathan Quong, Denis Phillips, Hillel Steiner, Paul Standish and Jonathan Wolff. There certainly are many others, and I apologize for any omission.

This book was completed during a Fellowship at the Centre for Public Policy Research at King's College London. I most thankfully acknowledge the generous HFCE research fellowship granted by Roehampton University. I am grateful to both universities and to the named funding institution for the invaluable opportunities they provided.

Finally, special thanks are due to my editors at Continuum, Alexandra Webster, who believed in this project and supported it with her enthusiasm and expertise, and Kirsty Schaper, for her patience and help on many occasions.

This book is dedicated to Marco, when he was a child.

I would like to thank Blackwell, Palgrave and Sage for permission to use material from the following articles:

Terzi, L. (2004), 'The Social Model of Disability: A Philosophical Critique'. *Journal of Applied Philosophy*, 21, (2), pp.141–57.

Terzi, L. (2005), 'Beyond the Dilemma of Difference: The capability approach on disability and special educational needs', *Journal of Philosophy of Education*, 39 (3), pp.443–59.

Terzi, L. (2005), 'A Capability Perspective on Impairment, Disability and Special Educational Needs: Towards social justice in education', *Theory and Research in Education*, 3 (2), pp.197–223.

Terzi, L. (2007b), 'The Capability to be Educated', in Walker and Unterhalter, *Amartya Sen's Capability Approach and Social Justice in Education*. Palgrave Macmillan, reproduced with permission of Palgrave Macmillan.

Terzi, L. (2007c), 'Capability and Educational Equality: The just distribution of resources to students with disabilities and special educational needs', *Journal of Philosophy of Education*, 41 (4), pp. 757–73.

Foreword

Harry Brighouse

Moral philosophy has two central roles. One is to describe moral reality: to distinguish which values are morally important, to discern how important they are relative to one another in the abstract and, ultimately, in particular circumstances. The other is to guide action: to provide the moral compass which agents need in order to ensure that they act rightly.

A great deal of research and writing on education makes implicit appeals to assumptions about the moral truth; similarly, all educational policy and practice makes normative assumptions. But too often these assumptions are left implicit or even, at worst, denied by the people making them. Some researchers like to think that their work is value-neutral, and some policy-makers, and even teachers, like to think that they are guided only by 'what works'. Of course some empirical research really is value-neutral, in the sense that it describes an empirical reality and discerns causal mechanisms. But even this work is usually guided by a sense of what *matters*; and whether some aspect of the educational system matters is, in part, a normative judgment. And what works depends on what the goal is, and our goals are open to normative evaluation.

Some moral and political philosophy, especially that which is concerned only with the description of moral reality, is conducted at a very high level of abstraction. But any work that aims to guide action or practice must concern itself both with the abstract and with the empirical and institutional realities of the agents whose behaviour it hopes to guide. Lorella Terzi's book is a brilliant exemplar of this latter kind of work. She is lucid and comfortable in the realm of the abstract moral philosophizing which is essential to her task, but equally compelling in the application of that philosophizing to the real world of educational policy and practice.

The problem Terzi sets herself is straightforward: what is owed to students with disabilities? This requires her to bridge four hitherto quite separate sets of discussions. The first concerns the place of disability within a theory of distributive justice. The second concerns the just distribution of specifically educational resources among children. The third concerns sociological theories of disability and the fourth concerns the policies and practices of contemporary education systems in the developed world with respect to children with disabilities, including the sociologically influenced but often philosophically neglectful literature on inclusion.

The result is a rich, and compelling, study. Terzi presents a careful and nuanced argument against the social model of disability which has become the standard model among disability rights theorists and social theorists of disability. She argues that even though some aspects of disability are socially constructed not all are, and that the non-socially constructed aspects are, even though not socially constructed, still objects of moral concern. Society cannot evade its responsibilities to people with disabilities by noting that their situation is not entirely socially caused. She then explores the way that the capabilities approach, first developed by Amartya Sen and Martha Nussbaum as an account of the metric of distributive justice, copes with our obligations to provide high-quality education for children with disabilities, and the specific guidance that it provides for policy-makers, administrators and educators. She then explores the more general implications of the capabilities approach as a guide to the distribution and aims of education. She sets her argument in an overview of the general advantages of the capabilities approach over rival accounts that have been posed by contemporary political theorists who think of justice as a matter of the distribution of resources or subjective satisfaction.

The principle that all children (those with or without disabilities) should have an equal education is much more generally accepted than more ambitious principles of equality, not least because no one seriously thinks that children are responsible for the quality of the education they get. But the principle is susceptible of many different interpretations and, despite being more widely accepted than other principles of equality, has been subject to numerous attacks and objections. Terzi's book offers a philosophically rich elucidation and defence of the principle of educational equality, but also practical guidance concerning the education of children with disabilities. She concludes the book by responding convincingly to several of the most powerful objections to educational equality.

Anyone interested in political philosophy as it applies to education or in the philosophy of education more generally will want to read the following pages. Anyone who wants to think carefully about inclusion, disability rights, or the sociology of disability, *has* to.

Introduction

Educational equality is a fundamental principle of social justice. Yet despite the centrality of social justice and its extensive analysis in the theory and research of education, the concept of equality is conversely rather unspecified or vaguely theorized, and there is a lack of consensus on its implications for policy-making. However, the ideal of equality has a crucial normative role to play at two interconnected levels in education: the theoretical level, concerned with values and aims, and the level of provision, relating to the enactment of these ideals into policy and practice. Consider the following two examples.

A broad understanding of equality as equal entitlement to education informs many state systems of schooling. Yet while the idea that all children are equally entitled to education is generally accepted, the precise content of this goal is not only difficult to determine but also a source of controversy in itself. On the one hand, an equal entitlement to education can be seen as implying an equal provision of schooling, for example through a national curriculum. On the other hand, it can be understood as giving everybody an equal chance to develop and fulfil personal interests and talents, regardless of any common provision. Furthermore, an equal entitlement to education is a different concept from an entitlement to an equal education. While the former idea broadly relates to an equal right to learning, the latter often refers instead to the same quality education.

Second, consider the relevance of equality in the provision of education, and hence, for instance, in terms of the design and implementation of school funding systems. Many funding formulae are the result of policies aimed at justice and claiming to apply equitable measures. However, both the understanding of justice in the distribution of resources, and the meaning of equity at policy level are often generic and imprecise. The current funding system in England exemplifies this situation. While 'the existing arrangements for the distribution of resources are complex and vary widely throughout the country' (DfES, 2001b: 1), the system is explicitly committed to adopting transparent procedures and equitable allocations of funding, in particular in the finance of inclusive and special education. However, there is a lack of clear reference to what constitutes an equitable distribution of resources, apart from the indication that arrangements should be flexible enough to meet the demands of children with complex and severe needs, and sustain their achievement (DfES, 2001b: 3–4 and 9). As various studies attest, the different procedures of this system result in pervasive unequal distributions of funding, and in extremely unequal educational provision throughout the country (Marsh, 2003). Certainly, establishing the causes of these inequalities entails a thorough analysis of the policy design and its implementation in particular contexts. However, the under-specified status of the principles underpinning the policy is perhaps a crucial factor in the outcomes. Knowing more precisely what we mean by an equitable distribution – whether, for instance, it should be a fair distribution of resources in order to increase average achievement, or, conversely, in order to maximize the achievement of the lowest achieving students (Brighouse, 2004: 7) – would certainly make a difference to the policy design. The intuition at work here is that, although the relation between educational ideals and the non-ideal conditions of policy is complex and indirect, clarity at the level of principles is important in informing policies aimed at enacting these very principles.

These examples show not only the complex nature of the concept of educational equality, but also that equality matters in a fundamental way, both normatively, at the level of ideals, and for the more practically oriented concerns of policy-making and implementation. Thus, clarifying the meaning of equality in education, and hence specifying its status at normative level, is an important ethical and political goal. In short, we need to provide a correct theoretical structure. Further, these examples highlight that there is an inherent distributive dimension to educational equality. Asserting, on the one hand, the right to an equal education, and, on the other, the importance of fairness in the funding of schooling, implies an understanding of educational equality in terms of an equal distribution of educational goods, however defined. As we shall see, this relates directly the understanding of educational equality to egalitarian theories of distributive justice.

My aim in this book is to contribute to the debate on justice and equality in education by dealing with the timely and contentious issue of provision for students with disabilities and special educational needs. The question of a fair provision for these students is currently extremely controversial in almost all developed countries. The debate involves arguments related to public policy, as well as considerations of educational theory and practice.

However, there is a crucial but neglected philosophical core to the issue, which I aim to analyse in this book by addressing the following, fundamental question: what constitutes a just educational provision for students with disabilities and special educational needs, and, more specifically, what distribution of resources is fair to these students?

Subsumed into this main question is a further, controversial problem, namely how to understand and define disability and special educational needs. The relevance of this issue is clearly related to a project of fair distribution, since how we identify children who might require different amounts of resources will have wide implications for the distribution – in setting priorities, for example – and in particular in its guidance for policy. However, as we shall see, current understandings of disability and special educational needs present partial and, to a certain extent, flawed views, which fail to provide appropriate theoretical bases for correct distributive principles. A more justified perspective is therefore needed.

In this book, I respond to these two fundamental questions by deploying a version of liberal egalitarianism. More specifically, I argue for a principled framework in the distribution of resources, which entails a re-definition of disability and special educational needs, and an understanding of educational equality in terms of the capability approach, as developed by Amartya Sen and further articulated by Martha Nussbaum and other scholars. The central concern of the capability approach is evaluating how well people's lives are going with reference to their 'capability to function', that is, their real opportunities to be and to do what they value being and doing. It is within this framework, and in particular through the concepts of capability (effective opportunities for functionings) and functionings (beings and doings as, for instance, being educated, reading, or participating in political activities), that a philosophical understanding of disability and special educational needs, and a conception of educational equality can be appropriately thought, in order to provide justified answers to my starting questions.

However, before outlining further insights relating to this project, it is perhaps worth anticipating here a possible contention. This will also be analysed further on in the book. Recent debates have addressed the question of whether egalitarian theories should provide correct distributive principles, or whether they should instead be concerned with equality in the social structure which determines relations among people. This is also a recurrent theme in educational theory, where the understanding of justice is often argued in terms of disestablishing oppressive structures, and establishing instead relations of respect and valorization of differences, as well as in terms of enabling individuals to participate in the

educational process. Attention to the distributive aspect of equality, especially as equal distribution of opportunities, is seen as misplacing concerns
that are more fundamental to education. In my view, this divide is not
entirely founded, and, as I aim to show in this book, a proper conception
of distributive equality can respond to the demands of equal distribution
of what goods are considered important, while providing conditions for
the establishment of equal relations. My view is that the capability
approach provides important insights towards that fundamental goal.

The chapters in this book develop and articulate the argument in
support of the principled position I suggest. In what follows, however, I
shall outline the broader concerns and the theoretical framework that
underlie my perspective, while progressively unfolding some of the
complex aspects of the task at hand.

1. Liberal Egalitarianism and Educational Equality

The distributive dimension of the ideal of educational equality relates it
directly to liberal egalitarian theories of justice. Liberal egalitarians, as we
shall analyse in more depth in Chapter 6, are concerned with the just
design of social and institutional arrangements, and the consequent distribution of benefits and burdens among individuals. They maintain that
in a society of equals, social and institutional arrangements should be
designed to show equal consideration and respect for all. Although they
differ on its precise meaning, egalitarian theories understand equality as a
fundamental principle of social justice. These theories, and the principles
they articulate and defend, set therefore an important philosophical
framework for the analysis of educational equality. One such theory, in
particular, provides specific insights towards an understanding of equality
for students with disabilities and special educational needs, and it is
perhaps worth analysing it here in more detail.

In his monograph *School Choice and Social Justice* (2000b), Harry Brighouse presents a compelling theory of educational equality. In line with
broad egalitarian positions, Brighouse maintains that the value of educational equality rests on the fundamental ideal of the equal respect due to
individuals. He further maintains that the case for educational equality has
to be considered as interrelated to the two functions that education plays
for the individual. Here the reference is to the distinction between the
instrumental and the intrinsic value of education. On the one hand,
education provides competitive advantages in economies, which distribute
benefits and burdens unequally. Thus being better educated, other things
being equal, is instrumental in enhancing the opportunities of attaining

better positions, and therefore enjoying the benefits of the unequal rewards of the labour market, at least as it is currently organized in most developed countries. On the other hand, education provides fulfilling life experiences, for example an interest in literature or the natural world, and is therefore intrinsically good (Brighouse, 2000b: 121–2). On these bases, according to Brighouse, supporting equality in education implies two general concerns. First, children should not have significant advantages in education due to family circumstances, such as wealth and social position. Second, and importantly for my analysis, children should not have significant advantages in terms of better education because of their natural talents or abilities (2000b: 112).

Consequently, Brighouse argues that educational equality, in taking into account these two concerns, should be based on two principles. First, no one should be advantaged or disadvantaged because of the personal, social and economical circumstances they were born in (2000b: 112). Second, resources should be allocated and used effectively, and allowing for more resources to be devoted to children with disabilities (2000b: 138–9). Note that, while playing a fundamental role in egalitarian theories, the question of resource distribution is central to principles of educational equality, and specified here in relation to students with disabilities and special educational needs. This is reflected in Brighouse's position, when he argues,

> A full and principled account of educational equality would say something about how much more must be devoted to children with disabilities than to ordinarily-abled children. (. . .) So the account must also be able to guide the distribution of resources among more or less able children within the ordinary-abled group. If the same resources should be devoted, the account needs to explain why, and why such differences do not merit the same responses as the differences between the ordinarily-abled and disabled. If, on the other hand, differential resources should be devoted, this needs to be explained.
>
> (2000b: 138)

According to Brighouse, therefore, educational equality entails a differential distribution of resources to children with different abilities on grounds of fairness. But his analysis goes further, and sets the requirement of specifying exactly what the differential distribution should amount to, and of justifying the reasons behind these differences. Moreover, his analysis gives a full account of how to understand resources in this context. Brighouse understands resources in terms of educational opportunities, and rules out the possibility of interpreting a just resource distribution in education as the distribution of equal educational resources. If the latter understanding were applied, he maintains, it would lead to unfairness to all children with abilities not met by that specific resource distribution. Providing all children with equal literacy resources, to mention a common interpretation, would intuitively be unfair to children with dyslexia, just as providing the same resources to every child would prove evidently unfair, for example in the case of children with hearing or visual impairment, since these students would require respectively signing interpretation or Braille resources.

Educational equality, ultimately, is inscribed in a theory that considers equality in terms of equality of opportunities, thus generally in terms of equality of input (rather than the more commonly agreed understanding of equality of outcome, broadly informing much educational theory), and principles of fair distribution of resources as fundamental elements of social justice.

While providing insights towards a notion of educational equality for students with disabilities and special educational needs, this position raises some fundamental questions, which are nevertheless left unanswered. In particular, the theory highlights the importance of providing a full account not only of what level of resources should exactly be devoted to these students, but also of the reasons that legitimate the different amounts of resources. These are fundamental aspects of a conception of educational equality, and the principled framework I suggest aims at providing a legitimate response to them. There is, furthermore, a second dimension, which is not fully analysed in Brighouse's theory. In common with other liberal egalitarian perspectives, Brighouse assumes a generic and rather a-critical understanding of disabilities in education. As I have mentioned above, definitions of disability and special educational needs are highly contentious, and generally subsume different, if not polarized views and perspectives. These definitions, in turn, have implications for the articulation of distributive principles, and should therefore be more specifically addressed. While the latter is among my tasks in this book, in the next section I turn my attention to a brief introduction of these perspectives, and their respective limitations, which will be discussed more extensively in further chapters.

2. Impairment, Disability and Special Educational Needs: Individual or Social?

The emergence of the social model of disability in the last thirty years has radically changed perspectives and views of impairment and disability. Proposed by disabled people as an expression of their experience, the social model sees disability as socially constructed, that is, as the result of discriminating and oppressive social and institutional arrangements. This view has challenged previous understandings of disability as an individual deficit, mainly based on medical perspectives. In locating disability within the design of social and institutional arrangements, the social model advocates the removal of all forms of barriers to participation in society for disabled people. Yet, as I shall argue in Chapter 2, this model, in understanding disability as entirely socially constructed, presents over-socialized, and to a certain extent flawed conceptions, which are not conducive to the very aim of inclusion and equal entitlement advocated by disabled people's movements. While many disabilities have a social component, many others do not, or not as unilaterally as the social model maintains. However, as we shall see in Chapter 3, the model has highly influenced perspectives in education which support an understanding of disabilities as caused by the design of schooling systems, together with the rejection of any form of medical understandings, including the concept of special educational needs.

But the debate in education is characterized also by positions that reject the assumptions of the social model of disability, and propose instead views of disability and special educational needs relating to medical and psychological understandings. These positions locate the difficulty experienced by some children in education within the individual child, and see the use of classifications as a valuable means not only of providing and securing necessary support, but also of allowing an appropriate response to the identified needs. While these are legitimate concerns, what these perspectives overlook, as we shall see in Chapters 1 and 5, is the important effects of the design of schools in determining difficulties. These perspectives, too, therefore, fail to a certain extent to provide justified understandings of disability and special educational needs. Furthermore, as I shall analyse in Chapter 1, the adoption by educational policies and legislation of unworkable concepts and classifications of disability and special educational needs has given rise to profound inequalities, both in the identification of students with disabilities, and in the allocation of additional funding. This situation highlights the necessity of a different and more comprehensive conception of disability and special educational needs, i.e. a conception that encompasses both social and individual factors of disability. The capability approach, as we shall see, provides an important theoretical framework towards that end.

There is, finally, a further important element relating to the concerns expressed above. This pertains to the contentious use of language in educational theory, policy and practice. It is worth addressing this issue here, as it explains the specific expressions that I will use throughout the book. Many educators[1] have drawn attention to the limits of using categories in general, but specifically categories of special educational needs and disadvantage. Definitions such as 'special educational needs', 'learning difficulties' or 'learning disability', while mainly introduced to describe situations, can be, and indeed are, also used to 'label' and produce negative stereotypes (Wilson, 2000: 817). Moreover, in education, as in other contexts, the use of categories varies considerably over time, and reflects a particular theory or view behind it. The terminology currently used to describe what refers to 'learning difficulties', for instance, has changed to a great extent in the last century, from the use of terms like 'mental retardation' or 'educational subnormality', to current definitions such as 'Severe Learning Difficulties'. Some authors point out how the 'labelling' use of these categories implies a 'bad-mouthing process', whereby the categories used in the past become the insults of the present (Corbett, 1996; and also Tomlinson, 1982). The use of categories and the related understandings constitutes one of the theoretical and moral dilemmas characterizing the debate in inclusive and special education, which is discussed in Chapters 1, 3 and 5. In acknowledging these views, therefore, in this book I shall make use of the definitions and distinctions proposed by disabled peoples' movements and scholars. However, the theoretical necessity of referring to current policy and practice in inclusive and special education, as well as to official documents, requires also the introduction of the concept of 'special educational needs', widely adopted in the relevant literature, and conceptually distinct from disability, especially in the UK debate. Consequently, throughout this book I shall refer to 'children with disabilities and special educational needs', as well as to 'disabled people', and 'people with disabilities'. I am fully, and painfully, aware of how this may appear redundant to the reader, and, more importantly, of the limits and the contingent and problematic meanings these terms subsume. At present, however, no better solution seems available.

As I have noted at the outset, finally, the argument I develop in this study deploys a specific perspective within liberal egalitarianism. Given the controversies surrounding definitions and understandings of disability, it is therefore necessary to outline briefly the place of disability within theories of justice.

3. Liberal Egalitarianism and Disability

Equality, as we have seen, is central to egalitarian theories of justice. But why is the egalitarian concern for equality important? Although egalitarians differ on the kind of equality they propose, they generally agree on the importance of the ideal. In his influential work, Ronald Dworkin defends equality as a valuable political ideal by stating that its virtue resides in being both intrinsically good, and instrumentally necessary as a precondition of political legitimacy. Equality matters, says Dworkin, because 'no government is legitimate that does not show equal concern for the fate of all those citizens over whom it claims dominion and from whom it claims allegiance. Equal concern is the sovereign virtue of political community' (Dworkin, 2000: 1). In linking the legitimacy of state authority to the moral ideal of equal concern, Dworkin extends the demands of equality to all participants in the political community, while at the same time asserting the equal moral worth of citizens.

A deep commitment to the moral ideal of equal concern and respect is the fundamental underpinning of liberal egalitarian theories of justice. Equal concern for each and every individual is the liberal principle invoked by egalitarians as the one that should inform the design of social and institutional arrangements, as we have seen in relation to educational equality. What is important to address very briefly at this stage of the discussion is how the principle of equal concern and respect is enacted in relation to disability.

One fundamental aspect of the debate concerns what kind of equality should be sought, and the different variables that should be deployed in interpersonal comparisons aimed at adjudicating people's relative advantages or disadvantages. And it is in relation to the evaluation of disadvantage that disability is generally considered within distributive theories. More specifically, these theories engage with the question of what individual traits constitute personal advantages or disadvantages, whether these are naturally or socially caused, and why and how diverse personal traits do or do not have to be considered in determining a just distributive scheme. Within this evaluative process, disability is generally considered a personal deficit, and a morally relevant inequality. What justice demands in relation to this inequality is a further matter, mainly addressed in terms of correction or compensation. As we shall see in Chapter 6, different metrics for interpersonal comparison are differently sensitive to the demands of disability, and the debate on this issue is far from being settled. However, I shall anticipate here an element of this debate by touching upon John Rawls's theory and its critique by Sen and Nussbaum. This will serve the aim of presenting briefly some arguments that support the capability approach, and its metric, as a coherent expression of egalitarian concerns in relation to disability.

John Rawls's theory is one of the leading examples of liberal egalitarian theories of justice (Brighouse, 2001: 537). Rawls provides us with an index of comparable social primary goods to measure our well-being: liberties, opportunities, powers and prerogatives of office, and income and wealth. According to Rawls, people's relative positions have to be evaluated in the space of these social primary goods. His theory of justice consists in two principles: the Liberty Principle, which guarantees a set of basic liberties equally to all, and the Difference Principle, which stipulates that opportunities must be equally distributed and that inequalities of income and wealth are to benefit the least advantaged members in society (Rawls, 2001: 42–3). Within these two principles, Rawls defines fair equality of opportunity in terms of a fair chance, by stating,

> Supposing that there is a distribution of native endowments, those who have the same level of talent and ability and the same willingness to use these gifts should have the same prospects of success regardless of their social class of origin.
>
> (Rawls, 2001: 44)

Rawls's theory has often been critiqued for not entailing considerations for disabled people. In particular, the charge levelled at it by proponents of the capability approach is that, by comparing people's well-being on the basis of primary goods, therefore ultimately on the shares of resources they hold, the Rawlsian model fundamentally neglects the crucial heterogeneity of human beings (Sen, 1992; and Nussbaum, 2000: 68, and more extensively, 2006a) and therefore ends up overlooking important elements. Rawls openly formulated his theory aiming at covering the 'fundamental case', thus leaving any possible extension to further developments. He maintains,

> Our aim is to ascertain the conception of justice most appropriate for a democratic society in which citizens conceive of themselves in a certain way. So let's add that all citizens are fully cooperating members of society over the course of a complete life. This means that everyone has sufficient intellectual powers to play a normal part in society, and no one suffers from unusual needs that are especially difficult to fulfil, for example, unusual and costly medical requirements.
>
> (Rawls, 1980: 545–6)

Rawls did not proceed to provide an extension of his theory and to reflect on the position of disabled people in his conception of justice, but several authors have pointed out how his positions can appropriately be extended to include physical disability, albeit perhaps not cognitive ones (Brighouse, 2001; Daniels, 2003; and Kittay, 1999, 2001). I will not pursue this line of argument here, but further outline instead Sen's and Nussbaum's critique of the primary goods.

As we shall see specifically in Chapter 4, both Sen and Nussbaum argue that, given the fundamental fact of human diversity, the design of social arrangements should be evaluated, not in the space of primary goods, but in the more appropriate space of capabilities, that is, in the space of people's real freedoms to achieve valued functionings. According to Sen in particular, what is fundamental in assessing equality is not an equal share of the means to freedoms, but rather an equal share of opportunities for valuable functionings. For example, a disabled person and an able-bodied one may have an equal share of primary goods, but this does not necessarily equalize their positions, as the disabled person may convert resources into valuable functionings very differently from, and perhaps not as effectively as, an able-bodied person. And this consideration opens the possibility of theoretical understandings of disability and capability equality which are sensitive to the just position of disabled people in social arrangements.

The important insights that I shall explore in this book concern exactly how the capability approach, in placing human heterogeneity as central to considerations of justice and equality, and in evaluating people's reciprocal positions in the space of the real freedoms they have to achieve valuable aims, allows for a re-examination of impairment, disability and special educational needs within a perspective of equality and justice. Thus, the approach provides valuable insights for reconsidering disability within distributive theories.

The theoretical framework outlined so far constitutes the philosophical underpinning of my analysis and will be more fully developed in the book. I now turn my attention to the method that informs it.

4. Methodology

As I have stated at the outset, my central aim in this book is to develop a principled framework that, primarily, adjudicates what students with disabilities and special educational needs are entitled to in education, and the reasons that justify that entitlement. There are important grounds in support of this goal. The first is a fundamental and inescapable moral reason, relating to the formulation of egalitarian principles that accord full consideration for the moral worth of all individuals. The second is a theoretical motive, in that theories, and the principles underpinning them, ought to be right, or as approximating as much as possible the level of rightness we can formulate. The final reason is connected to the relation between theory and practice, in that clarity at theoretical level should help in informing decisions at policy level. The principled framework I develop in this book aims to provide not only the theoretical foundations for a fair distribution of resources, but also more policy-oriented guidance to that aim, in that it sets out a theoretical groundwork for the evaluation of the fairness of current models of distribution and the design of policies that are more just.

However, in order to arrive at a justified conception of educational equality, we need a process of adjudicating between different judgements and understandings. Here the standard processes of political philosophy prove fundamental to this purpose. In particular, in my analysis I shall apply what John Rawls has called 'reflective equilibrium'. This consists in presenting our arguments for a normative position, testing them against our moral intuitions, and subsequently adjudicating the conflicts between principles and intuitions when they arise. For example, one of our intuitions might be that inequalities in education due to family circumstances or to individual abilities are wrong. We therefore analyse how various conceptions respond to that intuition, and we may support a specific approach as the best response to that initial intuition. We finally move towards a position that shows consistency and accommodates our judgements, and those of others, in a shared political consensus. In applying reflective equilibrium to the ideal of equality in education, we refer not only to philosophical principles, but also take into account the specificity of education. We therefore test our considered judgements in the light of educational positions and perspectives, many of which result from empirical and evidence-based research. In exploring the ideal of educational equality, this book draws valuable connections between political philosophy and educational theories, thus showing how the debate in philosophy can contribute to educational understanding and vice versa. Not only that, but while educational theories are enhanced by the clarifying process of philosophical analysis, philosophical reflection is conversely enriched by the valuable input of the empirical and more practice-based part of education itself. Ultimately, in exploring what educational equality means, we not only clarify its meaning(s), but also think of how to operationalize it, thus considering the various elements, many of empirical nature, which can promote or obstruct its accomplishment as an educational aim. This point highlights the connection between theory and practice, and underlines its relevance for philosophical studies in education.

5. The Structure of the Book

In concluding these introductory notes, it is worth summarizing the plan of the book. In this introduction, I have set out the theoretical framework of the book, and its main aims. Chapter 1 addresses current policies in special needs education and the dilemmas at the core of the debate in this area, while showing how the variety of policies and practices, for example in England and in the USA, leads to pervasive and widespread inequalities. Chapter 2 critically engages, from a philosophical position, the social model of disability. It shows the theoretical limits of the social model in providing proper grounding for its own claims of equal entitlement and consideration for disabled people. This argument is further pursued in Chapter 3, which shows how educational positions based on the social model of disability operate in the absence of a principled framework, thus possibly hindering the achievement of their own aims of equal entitlement for disabled children. These chapters highlight the compelling need for a principled framework informing both conceptions of disability and special educational needs as well as the provision of education.

Chapter 4 introduces the capability approach as an innovative perspective. It suggests that the specific understanding of human diversity proposed by the approach, as well as the democratic decisional process promoted and the normative dimension entailed, are all fundamental elements for informing the principled framework I develop. It also addresses some critical problems with the approach. Chapter 5 applies the capability perspective on disability to the context of education, and presents a conception of disability and special educational needs in terms of functionings and capabilities. It furthermore discusses and counter-argues two critiques of the framework proposed. Finally, Chapters 6 and 7 explore the debate on equality and outline the normative dimension of the principled framework I develop. Chapter 8 presents and counter-argues some of the most powerful objections to educational equality. The book ends with some final, critical comments.

Chapter 1

Inclusive and Special Education: Incoherence in Practice and Dilemmas in Theory

The educational provision for children with disabilities and special educational needs is a key area not just for those involved in it, students, parents and professionals, but also for all those interested in the field of education more broadly conceived, as well as for society as a whole (Riddell, 2002: 1). Considering the provision for these students, and the related debates on how to characterize their educational interests, implies addressing two interrelated levels of analysis: the level of policy and practice in inclusive and special education, and the level of the theoretical frameworks and 'models' informing this field.

At the first level, the current provision for students with disabilities and special educational needs is mainly characterized by systems of schooling which involve the coexistence of special institutions, specialized additional provision in mainstream settings and more inclusive schools. For instance, in England,[1] the educational system is organized in special schools operating alongside the inclusion of students with disabilities and special educational needs into mainstream education, 'wherever possible' (Lunt, 2002: 38). Similarly, in the United States provision is organized in a continuum from full inclusive schools to special ones, on the basis of the principle of the Least Restrictive Environment (LRE) set out in the 1997 Individual with Disabilities Education Act (IDEA). Likewise, provision within the European Union varies considerably according to the features outlined above. In some countries, for example Sweden, Italy or Spain, policies are geared towards the inclusion of almost all students within mainstream schooling. In other countries, for instance France, Denmark, Austria, Finland and Slovenia, provision encompasses inclusion in mainstream schools alongside special ones (Meijer *et al.*, 2003).

The picture emerging from this brief overview reveals some current important tendencies in the provision of special needs education. First, it highlights that '[I]nclusive education is now firmly established as the main policy imperative with respect to children who have special educational needs (SEN) or disabilities' (Lindsay, 2003: 3). Second, it shows that the movement towards the inclusion of all students in mainstream schools, while being widespread, is nevertheless at different stages in different countries. Finally, and importantly, it points out how the provision for these students encompasses different settings, from special to more inclusive ones. This leads to a complex and heterogeneous situation, which sees a variety of differently articulated policies and practices within the same country and among different countries.

A fundamental element of the policies informing these different systems of provision is the set of definitions and classifications of disabilities and special educational needs they adopt. Here again, there are widespread variations. For instance, in England, following the recommendations of the 1978 Warnock Report (DES), definitions of disability have been abolished, and policies and official acts refer to the notion of 'special educational needs'. More recently, however, references to medical and psychological notions have been reintroduced as a necessary specification of this broader concept (DfES, Code of Practice, 2001a). Conversely, policies in the United States adopt categories of disabilities, mainly relating to medical and psychological notions, for example 'visual impairment' or 'mental retardation'. The situation is similarly differentiated in the European Union, with countries adopting various systems of classifications, from medical and psychological definitions, to broader ones, including reference to health and social factors, such as chronic illness or immigration (OECD, 2000, 2005, 2007).

If consistent variations characterize the level of provision, the theoretical level presents tensions, and different and often contrasting positions on how to respond to the educational demands of children with special educational needs. The debate in inclusive and special education presents wide arrays of theoretical perspectives, which are seen by scholars in the field as reflecting the problematic and complex nature of the issues involved. Brahm Norwich, among others, has outlined the inherent tensions and the dilemma at play when trying to characterize the educational interests of children with disabilities and special educational needs (Norwich, 2002). In his view, these tensions are expressed by

> the issue of whether we talk about special or inclusive education. Do we assume that there is something additional or different about special education compared to mainstream or general education? Or do we assume that the mainstream education is to be extended and enhanced to accommodate or include the diversity of learners? Is reference to anything additional or different a form of discrimination? Or does talk about inclusive education just perpetuate the apartness of

special provision which critics have identified in reference to special educational needs?

(Norwich, 2002: 482–3)

Addressing these issues implies not only reference to current theoretical models in the field, but also recognizing and analysing the 'dilemma of difference'. According to Norwich, dilemmas are inherent to the conceptualization of differences in education and are related to the possible negative connotation of concepts of disability and special needs. Thus, dilemmas arise between, on the one hand, identifying differences relating to disability and special educational needs in order to establish an appropriate educational provision, but with the possibility of attributing negative connotations to differences. Or, on the other hand, emphasizing what is common among children, with the risk of not responding to the educational interests of some of them (Norwich, 2002: 495).

In this chapter, I outline the current situation in the educational provision for children with disabilities and special educational needs, with respect to policies in England and the United States, and, to a lesser extent, to developments in the international scene. I furthermore relate issues of provision to theoretical debates and frameworks in the field of inclusive and special education. My aim is to show that the situation at the level of provision leads to inequitable widespread conditions. This can be related to the tensions and the dilemma at the core of inclusive and special education, and referred primarily and substantially to the absence of a principled framework informing this field. More specifically, my main claim is that the current incoherent and inequitable provision of education for children with disabilities and special educational needs stems from the absence of a framework, both in terms of definitions and provision, guiding and informing educational policies and, in particular, the just distribution of educational resources to these students.

While this analysis does not constitute an attempt to make a specific comparative study between the United Kingdom, and specifically England, and the United States, or indeed among these and other countries, I maintain that referring to policies and practices of these two countries is useful, since it provides wider perspectives and broader insights on the issues at stake. Moreover, recent studies have emphasized how, in education, 'the two countries [*the UK and the USA*] have influenced each other's reforms, and yet their individual policies and practices vary enough to provide interesting contrasts', while, at the same time, exerting a considerable influence on other countries,

too (McLaughlin and Rouse, 2000: 1; and Rouse and McLaughlin 2007: 86).

The chapter is organized in three sections. The first explores the wide variations in the provision of inclusive and special education, in light of recent developments and with reference to main legislation and policy issues. The second section analyses current policies for the funding of special and inclusive education and outlines the profound inequalities resulting from the implementation of these policies. Finally, the third part outlines the main terms of the dilemma of difference, and addresses some conceptual tensions inherent to current perspectives in the field.

1. Variations in Provision: Special, Integrated and Inclusive Education

In most Western countries the last three decades have been characterized by substantive developments in the provision of education for children with disabilities and special educational needs, and by parallel theoretical debates about the aims, practice and location of special education (e.g. Dyson and Millward, 2000; Rouse and Florian, 1997; Ainscow, 1999; Armstrong and Barton, 2007). As Hegarty notices, '[I]n 30 years we have moved from a segregation paradigm, through integration to inclusion' (2001: 243).

The historical legacy of separate special schools – a feature common to developed and developing countries, which refers to an initial provision, often organized by religious or philanthropic bodies, and subsequently expanded by national systems of public education (Ainscow, 1999: 180–1) – has gradually been challenged by different approaches. More specifically, perspectives based on human rights have questioned the practice of segregated institutions and expressed moral concerns for the placement of children in special schools. At the same time, professionals in the field of special education have voiced concerns for the effectiveness of segregated provision. This has led to a move that has involved the whole of the developed countries and, although to a different extent, also developing countries. The move has progressively shifted provision from segregated institutions towards more 'integrated' settings, thus towards educating children with disabilities and special educational needs within mainstream schools (Pijl and Meijer, 1994: xi; Ainscow, 1999: 181).

In their important study of integration in six countries conducted at the beginning of the 1990s, Pijl and Meijer define integration as 'a collective noun for all attempts to avoid the segregated and isolated education of students with special needs', and furthermore specify integration as 'conceived in terms of the organisational structure and in terms of the nature of integration' (1994: 4). According to their study, integration can be characterized along three parameters. The first refers to the actual 'place' of education, its 'location', which, for students with special educational needs, could be either in special classes or units within mainstream schools, or in mainstream classes with additional provision. The second parameter relates to elements of social interactions, in terms of the possibility of social contacts between children. Finally, the third refers to curricular elements, and is defined by the use of the same broad curricular frameworks for the education of all children (1994: 6). The results of Pijl and Meijer's study demonstrate that integrated provision has taken many different forms and has led to substantially diverse outcomes in different countries. Nevertheless, this study also importantly suggests that the vast majority of Western countries, during their 'integrationist phase', have made substantive changes in their educational systems in order to accommodate children with disabilities and special educational needs within mainstream, neighbourhood schools.

In the last decade, however, the concept of inclusion has consistently replaced integration, which, in turn, has been seen as limited and unsatisfactory (Ainscow, 1999: 182; Rouse and Florian, 1997: 326). Two main interrelated factors have contributed to this change. First, professionals in the field of special education have started to express concerns about the often too narrow interpretation of integration as simple 'placement' of children with special educational needs in mainstream schools, without any attention to the quality of the education provided. In many cases integration has resulted in the actual transfer of special educational practices and methods to the new setting, with a correspondent provision in terms of a 'watered-down variant of the regular curriculum' (Pijl, Meijer and Hegarty, 1997: 2). Hence, integration has often taken the form of a means to avoid segregation, but with little improvement in terms of the actual content and practice of education. Furthermore, professionals in the field of special education have critiqued the practice of identifying children with disabilities or special educational needs, and have brought attention to the social element inscribed in any form of classification, as well as the relation between special educational needs and the design of schooling systems. This has led to questioning the 'simple' integration of children into regular schools and classes, and called upon a change of educational systems to accommodate the diversity of children (Ainscow, 1999: 182).

The second, important factor that has influenced the move from integration to inclusion in education relates to the progressively stronger influence exercised by disabled people's movements and by associations of parents of children with disabilities, who have advanced their pressing requests for equal consideration and entitlement. The social model of disability, in particular, as the theoretical model providing the meaning of disability from disabled people's own perspective, emphasizes ways in which existing social structures and policies should be fundamentally changed to ensure the removal of all forms of institutional and physical barriers to the full participation of disabled people in political and social life. Correlatively, inclusive education is often proposed by the same movements as a means to remove barriers and discrimination, and to ensure the full participation of all children in education. These movements have resulted in the recognition of the rights of disabled people as well as in the affirmation of the rights of children with disabilities and special educational needs to be educated in 'regular' schools.

This new emphasis on rights and opportunities for equal participation is reflected in important and influential documents at international and national level. At the international level, for instance, the 1982 United Nations World Program of Action Concerning Disabled Persons states the equalizations of opportunities as one of the main goals to be achieved worldwide (UN, 1982: 2). Likewise, at the national level, different countries have devised laws and policies aimed at ensuring disabled people have equal rights and opportunities, as, for instance, in the UK the 1995 Disability and Discrimination Act, and the more recent 2006 Disability Equality Duty, and in the US the 1990 American with Disabilities Act (ADA). The provision of education for children with disabilities as an integral part of education systems is stated at the international level in the Standard Rules on the Equalisation of Opportunities for Persons with Disabilities, adopted by the United Nations General Assembly in 1993, which emphasizes access to ordinary schools as a fundamental process for the equalization of opportunities. This has been recently reaffirmed in the new Convention on the Rights of Persons with Disabilities, adopted by the United Nations in December 2006, which states the right to access to an inclusive education at all levels.

The same emphasis on rights and equal opportunity has informed the move from integration to inclusion in education, which is now central to the debate in special needs education. This centrality is expressed by several documents and policies both at the international and the national level. The main document based on human rights perspectives and stating the aims of inclusive education at international level has emerged from the 1994 Salamanca World Conference on Special Needs Education and is expressed in the 'Salamanca Statement', proclaimed by delegates representing 92 governments and 25 international organizations (Lindsay,

2003: 3). The Statement highlights 'the necessity and urgency of providing education for children, youths and adults with special educational needs within the regular education system' (UNESCO, 1994: 9) and claims, specifically, that

> Every child has a fundamental right to education, and must be given the opportunity to achieve and maintain an acceptable level of learning . . . those with special educational needs must have access to regular schools which should accommodate them within a child centred pedagogy capable of meeting these needs.
>
> (UNESCO, 1994: 10)

While reaffirming the aim of educating children with disabilities and special educational needs in regular schools, the Statement endorses a 'Framework for Action on Special Needs Education', which is intended to provide guidance for governments and organizations. The guiding principles informing the Framework specify several fundamental aspects of inclusive education. Among them, three parameters are specifically relevant both for policy implementations and for their centrality in the debate on inclusion in education: identifying and defining special educational needs, the location of education, and the importance of additional provision in terms of resource allocation to secure the process of inclusion.

With regard to the first aspect, identifying and defining disability and special educational needs, the Framework affirms, primarily, that, 'schools should accommodate **all children** regardless of their physical, intellectual, social, emotional, linguistic or other conditions' (UNESCO, 1994: 59). It then defines 'special educational needs' by stating:

> In the context of this Framework, the term 'special educational needs' refers to all those children and youth whose needs arise from disabilities or learning difficulties. Many children experience learning difficulties and thus have special educational needs at some time during their schooling. Schools have to find ways of successfully educating all children, including those who have serious disadvantages and disabilities.
>
> (UNESCO, 1994: 59)

This definition identifies both disabilities and learning difficulties as aspects of special needs. In doing so, the definition incorporates elements deriving from considerations of physical disability and mainly referring to medical perspectives, together with elements referring to the concept of learning difficulties. In the context of the framework, moreover, special educational needs are defined both with reference to the different demands posed by individual children to the school system in the process of learning, and to general considerations of disadvantage and serious disability. The Framework explicitly states:

> This *definition* should include disabled and gifted children, street and working children, children from remote or nomadic populations, children from linguistic, ethnic or cultural minorities and children from other disadvantaged or marginalized areas or groups.
>
> (UNESCO, 1994: 59)

Although aiming at including a wide variety of 'needs', the definition provided is nevertheless unspecified in its considerations of the different dimensions of needs, from those related to impairment and disability, to learning difficulties and needs deriving from social causes, such as poverty and deprivation. The definition does not specify whether children with disabilities and special educational needs, or children from under-represented groups and gifted children, actually experience different educational needs, thus assimilating a wide range of different demands within a broad conception. This unspecified aspect of the definition, while important in urging governmental action upon a wide range of causes of exclusion from education, is rather less effective in terms of its possible operationalization in policy development.

The second element considered in the Statement is the location of education. In proposing mainstream education as a fundamental right of children with disabilities and special educational needs, the Statement advocates the confinement of special settings and institutions to past practices. The statement outlines that access to ordinary schools is an integral part of the process of equalization of opportunities:

> Inclusion and participation are essential to human dignity and to the enjoyment and exercise of human rights. Within the field of education, this is reflected in the development of strategies that seek to bring about a genuine equalization of opportunity.
>
> (UNESCO, 1994: 61)

According to proponents of the Statement, moreover, not only are inclusive institutions the most effective means of combating discriminatory attitudes, creating welcoming communities, building an inclusive society and achieving education for all; moreover, they provide an effective education to the majority of children and improve the efficiency and ultimately the cost-effectiveness of the entire education system.

(UNESCO, 1994: 10)

It is important to highlight here the social and economic dimensions implied by this position. On the one hand, the statement emphasizes the anti-discriminatory and participatory aims of inclusive institutions, while, on the other, introducing elements of cost-effectiveness and efficiency.[2] This last point links the recommendation on inclusion to the accent on resource provision advocated by the statement. This is the third important element relevant for policy implementation and for the debate on inclusion in education.

Considerations of resource requirements are a fundamental and complex element of the process of inclusion in education. The Salamanca Statement expresses the importance of this aspect by stating:

The development of inclusive schools as the most effective means for achieving education for all must be recognized as a key government policy and accorded a privileged place on the nation's development agenda. It is only in this way that *adequate resources* can be obtained. Changes in policies and priorities cannot be effective unless *adequate resource* requirements are met. Political commitment, at both national and community level, is needed both to obtain additional resources and to redeploy existing ones.

(UNESCO, 1994: 78, Italics added)

Moreover, the Statement recommends that '[T]he distribution of resources to schools should take realistic account of the differences in expenditure required to provide appropriate education for all children, bearing in mind their needs and circumstances' (UNESCO, 1994: 78). This appeal to additional funding for inclusive education represents a fundamental claim, and introduces considerations of resource distribution at the core of the process of inclusion. However, the statement leaves unspecified both the concept of resources and the differential amount that should be provided for the education of children with special educational needs, thus resulting in a declaration of intentions that needs further specification in order to be enacted at policy level.

Despite the often under-specified nature of the definitions and concepts

introduced, the Salamanca Statement represents an important international declaration at policy level, upon which governments and international agencies are called to act in order to promote and establish
inclusion in education. In this sense the Salamanca Statement has encouraged the overall worldwide trend towards providing different responses to
the educational demands of children with disabilities and special educational needs, from those traditionally associated with segregated and
special provision (Ainscow, 1999: 183). Notwithstanding these important
trends and correlated policy measures, however, different countries are at
different stages in this process towards inclusion, and in the vast majority
of cases education systems still reflect the ongoing transition from special,
segregated institutions, through integrated settings and towards inclusive
schooling. The situation of special and inclusive education in England and
in the USA reflects this state of affairs, and it is therefore worth exploring
it in some more detail by way of example.

1.1 Inclusive and Special Education in England

According to Lindsay, 'Within the UK the development of policy towards
inclusion is well advanced, but not all-encompassing' (Lindsay, 2003: 4).
Anticipations of the move towards educating all children in normal
schools are traceable back to the 1928 Wood Committee, which emphasized the unity of special and ordinary education, and to the 1944 Education Act, which recognized that education for children with special
requirements should take place in ordinary schools (Lindsay, 2003: 4).
However, it was the 1978 Warnock Report (DES, 1978) which marked a
watershed in the educational provision for children with disabilities and
special educational needs (Riddell, 2002: 6). The Report importantly and
substantially pointed out the commonality of educational aims for all
children, and the rights of children with special educational needs to be
educated in mainstream schools, providing their needs could be met, and
stipulating additional support to this purpose. The Report also introduced
the concept of 'special educational needs', while highlighting the interactive nature of learning difficulties, seen as related to the context of the
student and to different variables, not all pertaining to the individual
child. It recognized that 20 per cent of children experience difficulties at
some time during their education, and that for only 2 per cent of children
these difficulties are so significant as to require their assessment by a multi-
disciplinary team, and their condition protected through a formal statement. Hence the Warnock Report asserted the possibility of meeting
children's needs through additional resources and specialist services,

without the recourse to special school provision (Dyson and Millward, 2000: 1).

The recommendations of the Report were subsequently implemented by the 1981 Education Act,[3] which mainly set the frameworks of the current provision in special and inclusive education (Norwich, 2002: 485). The Act legally formalized the concept of special educational needs and endorsed the principle of educating all children in mainstream settings. It furthermore introduced the statutory multi-disciplinary assessment, conducted by the competent Local Authority,[4] and stipulated that Local Authorities and schools should provide the appropriate support necessary to meet the needs of children experiencing learning difficulties. The Act also increased spending on special education and encouraged school level initiatives in order to develop policies for meeting special educational needs. Norwich (2002) outlines how, as a consequence of this Act, there are now three main groups of children with special educational needs.[5] The first includes children with the most severe learning difficulties ascertained by a statement and educated in special schools, estimated to be around 1.3 per cent of all students. The second includes children with statements but educated in mainstream schools, currently representing more than half the children with statements; and, finally, a third group of children with no statement, but whose special educational needs are met through additional specialized support within mainstream schools. These groups represent the 20 per cent mentioned in the Warnock Report (Norwich, 2002: 485).

A more decisive focus on inclusion in special education has emerged as a consequence of the 1997 Green Paper *Excellence for All Children: Meeting Special Educational Needs* (DfEE, 1997), and the 2001 Special Educational Needs Code of Practice (revised) (DfES, 2001a). In particular, the Green Paper officially endorses the Salamanca Statement and affirms the support of the government for the inclusion of pupils with special educational needs in mainstream primary and secondary schools, thus implying provision for a variety of needs within regular schools (DfEE, 1997: 44). The more recent 2001 Special Educational Needs and Disability Act (SENDA) further emphasizes the support for inclusive education by requiring children with special educational needs to be educated in mainstream schools, unless this is against the wishes of the parents or incompatible with the efficient education of other children (Lindsay, 2003: 4). Moreover, the Act extends provision in mainstream settings also at the level of secondary and higher education, stipulating that institutions have to make all the 'reasonable adjustments' in order to anticipate and accommodate the broad variety of educational needs. Finally, key among the more recent initiatives in support of inclusive education are the Green Paper *Every Child Matters* (DfES, 2003), which expresses a commitment to the promotion of every child's well-being and to a more comprehensive and unified approach to the protection and support for vulnerable children, and the 2004 'Removing Barriers to Achievement: *the Government's Strategy for SEN*' (DfES, 2004). The Strategy highlights four essential areas of intervention in order to promote the learning opportunities of children with special educational needs: early intervention, the removal of all barriers to learning, the improvement of expectations and achievement as well as an integrated approach in support of students with special educational needs. In emphasizing the removal of barriers to learning, the Strategy adopts the social construction view on disability and the concerns expressed by disabled people's movements (this is addressed below and in Chapter 2).

Ultimately, educational policy in England shows an explicit promotion of inclusion and a commitment to extend it to all sectors of education. At the same time, the educational provision is characterized by a variety of organizational settings, which encompass special schools, integrated settings and 'more' inclusive provision. This has led some authors to question the government's politics of inclusion and to express concerns about its real commitment to it (see, for instance, Armstrong, 2005 and Armstrong and Barton, 2007). Correlatively, the educational debate is characterized by a prominent focus on the language of inclusion and by greater attempts by some of its proponents to abandon the language of needs (Norwich, 2002: 484; and Keil *et al.*, 2006). As we shall see, these differences in educational provision, together with difficulties in operationalizing the concept of special educational needs, and unclear conceptual frameworks, lead to wide inequitable conditions in the education of children with disabilities and special educational needs (more on this below). Before addressing these issues, however, I shall analyse the situation in the USA in more detail.

1.2 Inclusive and Special Education in the USA

According to Lipsky and Gartner (1996: 46) the history of public education in the United States is characterized by the progressive inclusion of under-represented groups of students into mainstream education. In particular, the educational provision for students with disabilities has developed along the three stages of exclusion, formal integration or inclusion on the basis of judicial or legislative requirements, and a progress towards more precise definitions of the nature of inclusion.

Until the 1960s, children with severe disabilities were either home educated or placed in private institutions, while children with less complex disabilities were educated in special schools or in residential centres. As a result of the pressures from the civil rights movement and from parents of children with disabilities in the late 1960s and early 1970s, the state education of these students began to be addressed by federal and state regulations and legal mandates, which have since played a substantial role in special education in the United States (Florian and Pullin, 2000: 19). This struggle resulted in the passage in 1975 of PL 94–142: The Education of All Handicapped Children Act, which stated that all children with disabilities were entitled to a 'free appropriate public education' (FAPE). The main concern of Congress in passing this law was to affirm the educability of all children with disabilities and the provision for their education in the regular neighbourhood school (Lipsky and Gartner, 1996: 147). While adopting categories of disability mainly based on medical definitions and still currently in use, the law identifies children on the basis of a medically defined disability, and the associated educational needs resulting from the adverse effect of the disability. It further establishes financial assistance to the states for the pursuit of these goals, and also encompasses 'detailed procedural protections for children and their families to ensure compliance with the law, including the right to use the federal court system to obtain enforcement of these legal rights, if necessary' (Florian and Pullin, 2000: 19). At around the same time of the enactment of the federal law, each state passed similar sets of requirements, thus establishing the educational provision for children with disabilities across the whole of the country.

The 1975 Act has been amended several times and re-authorized in the 1997 Individual with Disabilities Education Act (IDEA), which maintains the original requirements of a 'free and appropriate public education', to be provided in the 'least restrictive environment' (LRE). The Act outlines the precise meaning and content of both 'free and appropriate public education' and 'least restrictive environment', linking compliance with their implementation to the provision of additional federal funding to state and school districts. Thus, a 'free appropriate public education' is intended as

special education and related services that – A) have been provided at public expense, under public supervision and direction, and without charge; B) meet the standards of the State educational agency; C) include an appropriate pre-school, elementary, or secondary education in the State involved; D) are provided in conformity with the individualized education program required under IDEA.

(IDEA, quoted in Florian and Pullin, 2000: 20)

The US Supreme Court has subsequently specified the concept of appropriate education by indicating that 'special education and related services'
have to be provided in conformity with the IDEA procedure and have to
ensure educational benefits to children with disabilities. The other
primary principle of IDEA, the right to be educated in the 'least restrictive
environment', sometimes referred to as mainstreaming, requires that
children with disabilities should be educated, to the maximum extent
possible, with children who are not disabled. The 1997 enactment extends
this principle to include the possibility for students with disabilities to be
educated in private institutions, when the program or the design of public
ones does not respond to the criteria set forth by the law or to the parents'
choice.

   More recent developments include the 2001 Elementary and Secondary
Education Act (No Child Left Behind Act, PL 107–110) and the 2004
Individual with Disabilities Education Improvement Act (IDEA, PL
108–446). As Rouse and McLaughlin notice, these two very powerful laws
are currently shaping provision for students with disabilities in the USA
(Rouse and McLaughlin, 2007: 88). These acts are informed by concerns
about accountability and improving standards of achievements for all
students, thus requiring access to the general educational curriculum also
for students with disabilities. In particular, the No Child Left Behind Act
specifies set annual goals that schools have to meet in order to close the
achievement gap among different subgroups of students, including
students with disabilities (but with alternate assessment for students with
the more severe cognitive disabilities). While evidence on the implications
of these changes is at present limited, given their recent implementation,
concerns have been expressed about the difficulties of maintaining
uniform performance and progress goals for all students (Rouse and
McLaughlin, 2007: 93).

   Although the American education system has seen a progressive development towards more inclusive institutions, inclusion does not represent
a legal requirement. According to Lipsky and Gartner, the concepts of
mainstreaming and the principle of the 'least restrictive environment' de
facto still stipulate the existence of two systems of provision, special and
regular ones, in which students with disabilities subdivide their educational time. Hence, they maintain, despite developments towards more
inclusive practice, most students with disabilities continue to be educated
in separate settings, which could be separate classes within mainstream
schools or special units, and interact with their non-disabled peers mainly
in socializing activities (1996: 151). Furthermore and importantly, Lipsky
and Gartner maintain that 'there can be little doubt that the current

system is not working' in spite of an annual cost of approximately $30 billion (1996: 148). To support their claim, these authors report the poor educational outcomes of students with disabilities, including high drop out rates, low graduation rates and limited success in post-secondary education (1996: 148). In addition to this, as I shall address in more detail in the next section, the current funding of special education in the USA encompasses varying rules, regulations and practices at state level, which result in wide variations in both placement of children and expenditure within states and among states, thus fundamentally proving the substantial inequitable situation in the educational provision for these students.

This brief overview of developments in England and in the USA highlights, on the one hand, the transitory situation in the provision of inclusive and special education, and the current uneven achievement of inclusion. On the other hand, it presents evidence of the widespread variations in the educational provision for students with disabilities and special educational needs. As Hegarty suggests, although such uneven results may be related to the magnitude of the changes underway in educational systems the world over, it may nevertheless be prudent to allow for other possible explanations of these variations, not least that the aims being pursued are not well-formulated, or are the wrong ones (Hegarty, 2001: 244). Taking Hegarty's insights further, I maintain that these variations, which result in widespread inequitable conditions, may be related to the absence of principled frameworks underpinning and informing policy and practice in inclusive and special education. The next section addresses the variations in the funding of education, and the resulting inequalities, through a general outline of the situations in England and in the USA.

2. Inequalities in Practice:
The Funding of Inclusive and Special Education

The current financial provision for children with disabilities and special educational needs in England and in the United States can be taken as an example of a more widespread situation in the funding of inclusive and special education. The pervasive inequalities resulting from these funding systems are reflected in the trends identified by recent studies conducted by the OECD among its member countries (OECD, 2000, 2005, 2007; Evans, 2001). In general, the picture emerging from research and data available shows a general increase in the funding of inclusive and special education, together with wide and substantial differences in the amount of resources being allocated, which, in turn, result in substantial inequalities of provision. I start my analysis by outlining the situation in England, and then turn to the finance of special education in the USA.

A series of reforms in the financing of education during the 1980s in England delegated the administration of school budgets to the individual schools, enabling them to manage their own finances (Evans *et al.*, 2001: 1). The major legislation embodying this change is the 1988 Education Reform Act (ERA), which introduced also a unified National Curriculum and national testing and assessment. Furthermore, schools were deemed to be competing for students under an open enrolment scheme, and parental choice to be enhanced by the publication of school performance tables. The 1988 Act is unanimously considered one of the most important and far-reaching pieces of legislation for England, and its effects on the school system in general, and on the provision for children with disabilities and special educational needs in particular, are today subjects of research and discussion. More specifically, several authors have pointed out how the market-oriented elements formalized by the Act in terms of school choice, competition and local management of schools have yielded negative consequences for students with disabilities and special educational needs.[6]

Particularly relevant to my analysis is the introduction of the local management of schools (LMS), which required Local Authorities to delegate finance to single schools and to determine a funding formula for the allocation of the school budget. Under Section 38 of the Act, the formula must apply 'a consistent set of criteria for distributing resources' (Marsh, 2003: 72). In addition to the notional principle of allocating resources according to the number of pupils enrolled at the school (Age-Weighted Pupils Numbers), it may take into account any other relevant factors which could affect the requirements of individual schools, for instance the number of pupils having special educational needs (Marsh, 2003: 72).

Further governmental guidance about school finance is contained in the Fair Funding document published in 1998 (DfEE, 1988) and implemented in 1999. Under the system of 'Fair Funding',

> Local Authorities in England and Wales are currently required . . . to delegate at least 80 per cent of their budget for funding schools to the schools, leaving 20 per cent to fund central administration and services to support school, such as psychological services, advisors to support school improvement, and funding for making provision for pupils with statements of special educational needs.
>
> (Evans *et al.*, 2000: 1)

As Evans *et al.* note, in this way the funding of special needs education is characterized by a two-tier system, with resources being provided by the Local Authorities from central funds on the one hand, and resources given directly to schools on the other (2001: 2). Furthermore, the same two-tier system regulates the responsibility for children with special educational needs, since children identified with a formal statement are under direct Local Authority responsibility, although shared with the school, whereas children identified by the schools, but without a formal statement, remain under the responsibility of the school. This organization is also related to the implementation of the Code of Practice on the Identification and Assessment of Special Educational Needs, following the 1993 Education Act (see above) and the current revised 2001 Code of Practice (DfES, 2001a). The original Code established a five-stage model of assessment and provision, with the first three stages under the responsibility of the school, but with a direct involvement of the Local Authority at stage three, and the last two stages under shared responsibility. The conduct of a statutory assessment and the drawing up of the formal statement of special educational needs lay with the Local Authority. The revised current Code of Practice has a graduated model of assessment and provision organized in only three stages. However, this change does not substantially alter the two-tier system of provision. Under the revised Code of Practice schools are primarily responsible for the provision at the first two stages, namely 'School Action' and 'School Action Plus'. Once a request for statutory assessment is made, at stage three, the Local Authority becomes responsible both for the conduct of the assessment and for the drawing up of the statement of special educational needs.

Several studies have addressed how the implementation of the local management of schools and subsequently the Fair Funding system have resulted in substantial differences from one Local Authority to another in the provision for students with special educational needs (Vincent *et al.*, 1994; Evans and Lunt, 1994; Evans *et al.*, 2001; Marsh, 2003). Three main difficulties are mentioned as causing these widespread differences. First, difficulties arise in operationalizing the concept of special educational needs for the identification of children. Lunt and Evans (1994) note how 'the 1981 Education Act produced an unclear set of descriptors in its definition of the term "special educational needs" . . . which was effectively impossible for LEAs to operationalise' (1994: 9). The set of descriptors implied both a relation to a concept of normality, which was differently conceptualized by different schools, and a relation to the school's learning environment, which is another aspect particularly subject to different conceptualizations. This has resulted in the possibility for a child, legally, to have special educational needs in one school but not in another (Florian and Pullin, 2000: 18).

Secondly, determining the funding formula for the allocation of the budget to schools has proven difficult for Local Authorities. In particular, due to the absence of clearly stated and shared criteria for the identification of special educational needs, the task of devising an acceptable formula, which could account for students with no statement of special educational needs, has caused numerous problems. Local Authorities used at first indicators such as the percentage of children entitled to free school meals (FSM). Recent studies demonstrate that, over a ten-year period, from 1992 to 2002, the number of Local Authorities adopting the 'free school meal' criteria rose from 81 to 96 per cent (Marsh, 2003). More recently, Local Authorities, in order to determine the percentage of school delegated budget with respect to children with special educational needs but no statement, appear to be using a combination of indicators, such as the 'free school meals', and audit systems like test results and professional consultation (Marsh, 2003: 73). Furthermore, as a consequence of the Fair Funding procedure, and the subsequent 2001 DfES guidance to Local Authorities on the distribution of resources to support inclusion, increased amounts of funding have been delegated to schools: 'the Audit Commission estimated that the amount of funds transferred to school as a result of that increased by over £600 million' (Marsh, 2003: 73). As a result of these mechanisms, 'the expenditure in Local Education Authorities on additional and special educational needs ranges from £8 per pupil to £270 per pupil' (Marsh, 2003: 74).

Finally, the two-tier system of funding has worked as an incentive to formally assess children, in order to secure additional funding, and has resulted in a consistent increase in the number of children with formal statements and in the total cost of special needs education. As Marsh notes,

> The total SEN spend has increased by 50 per cent, from £2.5 billion in 1996 to £3.8 billion in 2001/02, of which £1 billion is now delegated by English LEAs for AEN [*additional educational needs, such as difficulties related to social deprivation*] and SEN.
>
> (Marsh, 2003: 81)

A recent study undertaken by the National Foundation for Educational Research (Evans *et al.*, 2001) on the impact of the system of Fair Funding on 56 English Local Authorities confirms the widespread differences in funding noted by previous researches. In particular, according to the findings of the study, most Local Authorities 'allocated between 3 per cent and 7 per cent of the Local School Budget to special education' and, furthermore, 'all categorised spending differently and allocated different proportions of special education spending to each of the eight subheadings in the budget statement' (Evans *et al.*, 2001: ii). The authors of the study conclude that the overall picture emerging is one of diversity and difference within and among Local Authorities, with 'no clear trends . . . which account for the range of policies and practices regarding . . . SEN funding' (Evans *et al.*, 2001: 67). Finally, the research also confirms that the national variation in the funding of special education noted in previous researches 'has been maintained and is as great as it was at the inception of local management' (Evans *et al.*, 2001: 68). More recent developments in England indicate that emphasis is to be placed both on 'personalized learning', with an explicit focus on the 'unique talents of every pupils' (Miliband, 2004, cited in Evans, 2007: 53), and on a comprehensive approach to funding, ultimately aimed at ensuring children's well-being. As Evans notices (2007: 53), 'If all children are to be entitled to "personalised learning" . . . then . . . School budgets will have to be used in flexible ways to ensure the most effective approach for each child'. These elements seem to point in the direction of a shift in the culture of provision for inclusive and special education. Further, the recent 'Equalities Review' expresses concerns about the unequal educational provision for students with disabilities and special educational needs, both at primary and secondary school level, and points out how these students 'are not achieving their true potential' (The Equalities Review, 2007: 8, 58), thus urging a reconsideration of policy and legislation on the basis of a renewed emphasis on equality. While these developments appear to be promising, their effects on policy and practice will require further analysis and evaluation.

If the funding of special needs education in England presents such pervasive differences and, ultimately, inequalities, the situation in the United States shows no better picture. With the passage of the Education for All Handicapped Children Act – PL 94–142 – in 1975 and its re-authorization in the Individual with Disabilities Education Act (IDEA) in 1997, provision for children with disabilities has become an integral part of the American public education system (see above). Parrish notes that there has been a recent increased interest in the funding of special education, due largely to its high level of total estimated annual expenditure, in the range of $32 billion, but also due to questions being raised about the rapid growth in costs for special education and its possible negative effects on the resources of the entire public education system (2000: 432–3; 2004: 57).

The funding of special education in the United States is organized through a complex set of provision at federal, state and local level of government, with the federal government accounting for about 8 per cent of the total expenditure, and the remaining equally provided by the state and the local level of school districts (Parrish, 2000: 180). The federal funding has been mainly based on the count of children with disabilities receiving special educational services in each state, with no distinctions made with respect to the variations of type of disabilities or their level of severity. More recently, however, as a consequence of the 1997 IDEA amendments, the federal funding is gradually moving towards a census-based system, centred on total enrolment rather than on the number of children with disabilities. Under census-based funding, the federal government provides funds for the total number of students registered in each state, regardless of the number of students with disabilities, the severity of the disability or their different placement. Under this system, therefore, two states with the same number of students would receive the same amount of funding, regardless of their respective numbers of students with disabilities. Census-based funding, introduced essentially to limit the increase in the identification of disabled students in order to secure more funds, is also adopted in various forms by six of the fifty states for their level of funding (Parrish, 2000: 432; 2004: 59). In addition to the progressive introduction of the census-based funding, the 1997 IDEA contains another important element for the provision of special education. This consists in the possible adjustment upward of the amount allocated to each state, on the basis of the percentage of students in poverty in each state (Special Education Poverty Adjustment Funding) (Parrish, 2000: 442).

However, the major responsibility for the funding of special education lies at state level. Although 'All 50 states have special provision in their funding formulas that acknowledge the excess cost of special education' (Parrish, 2000: 433), there are substantial differences in the ways in which they account for their expenditures. These vary from reimbursing a fixed percentage of the actual expenditure for special education, a system adopted by 11 states, to pupil-weighted systems in 18 states. Moreover, six states use systems that fund directly the number of special education teachers and another 10 use a system of fixed dollar grants to each student. These different systems of funding relate to consistent differences across the states and within each state. Moreover, these differences are subject also to the 1997 IDEA amendment in favour of school choice extended to parents of children with disabilities. Under this amendment,

When parents place their child in a school chartered by the state or the local educational agency, the public agency remains obligated to provide special educational services and funding to students with disabilities in the same manner that the local agency provides support to its other public school programs.

(Rothstein, 1999: 336)

Although local educational agencies, on the basis of financial considerations, try to respond to the educational demands of students with disabilities within their own public program, the elements of 'placement' and school choice add complexity to the funding formula of each state.

Despite the fact that the exact amount of current expenditure for special education is estimated, since states were last requested to report these expenditures for the 1987/88 school year and recent statistics are hard to come by, the current estimated cost of special education in the United States, as mentioned above, is in the range of $50 billion per year. The Center for Special Education Finance (CSEF) at Stanford University has addressed this lack of nationally representative data on the funding of special education through several surveys of states' expenditures. The data collected between 1994 and 1996[7] show considerable variations across states in the average special education expenditure per student (Parrish and Wolman, 1999: 215). This is confirmed by more recent research showing that

State support for special education varies considerably across the nation's 50 states, ranging from 3 per cent in Oklahoma to 90 per cent in Wyoming . . . [T]he average amount of funding . . . that states reported also varied dramatically per special educational student, ranging from less than $1 in Mississippi, to $597 in Vermont.

(Parrish and Wolman, 2004: 59)

Furthermore, the percentage of students identified as disabled has grown every year since the passage of the 1975 special education law. 'On a state-by-state count, however, this percentage varies considerably across the nation, with 10.7 per cent being identified in Massachusetts as compared to 5 per cent in Hawaii' (Bowers and Parrish, 2000: 180), with these variations being related to the varying practices and regulations in place in different states.

In conclusion, the funding of special education in the United States presents pervasive differences, which parallel the inequalities at provisional level noted in England. Moreover, recent studies conducted by the OECD across its state members show similar patterns in the provision for special needs education, thus confirming the problematic situation noticed for England and the USA (OECD, 2000, 2005, 2007; Evans, P., 2000). The picture emerging from the analysis of the provisional level in terms of enactment of equal entitlement to education for children with disabilities and special educational needs is therefore a rather discouraging one. The different and often contrasting 'models' informing the level of theories in inclusive and special education, however, further complicate this picture. The next section outlines elements of the 'dilemma' central to this field.

3. The Dilemma of Difference

In *Special Educational Needs: A New Look* (2005), Mary Warnock called for a radical review of special needs education and a substantial reconsideration of the assumptions upon which the current educational framework is based. The latter, she maintains, is hindered by a tension between the intention to treat all learners as the same, and that of responding adequately to the needs arising from their individual differences (Warnock, 2005: 13). The tension highlighted by Warnock, which is central to the debate in inclusive and special education, is also referred to as the 'dilemma of difference'. This consists in the seemingly unavoidable choice between, on the one hand identifying children's differences in order to provide for them differently, with the risk of labelling and dividing; or, on the other hand, accentuating the 'sameness' and offering a common provision, with the risk of not making available what is relevant to, and needed by, individual children (Dyson, 2001; Lunt, 2002; Norwich, 1993, 1996). The dilemma sees the interplay of two fundamental dimensions: a theoretical level, relating to issues of conceptualization, and a political one, which refers to the equal entitlement of *all* children to education. In what follows, I shall address specifically the theoretical level of the dilemma, while trying to outline the problematic elements inscribed in the positions proposed, and, consequently, their limitations in informing the political level.

Conceptualizing differences among children, and in particular differences related to disability and special needs, is a contentious educational problem. What counts as disability and special educational needs is not only much debated in education, but is also the subject of contrasting and often opposed views. However much they contrast, educational approaches to disability and special educational needs all address the relation between children's diversity and the school system. The debate is characterized, on the one hand, by perspectives that causally relate children's difficulties to their individual characteristics, often seen as individual limitations and deficits. These perspectives suggest the adoption of medical categories of disability and concepts of special educational needs. On the other hand, other positions locate the causes of children's learning difficulties within the inability of schooling institutions to meet children's differences. While opposing the adoption of any form of category or classification of children's differences, seen as inherently discriminatory, these positions promote instead 'the recognition and appreciation of all aspects of diversity within education' (Barton, 2003: 15).

The theoretical frameworks informing inclusive and special education, therefore, present a substantial duality between individual and social elements. I maintain that this duality, while being an artificial causal opposition, leads to limited and unsatisfactory conceptions of disability and special educational needs. More specifically, perspectives emphasizing individual limitations end up overshadowing the role played by the design of schooling institutions in determining learning difficulties. Conversely, perspectives that identify schooling factors as causes of learning difficulties tend to overlook elements related to individual characteristics. Let me proceed to substantiate these claims.

Educational perspectives that explain children's learning difficulties as causally linked to their personal features conceptualize disability as related to an individual impairment and limitation. These perspectives endorse the use of classificatory systems of disability and special educational needs, which are considered essential for identifying children's needs and for securing appropriate provision. Proponents of these views criticize perspectives based on the social model of disability – the model supported by disabled people's organizations – for failing to analyse the complexity of disability and for simplifying it under the 'neat umbrella of disability' as socially constructed (MacKay, 2002: 160). For instance, MacKay expresses concern about the fact 'that many cohorts of experienced teachers . . . have been taught that impaired hearing is not a barrier to learning, because real barriers have to be construed socially' (MacKay, 2002: 160).

These perspectives present limits in their understandings of children's difficulties. Impaired hearing, for example, can certainly become in itself a barrier to learning, and hence a disability, when teaching is not provided to accommodate children with that impairment. If teaching were conducted in diverse ways, for instance by specific methods of facilitating language development (see, for example, Gregory, 2005), then hearing impairment would remain an impairment, but would probably not result in a disability. Consequently, category-based positions end up emphasizing the 'individual' aspect of the relation between children's difficulties and school, thus seriously overlooking the relevance of the schooling factor in determining difficulties and, therefore, failing to express the complexity of disability and special educational needs as difference in education.

Similar considerations apply to the concept of special educational needs adopted in the UK following the Warnock Report (DES, 1978) and the 1981 Education Act. The concept of special educational needs was introduced with the aim of emphasizing the relational aspect of learning difficulties, while bringing the theory and practice of special education beyond the use of categories of disability. However, as Norwich points out, the concept of special educational needs not only remains inscribed in a 'within-child model', but also substantially introduces a new category, that of special needs. This category still presents special needs as essential to the individual child, and de facto separates children with special educational needs from the others (Norwich, 1993: 45). Furthermore, as we have seen in relation to funding arrangements, the concept of special educational needs appears theoretically unspecified and practically unworkable. This leads, on the one hand, to a conceptual proliferation of needs, for instance in ideas of exceptional needs (Norwich, 1996: 34), or notions of 'individual needs' (Ainscow and Muncey, 1989). On the other hand, the unspecified nature of the concept leads to the reintroduction of the categories it aimed to abolish, for example 'sensory impairment' or 'emotional and behavioural difficulties'. Thus, the notion of special educational needs remains conceptually a 'within-child model' and fails to capture the complexity of disability. Warnock herself has expressed the need for 'rethinking the concept of special educational needs' (Warnock, 2005: 28), thus urging a reconsideration of the related framework of identification and assessment.

Opposed to these views are perspectives that identify children's difficulties as caused by the limitations of the schooling systems in meeting individual differences. These positions maintain that disabilities and special educational needs are wholly socially constructed, thus not inherent or essential to the child. For some educationalists (for instance Booth and Dyson) difficulties and needs are caused by the inflexibility of the school system and by its inability to meet the diversity of children. Norwich notes that, although on this view difficulties are seen as arising from the relation between the diversity of children and the school system, critical attention is specifically directed only to the limitations of the school, rather than to a comprehensive understanding of how this relation takes place. Dyson, for instance, comments,

Special needs are not the needs that arise in a child with disabilities
with regard to a system that is fixed. Rather they are needs that arise
between the child and the educational system as a whole when the
system fails to adapt itself to the characteristics of the child.

(Dyson, cited in Norwich, 1993: 50)

As Norwich has rightly pointed out, there seems to be an inconsistency in
arguing for an interaction between child and school and then asserting
only the limitations on the part of the school (Norwich, 1993: 50).

Some sociologists of education influenced by the social model of disability maintain that disability and special educational needs are the
products of disabling barriers and of exclusionary and oppressive educational processes (Armstrong *et al.*, 2000; Barton, 2003; Corbett, 1996;
Oliver, 1996; Tomlinson, 1982).[8] They see disabilities and difficulties as
caused by institutional practices, which marginalize and discriminate
through the use of labelling procedures and disabling categories and
methods. These positions critique the use of categories of disability for
their arbitrary, socially situated and discriminatory effects. The use of
categories is seen as aimed at separating and, until recently, segregating
children on their presumed 'abnormality', and as labelling and devaluing
children with disabilities and special educational needs. Consequently,
and in line with the social model of disability, according to proponents of
this perspective, 'difference is not a euphemism for defect, for abnormality, for a problem to be worked out through technical and assimilationist
education policies. Diversity is a social fact' (Armstrong *et al.*, 2000: 34).
Differences and diversity, therefore, instead of posing a 'dilemma', have to
be promoted and celebrated.

This perspective shows relevant theoretical problems. First, stating that
difficulties and special educational needs are socially constructed presents
obvious elements of over-socialization and significantly overlooks the
individual factors related to impairments. To mention the example used
above, a hearing impairment has to be recognized and acknowledged if
provision has to be made in order to avoid educational barriers. Hence,
simply stating that hearing impairment is a difference to be celebrated
does not seem to be a sufficient means to the end of educating the child,
and even less so when the aim is the enactment of equal entitlements.[9]
This becomes more evident in the case of children with multiple disabilities. Second, the abandonment of any use of categories and classifications
of disability and special educational needs in favour of a generic celebration of differences is in itself a problematic and, to a certain extent, coun-
terproductive position. How can policies be designed to celebrate

differences, and specifically differences related to impairment and disability, in the absence of any specification of the concept of difference? Consequently, educational perspectives that advocate the abandonment of categories of disability and special educational needs and assert that they are solely socially constructed seriously overlook the relevance of individual factors and the importance of the relation between the latter and the design of schooling systems in determining difficulties. To anticipate one of my later themes, they also neglect a notion of functioning, which alone makes sense of a disability, whether socially or personally constituted.

The same polarization of perspectives is evident in the theorization of the second level of the dilemma, that is, the problem of what system of schooling better responds to the educational interests of children with disabilities and special educational needs. Here again, positions vary between, on the one hand, those advocating the 'special' element inherent to the education of students with special educational needs, and, on the other, those advocating a full inclusion in mainstream schools, and hence flexible schooling systems accommodating the full diversity of children. Furthermore, despite its centrality in policies and practices at national and international level, as well as in the educational debate, the notion of inclusive education is differently conceptualized and understood by various educational perspectives, and there is no agreement either on its meaning, or on its precise content (Mitchell, 2004: 1; Rouse and Florian, 1997: 323; Hegarty, 2001: 243). For instance, some perspectives describe inclusive education as the possibility for students with disabilities and special educational needs to attend the local school with appropriate supplementary aids and services (Lipsky and Gartner, 1999). Other perspectives conceptualize inclusive education in terms of accommodating children's differences, without any clear reference either to additional or to specific learning support (Ainscow, 1991; Barton, 1993; Thomas and Loxley, 2001).

Ultimately, current perspectives on disability and special educational needs present artificially fixed and limited positions, which, while reflecting main theoretical frameworks in socio-medicine and disability studies (more on this in the next chapter), do not account for the complexity of disability, and special educational needs. These limits point in the direction of different frameworks, which could reconsider both disability and special educational needs and their relation to the design of schooling systems.

Concluding Comments

This chapter has analysed the wide and pervasive differences characterizing the educational provision for children with disabilities and special educational needs in England and in the United States. It has shown how these differences result in substantial inequalities in the resources and opportunities available to these children. Furthermore, the chapter has presented and addressed elements of dilemmas at the core of the theoretical debate on disability and special educational needs, while trying to outline the limitations of the perspectives in the field. The picture emerging from this analysis confirms the need for a rigorous normative framework. However, before outlining elements of this framework, I will analyse the main conceptions of disability and, more specifically, the social model of disability, theorized by disabled scholars and supported by disabled people's movements, and widely influential in educational debates, too. The next chapter addresses the social model of disability from a philosophical perspective.

Chapter 2

The Social Model of Disability:
A Philosophical Critique

Despite the presence of people with accredited[1] impairments at all times and in all societies, a systematized political and theoretical reflection on impairment and disability by disabled people and scholars has emerged only in the last three decades. This contribution has mainly originated from the disabled people's movements and in opposition to the prevailing analyses based on medical or mainstream sociological frameworks.

The social model of disability, theorized primarily in the UK by the disabled scholar Michael Oliver, is a fundamental contribution not only to the discussion about the complexity of disability, but also to our understandings of disability as informed by disabled people's reflection on their own experience. An expression of disabled people's activism, the social model has influenced the political positions of disability movements, both in the UK and, in different forms, in the USA.[2] The model has also significantly influenced the field of disability studies as well as educational perspectives on inclusion. The social model defines disability as the product of specific social and economic structures and aims at addressing issues of oppression and discrimination of disabled people, caused by institutional forms of exclusion and by cultural attitudes embedded in social practices.

This chapter presents a philosophical critical account of the social model of disability. As such, my critique is conducted at a theoretical and political level, and identifies and addresses the conceptual problems of the model, rather than the experiential ones connected to the personal dimension of disability. In so doing, however, it aims at providing an alternative awareness of conceptual issues, which could inform the reflection on the personal experience of disability. My critique is conducted at two levels, one internal and one external to the social model itself. At the internal level, I address one intrinsic problem of the model, related to its theoretical framework, whereas at the external level I critically analyse the definition of impairment and disability proposed by the social model and highlight some of its limits.

Finally, as my critique is conducted from outside of the disabled people's movements and the direct experience of disability, it can be considered fundamentally external to the social model. Disabled theorists maintain that this position implies a number of problems, which are mainly related to issues of emancipatory research and to the necessarily external point of view it advances on disability and impairment. While these possible problems cannot be either addressed or overcome here, I acknowledge their relevance and their importance for disabled people in this debate.

1. Individual and Social Models of Disability

Disabled people and scholars, and among them primarily Oliver, have firmly rejected the theoretical framework underpinning medical and mainstream sociological theories of disability, which inform the definitions of the *International Classification of Impairment, Disability and Handicaps*[3] proposed by the World Health Organization (WHO). This classification, based on the distinction between impairment, disability and handicap, defines impairment as referring to

> [an] abnormality in the structure of the functioning of the body, whether through disease or trauma; disability [as] referred to the restriction in ability to perform tasks . . . ; and handicap [as] referred to the social disadvantage that could be associated with either impairment and/or disability.
>
> (Bury, 1996: 19)

This classification establishes a causal relation between individual impairment, seen as departure from human normality, and disability, seen as restriction in abilities to perform tasks. Therefore, causes of disability are attributable primarily to biological individual conditions, which depart from normal human functionings and determine handicap in terms of disadvantage. These definitions not only promote an understanding of disability primarily as an individual condition – and hence the labelling of 'individual model' of disability to this view by disabled people's movements – but also establish a natural cause related to disability and the associated disadvantage.

An example may clarify this view. According to this model, a visual impairment, being a departure from standard human repertoire, determines a restriction of activity and, consequently, causes disability, which then may result in handicap. Consider, for instance, some forms of congenital blindness. While being a clear departure from human average functioning, this condition determines a restriction in some activities, in that visually impaired people are, for instance, unable to drive, and this inability constitutes a disability, which, in turn, produces a social disadvantage. The latter takes the form of the preclusion from performing certain tasks, from everyday ones, like driving the children to school on the way to work, to broader ones, like choosing an occupation, for instance any profession involving a driving activity.

The set of definitions presented by the WHO classification ultimately subsumes a conception of human diversity as polarized in the opposition between normality, or normal average human functioning, and abnormality as divergence from this standard. Within this view, furthermore, disability is referred to as caused by an individual 'abnormality', linked to certain inabilities in performing tasks and, therefore, to disadvantages. Here, the relational aspect of disability, both to individual impairment and to handicap, is fundamentally grounded on the causal link established between natural impairment and disability, and the resulting disadvantage is attributed primarily to a specific individual condition.

A contrasting view is the social model of disability, mainly theorized by Oliver and initially conceptualized with reference to the *Fundamental Principles of Disability*, a document produced by the Union of the Physically Impaired Against Segregation in 1976 (UPIAS, 1976: 3–4). The aims and the theoretical perspectives of the social model are already inscribed in its origin within the disabled people's movements and in its development as their model. Oliver maintains that the genesis and articulation of the model are a rejection of the fundamental concepts underpinning the individual model (Oliver, 1996: 32) and that the model itself, despite several critical approaches to it, both within the disabled people's movement and from external positions, is still valuable in representing the view of disabled people.[4] The social model aims primarily at deconstructing and countering the individual model of disability with a perspective situated in the direct experience and understanding of disability by disabled people themselves. It also aims to address issues of marginalization, oppression and discrimination while trying to denounce and remove the disabling barriers produced by hegemonic social and cultural institutions (Oliver, 1990: 11).

Oliver claims that the social model of disability does not constitute a social theory and should not be considered as such (Oliver, 1996: 41; and 2004: 24). Nevertheless, the model provides a definition of disability inscribed in a sociological perspective informed by historical materialism, which guides his critique of the individual model. Furthermore, Oliver is aware of the limits proper to any model and recognizes that the social model itself cannot explain all the aspects of disability. He maintains that 'models are merely ways to help us to better understand the world, or those bits of it under scrutiny. If we expect models to explain, rather than aid understanding, they are bound to be found wanting' (Oliver, 1996: 40).

In Oliver's account the social model 'does not deny the problem of disability but locates it squarely within society' (Oliver, 1996: 32) and its definition of impairment and disability is an articulation of this perspective. The definition of disability provided by the social model refers back to the distinction originally drawn by UPIAS as one of the *Fundamental Principles of Disability*. Basically, disability is seen as something imposed on disabled people on top of their impairment by oppressive and discriminating social and institutional structure.

Thus *impairment* is defined as

> lacking part or all of a limb, or having a defective limb, organ or mechanism of the body; and *disability* as the disadvantage or restriction of activity caused by a contemporary social organisation which takes no or little account of people who have physical impairments and thus excludes them from participation in the mainstream of social activities.
>
> (Oliver, 1996: 22; italics added)

Disability, therefore, is all that imposes restrictions on disabled people and as such, 'disablement is nothing to do with the body' (Oliver, 1996: 35). Disablement is instead caused by the oppression of social and economic structure on disabled individuals who are, consequently, an oppressed group in society.

Two main issues of this definition are fundamental in the debate between the individual and social models. The first is an issue of causality. Oliver, as do other disabled scholars (Oliver, 1996: 39), underlines the importance of breaking the causal link between impairment and disability in trying to overcome oppression. In other words, if the individual model sees disability as a restriction of activity caused by impairment, the social model aims at breaking this link by maintaining that disability is caused by institutional and social discrimination. It is therefore not ultimately ascribable to an individual condition. The second issue, intertwined with the previous one, is connected to the 'divide' between illness and disability. Oliver suggests that asserting the complete separateness of illness and impairment or, on the contrary, their contiguity, might have more to do with terminology than with conceptual differences. Furthermore, he concedes that there might be some similarities between the two conditions and that some disabled people may have illness at some points in their lives. However, he also argues that

Disability as a long-term social state is not treatable medically and is
not certainly curable. Hence many disabled people experience much
medical intervention as, at best, inappropriate, and, at worst, oppressive.

(Oliver, 1996: 36)

This understanding of impairment and disability is set within a materialist
analysis of the economic and social forces of capitalism, which are considered as producing precisely the individualization of disability and the
oppression of disabled people. Oliver articulates three main dimensions in
the onset of individual perspectives on disability and the exclusion of
disabled people: the use of ideological normative categories of normality
and abnormality, in turn connected to the rise and dominance of the
medical profession, and the production of the hegemony of disability.

According to Oliver, therefore, under capitalism disability became individual pathology, and hence abnormality, and disabled people became
controlled through exclusion and through the medicalizing of disability.
He maintains that the whole ideology of normality originated within the
rise of capitalism, with its needs for a workforce defined by people's
capacity to be usefully trained and productively employed. It is in this
process, Oliver argues, that the construction of 'able-bodied' and 'able-
minded' individuals is significant 'with their physical capabilities of
operating the new machines and their willingness to submit to the new
work disciplines imposed by the factory' (Oliver, 1990: 45–6). Consequently, those individuals who could not be included in the category of
ability identified in terms of productivity became identified as 'dis-abled'
people. This process is, in turn, connected with the rise of the medical profession, its dominance and its power of controlling through defining and
prescribing (Oliver, 1990: 54). Oliver maintains that the power exercised
by the medical profession is connected to the medicalization of disability,
its individualization as pathological condition and its construction as
personal tragedy, a personal deficit in need of medical intervention.
Finally, the individualization and medicalization of disability are the
constitutive elements of disability as hegemony, and hence as a socially
constructed category, produced by dominant groups in capitalist societies
and perpetuated by discriminating and oppressive social structures.

Against these positions, the social model argues for the full inclusion of
disabled people in society and for their complete acceptance as citizens
with equal entitlements, rights and responsibilities (Oliver, 1996: 152).
Within that, consequently, the model aims at addressing the issues of
pressing concerns to many disabled people: independent living, poverty,

education, employment, communication, transportation, accessing built environments and civil rights (Thomas, 2002: 38–57 and 44). Finally, while claiming to counter the hegemony of disability through the empowerment of disabled people and their movements, the social model seeks to reinstate its own validity (Oliver, 1996: 42; and 2004: 25, 30).

While keeping these aims firmly in sight, in the following sections I shall outline a philosophical critique of the social model of disability, which highlights some of its theoretical limits and questions its feasibility to inform social theories and policies.

2. Internal Criticism: A Critique of the Materialist Framework

The social model examines the relationship between disability and society and, in determining why disabled people became excluded from economical and social structure, places the answer in the emergence of industrial capitalism and its specific organization of economic activities (Thomas, 2002: 46). Some of the leading social model scholars have addressed the position of disabled people within the capitalist society through differently oriented materialist paradigms. Finkelstein (1980) and Stone (1985), for instance, have based their analysis of disability on, respectively, historical materialism and a Weberian notion of rationalization.

In outlining the social model of disability, as we have seen, Oliver resumes a materialist framework. His aim is to explain, rather than describe, what happened to disabled people with the rise of capitalism and his analysis is conducted through a materialist view, which implies that 'the production of the category disability is no different from the production of motor cars or hamburgers' (Oliver, 1996: 127). Underpinning this view is 'a framework, which suggests that it [disability] is culturally produced and socially structured. Central to this framework is the mode of production' (Oliver, 1990: 22). It is in the articulation between the primacy of modes of production and cultural products that Oliver sees the position of disabled people in society and the emergence of the category of disability in terms of the unproductive and the dependent.

Two main criticisms at two levels emerge from applying a materialist analysis to the position of disabled people in society. First, within the disability movement, disabled theorists have addressed the need to update the materialist framework 'to take theoretical account of contemporary developments in capitalist economic systems' (Thomas, 2002: 47). Furthermore, postmodernist and feminist approaches within disability studies have noticed the significance of culture and cultural processes in the creation of disability and have criticized social model scholars for having relegated this as a marginal aspect of disability (see, for instance, Corker, 1999; Shakespeare, 1997; and Thomas, 2002). Second, two main considerations arise from an external perspective, one that entails considerations of justice. At this external level, the first question is the appropriateness of using a materialist paradigm in addressing disability issues and, secondly and consequently, the problem of what concept of distributive justice would best serve the interests of disabled people and their claim for an inclusive society.

The debate within disability studies encompasses different perspectives. Thomas, herself a disabled theorist endorsing a specific view of the social model, has expressed the need

> to examine whether economic arrangements characteristic of a global capitalism, or hyper capitalism . . . [are] changing, perhaps transforming, the social position of people with impairments, for better or worse.
>
> (Thomas, 2002: 47)

She questions whether new technologies are means to inclusion or, on the contrary, to further exclusion of disabled people from the labour market. Certainly Thomas's claim is a well-founded one; if we limit the field of enquiry to developed countries, for instance, the dominant co-operative framework is increasingly characterized by sophisticated information technology. It is evident that, in such a setting, visually impaired people or people with impairments in fine motor skills of the hands would be excluded from accessing most computing technologies, if the latter were designed only in a standardized form aimed at non-impaired people (Buchanan *et al.*, 2000). Furthermore, much needs to be addressed in terms of the position of disabled people with respect to new forms of labour implying the use of such technology. Thomas's request for a reconsideration of the materialist paradigm opens up the possibility of questioning the assumption underpinning the social model. If the means of production are rapidly changing and, correlatively, so are the abilities required to being productive, then the question arises as to what the implications for disabled people are. Moreover, as Thomas herself has noticed, some forms of impairments would stand in a different relationship towards the means of production than others, thus causing changes in the presumed creation of the category of disability by economic arrangements.

A second internal criticism of the disability movement concerns challenging the 'materialist prioritization of the economic roots of disability and the contemporary operation of structural barriers in the wider social environment' (Thomas, 2002: 48). Increasingly, feminist and postmodernist scholars within disability studies have pointed out different dimensions to disability, which, they claim, have been downplayed by the materialist framework. Central to their critique is the role of culture and cultural processes in shaping society and, ultimately, disabled people's position in it. The concept of difference comes to be included in the disabled people's agenda, with reference not only to general cultural settings, but also to the specific culture of difference connected to gender, ethnicity, sexuality and type of impairment. Evidently, it is argued, deaf people experience a very different form of exclusion from the one created by economic structures. Theirs is mainly related to language, communication and cultural systems, rather than to traditional barriers identified by the social model (accessing built environments, for instance) (Thomas, 2002: 48).

More radical is the critique, advanced by postmodernist scholars within disability studies, of the materialist bases of the social model. In postmodernist accounts,

> current approaches to theorising disability as a form of social oppression and their relationship to disabled people's experiences are hampered by a modernist conceptual framework, which is increasingly at odds with the contemporary social world and with developments in theory-making as a whole.
>
> (Corker, 1999: 627)

According to this view, no social phenomenon, including impairment and disability, exists independently from the 'discursive practice' that has created it. Therefore, rather than focusing on material relations of power, the social model of disability should draw attention to the cultural processes that shape impairment and disability and build a model to counter 'the disability-engendering role played by cultural ideas, always negative, about people with impairment' (Thomas, 2002: 49). As Corker has noticed, '[I]n order to bring disability theory closer . . . to the politics of new social movements, . . . the conceptual underpinnings of theory must be broadened beyond their current focus on structures' (Corker, 1999: 627).

Much of this is still an ongoing debate within disability studies; nevertheless, the call for a framework different from the materialist one in analysing disability is increasingly emerging not only as a vital part of this internal debate, but also, as external criticisms show, as a necessary step towards disability theory achieving a more cohesive and coherent framework.

Let us now turn to an external critical perspective, which, while entailing considerations of justice, addresses the materialist framework of the social model through a two-fold argument. On the one hand, it addresses considerations of the type of co-operative framework that would achieve greater inclusion while, on the other hand, looking at what concept of justice, if any, would support it. In addressing these points it is worth recalling the requirement, at theoretical level, 'to compare actuality with actuality, and in our particular historical circumstances' (Rawls, 2001: 178) and the implications that each co-operative framework has on concepts of citizens, society and their relationship.

Let us begin from the actuality of the framework. There, while it is clear that by placing the mode of production as central to his framework, Oliver and the social model scholars can show the discrimination of capitalist societies, it is more questionable why this model, and the consequent social structure it advocates, would best represent and defend the position of disabled people in society. As the model is indeed based on modes of production and on concepts of productivity, it seems to rest on a scheme of redistribution of resources based on what has been termed 'justice as reciprocity' (Buchanan, 1990: 228). Thus, the model considers proper subjects of justice those with the capacity to engage productively in social co-operation, that is, the 'deserving ones'. However, as impairment might entail the possibility or impossibility of participating in social co-operation, and at different levels and degrees, the same framework presents problems to the achievement of inclusion. Furthermore, it is quite clear that disabled people and their movement rightly aim at their full recognition as citizens, as '[C]itizenship determines the conditions for full membership and inclusion in a society' (Rioux, 2002: 216). Disability theorists have criticized the assumption that citizenship rests on the capacity of an individual to be productive. Consequently, for the above reasons, it is not evident why and how the materialist framework would best represent these demands. A final comment relates to the actualization of the society advocated by the materialist paradigm informing the social model. Oliver concedes that the realization of the communist society is rather unlikely and recognizes a struggle between some conceptual and theoretical basis of the model and the development of effective political strategies for change. Furthermore, he maintains that different schemes of redistribution and related policies will only be possible if capitalism itself is transcended, which he recognizes is unlikely in the foreseeable future (Oliver, 1990: 97).

In trying to unlock these issues, let us bring the analysis back to the theorization of types of societies. Then, two considerations emerge. As

> . . . [A] full communist society seems to be one beyond justice in the sense that the circumstances that give rise to the problem of distributive justice are surpassed and citizens need not be, and are not, concerned with it in everyday life . . .
>
> (Rawls, 2001: 177)

then the case for aiming at a full communist society as the more inclusive one might have a major appeal. In that case, presumably, disabled people would not face the exclusion inscribed in the capitalist setting and their equal share of resources could be secured.

However, if general considerations of citizenship are brought in, together with the recognition of the fundamental importance of the fair values of political liberties and of the reasonable pluralism of democratic arrangements (all issues claimed by disabled people's movements, both theoretically and in actuality), then a different theory looks more accommodating to the demands of disabled people. Justice as fairness, in the specific, assumes that

> the principles and political virtues falling under justice will always play a role in public political life. The evanescence of justice, even of distributive justice, is not possible, nor, I think, is it desirable.
>
> (Rawls, 2001: 177)

It is within justice as fairness that a concept of subject-centred justice would find its space. In that, justice requires that 'basic rights to resources are grounded not in the individual strategic capacities, but rather in other features of the individual herself – her needs or non-strategic capacities' (Buchanan, 1990: 231). Furthermore, these rights are based on the equal moral status of persons or, in other words, on 'the preeminent moral values of persons' (Buchanan, 1990: 235). According to Buchanan, '[T]o acknowledge the fundamental moral equality of persons is, first of all, to accord a certain kind of being *full moral status*' (Buchanan, 1990: 234).

This view supports and implies the conviction that we owe something to each person, even to the more incapacitated to reciprocate, in virtue of their moral equal worth. Moreover, these considerations require a reconceptualization of social co-operation, in order to recognize that different co-operative arrangements, in demanding different capacities to participate in the co-operation itself, imply different possibilities to contribute, thus setting the level at which each individual will contribute. For these reasons, social co-operation has to be evaluated in terms of justice and since, as in the concept of justice as fairness, fairness may be seen as encompassing more than just fairness among contributors, then justice as fairness allows a wider morality of inclusion.

In light of these considerations, ultimately, justice as fairness suggests a better framework. It is more extensive, in terms of both equal liberties and just distribution of resources, than the materialist framework underpinning the social model, and presents, therefore, a theory open to a greater and more complete level of inclusion for disabled people in the social co-operative framework.[5]

The liberal philosophical framework upon which I have based my internal critique of the social model also informs my external critique of it in the next section.

3. External Critique

There are two premises to my external critique of the social model of disability. First, liberal egalitarian concepts underpin my critical approach and my implicit suggestion of a possible, alternative framework for the understanding of disability. Secondly, the aim of inclusion, in a way a re-definition of the inclusive society advocated by disabled scholars and disabled people's movements, is kept firmly in sight as a necessary and valuable element of a liberal egalitarian position. My critique addresses two main issues: the question of defining impairment and disability in light of causality, responsibility and moral agency and, secondly, the place and use of normative categories.

3.1. Defining Impairment and Disability: Causality, Responsibility and Agency

The question of defining impairment and disability occupies a central and foundational place in any analysis or theory of disability and in any account of inclusion. Any given definition subsumes theoretical perspectives while, on the other hand, implying differently oriented policies, too. The social model definitions refer to a precise understanding of disability and, in turn, support political actions and policies that are different from those suggested by the individual model. The slogan 'change society not the individual', if taken as a basis for social policies, has evidently very different implications from those of the idea that it is the individual who needs to be modified with respect to certain norms. Thus, the centrality of providing a theoretically coherent definition of impairment and disability becomes self-evident. However, the task at hand is not an easy one, in view of the complexity of disability and impairment and the different perspectives on their dimensions. Nevertheless, my critique will articulate two main issues related to the social model definition: the issue of causation, and that of responsibility and moral agency.

It is worth here revisiting briefly the definition proposed by the social model theorists. The social model asserts,

> it is not the individual's impairment which causes disability (Impairment → Disability), or which *is* the disability (Impairment = Disability), and it is not the difficulty of individual functioning with physical, sensory or intellectual impairment which generates the problem of disability.
>
> (Thomas, 1999: 14)

Disability is the result of social arrangements that, by placing and acting as barriers, work to restrict the activities of people with impairments. Disability, ultimately, is 'socially caused (Social barriers → Disability)' (Thomas, 1999: 14).

The claim by Oliver and other theorists within Disability Studies that disablement is a consequence of social oppression and that it 'is nothing to do with the body' (Oliver, 1996: 35) stems exactly from the definition above. Furthermore, Oliver argues,

> What is at stake here is the issue of causation, and whereas previous definitions were ultimately reducible to the individual and attributable to biological pathology, the above definition locates the causes of disability squarely within society and social organisations.
>
> (Oliver, 1990: 11)

While agreeing with Oliver that causation is fundamental here, I suggest that the advocated break-up of the causal link between impairment and disability, and the consequent causality established between society and disability, needs further considerations. One immediate intuition, the idea that impairment and disability are related, proves prima facie difficult to deny. As the medical sociologist Bury notices,

> Without some underlying initial problem, social responses would, so to speak, have nothing to respond to. If labelling theory is invoked, some form of 'primary deviation' is necessary, if societal reactions are to have any meaning.
>
> (Bury, 1996: 30)

In other words, it would appear difficult to understand why society would oppress and discriminate against some individuals, if there were no relation at all with a, perhaps wrongly, perceived initial state which they share. True, this needn't be a causal relation, but it does not exclude it, either.

A major criticism that scholars within disability studies have raised of the social model is that is does not give any account of the element of impairment. French, among others, has convincingly described how her visual impairment imposes social restrictions, like not recognizing people or not reading social and non-verbal languages in social interactions, restrictions that are unaccounted for by the social model (Oliver, 1996: 37; see also French, 1993). Moreover, disability feminist scholars like Morris (1991), Thomas (1999) and Wendell (1996) have reconsidered impairment while accepting, in different degrees, the basic assumptions of the model. Thomas, for instance, maintains that

> In the everyday lives of disabled people there is a melding of the accumulated consequences of coming up against social barriers which restrict what one can do, of having to deal with emotional and psychological consequences of other people's reactions to the way we look or behave, as well as the wider cultural representations of being impaired, and (for many) of the difficulties of living with pain, discomfort, fatigue, limited functioning and other impairment effects.
>
> (Thomas, 1999: 81)

In her account of the social model, therefore, Thomas reinstates impairment considered as impairment effects and claims that the personal experience of living with disability and impairment and their interaction should be on the disability study agenda (Thomas, 1999: 125).

Why is impairment an important element? I suggest a hypothetical scenario related to Oliver's claim on social oppression as causing disablement and his decisive separation between impairment and disability. Thus, if we imagine a society where barriers and discrimination against disabled people were totally overcome and therefore non-existent, how would the experience of impaired people be configured? Would such a society imply that French's impairment would not be related at all to any restrictions in communication? I find it difficult to think of how French could actually overcome her restriction of activity, that is, recognizing non-verbal cues, if not by overcoming her impairment altogether. So, in my understanding, French would not be oppressed, as we have imagined that oppression has indeed disappeared, but her restriction of activity, her inability to read non-verbal messages would still be there. We might, in fact, extend the hypothesis so as to think that somehow, people would all be able to interact at different levels, verbal and non-verbal, thus allowing for French to communicate without experiencing any difference. Still, French would not be able to relate to other people through non-verbal language, unless she could overcome her impairment. Finally, even if oppression and discrimination were eliminated, where would the pain, the discomfort and the fatigue, acknowledged by Thomas as impairment effects, stand, according to social modellists? And how would they relate to restrictions of activities?

Disabled scholars have certainly considered the importance of analysing impairment as well as its effects, and, in light of that, they have proposed the theorization of a 'sociology of impairment' to complement their 'sociology of disability' (Oliver, 1996: 42). The framework would then be configured as follows. Disablement would be all that is referred to the systematic exclusion of impaired people from society, and consequently, disability would be all restrictions of activity caused by disabling arrangements. Impairments would have certain effects, among them restriction of activities or pain and discomfort, but that would be a completely separate matter from disability. Hence the need to define the latter 'impairment effects' and provide a sociology of impairment.

In my opinion, rather than supplementing one theory by another, a reconsideration of some problematic elements within the first theory would be preferable. However, let us proceed with the analysis of impairment as conducted by the disabled scholar Abberley, since his position, as does the social model, raises further theoretical issues in the articulation between impairment, disability and society.

Abberley has long claimed that social 'modellists' should not have left the analysis of impairment to biological theories and should have configured, instead, a social model of impairment (Thomas, 1999: 52). In his theory of the social origin of impairment and oppression, Abberley claims that, for the vast majority of the world's disabled people, 'impairment is very clearly primarily the consequence of social and political factors, not an unavoidable "fact of nature"' (Abberley, 1987: 11).

This claim is certainly well founded in some of the cases Abberley quotes, which are related to impairments as results of wars, or famine, or poverty, or hazardous occupations. Where he seems to conclude with arguable generalizations, however, is when he suggests that all impairments are socially caused. He provides, for instance, the example of the degenerative process connected to ostheo arthritis. In response, the claim that impairment is socially constructed can be partially accepted if modified into the statement that *some* impairments, for *some* individuals, *in some specific* circumstances can have social components. The degenerative process of arthritis when linked to specific occupations can certainly be considered as having a social element, but that does not extend to all cases and not to all people. Some people do develop arthritis independently from occupations or without having being exposed to the working conditions considered the social causes of the impairment.

Abberley presents a further argument in his analysis of impairment that may result from hereditary factors or from injury at birth (Abberley, 1987: 12). His example draws from the case of Phenilketonuria [PKU], a disorder associated with the hereditary inability to metabolize the amino-acid phenylanine, which, if undetected at birth, causes mental retardation. In Abberley's explanation, if prior to the detection and cure of the disorder it was reasonable to characterize it as congenital, it is now equally reasonable to characterize it as socially determined, as the effects of it are now emerging only in those settings in which the adequate detecting tests are not conducted. Consequently, Abberley concludes that

> It would thus seem impossible to adequately draw a dividing line between genetic and environmental, and thus ultimately social, factors. Rather, the designation of genetic factors as primarily causative is itself a judgement determined by knowledge, interest and intention, in other words, a political judgement.
>
> (Abberley, 1987: 12)

The claim of the difficulty of marking a clear divide between genetic and environmental origins for some traits seems well founded and points to the need to address empirically the fundamental question of how intrinsic features of an individual interact with features of the social environment to produce impairment and, in some cases, disability (Bickenbach *et al.*, 1999: 1174). More arguable, though, is the statement that PKU is, therefore, a socially caused impairment. In my understanding of the contention, if every child at birth presented PKU as a congenital character, and only some children were to be treated, it would certainly be true that, for those who did not receive any tests or treatment, and only for those, the origin of the impairment would rest on certain biological traits, but aggravated by a clear social component. However, as not all children present the congenital trait of Phenilketonuria, but only some and in a hereditary and therefore predictable way, Abberley's conclusion of its social cause is difficult to accept.

My questioning of the definition of impairment and disability provided by the social model does not aim at simply reintroducing a linear causal link between impairment and disability and in all cases. If we accept that society discriminates against impaired people, then we can also understand the claim of the disablement structure of society. What I hold, ultimately, is that there certainly is a causal relation between oppression and disability, when society plays a strong role in excluding and marginalizing impaired people. But in maintaining that disability is squarely socially caused, the social model theorists are over-socializing their position. Their model, then, as we have seen, needs clarifications and extensions (Bury, 2000; and Thomas, 2002: 44).

More specifically, the social model overlooks the impairment effects, in terms of their restriction of activities or the possible inabilities to perform different functions. In so doing, it downplays the importance of the relational nature of impairment, disability, and society.[6] Moreover, in asserting the total separation between impairment and disability, it opens up the chance of a 'proliferation' of terms other than disabilities, to denote inability or being unable to do things, which, if politically correct, appears less justified theoretically. One example to illustrate this position is related to some forms of congenital blindness, which, for instance, prevent people from performing certain actions, like driving a car. This form of impairment, which can be considered a clear inability and a disability if referred to driving (at present society is structured to have sighted drivers only), is certainly not a cause of inability or disability in many other possible activities, like enjoying music or cooking or acting as a state minister. It is now clearer, therefore, why some disabled scholars have voiced the need to reconsider impairment, and why medical sociologists have pointed at the relational aspect of some impairment with illness and disability. These considerations highlight the need for a different framework, providing a more coherent basis for the understanding of impairment, disability, society and their reciprocal implications. I suggest that a philosophical perspective based specifically on Amartya Sen's capability approach could take these issues in fruitful directions, and I shall develop this view in the following chapters. In particular, as we shall see, Sen's concepts of functionings and capability (opportunities for functionings), and the centrality of human diversity in his analysis, promote a relational view of disability as emerging from the interaction of individual and social elements, and fundamentally inscribed in an ethical framework aimed at equality.

A final critical point, on the relation between impairment, disability and society, concerns moral and social responsibility. In maintaining that disability is socially caused, the social model of disability attributes the responsibility of disablement completely to society. In his development of a social understanding of impairment, Abberley argues that impairment is socially caused; therefore asserting that society is responsible also for the impairment it produces. However, in light of the previous critical points and although the issue of responsibility is very complex, a few considerations emerge. First, if society causes discrimination, either politically or economically, and, therefore, restriction of activity or participation, then society is responsible for the disablement in an unacceptable way. The same applies when society causes impairment, as a consequence of war, for instance. But there are circumstances when impairment and its effects do not stem from social causes and many of the examples above have illustrated this claim. There are, consequently, different considerations related to responsibility with respect to impairment. How could a congenital impairment unrelated to any endemic condition be considered society's responsibility? Moreover, even if one fully endorsed the social model position, it would be quite problematical to assert how society could be held responsible in the case of disablement connected to the activity of driving by a person visually impaired owing to congenital blindness. Finally, there are impairments that are a consequence of a person's agency, in other words of her particular actions or activities, some of which may well be highly risky activities, voluntarily undertaken. When impairment arises from a hang-gliding accident, to mention an extreme case, considerations of society's responsibility are difficult to sustain. In that case, when the sport has been voluntarily chosen with full awareness of its potential risks, when all that could have been done to prevent the accident has been done and when rescue has been provided, where should society's responsibility be placed?

Here again, the social model of disability shows the element of over-socialization and improper generalization seen in the causal link established between society and disability, thus reconfirming the internal limitations highlighted so far.

3.2. Normality and Difference

The critique of the category of normality in terms of any human average functioning is a relevant aspect of the social model of disability. Social model theorists frame their position in a materialist approach that considers also postmodernist influences, mainly related to binary distinctions produced by the power/knowledge process (Thomas, 1999: 117) and to the role of health care systems in individual and social control (Oliver, 1996: 108).

'Normality', writes Oliver, 'is a construct imposed on a reality where there is only difference' (Oliver, 1996: 88) and the whole ideology of normal function and able-bodiedness stems from the capitalistic forces structuring society and controlling it through its institutions. Social model theorists oppose any idea of normality seen as ideologically constructed in order to control and exclude disabled people from the structure of a society that has no interest in accommodating them. Connected to the rejection of the concept of normality is the critical stand against issues of cure and rehabilitation, seen as oppressive powers used to convert created, individual, pathological states back into idealized states of normality.

My critique of this approach will first look at the internal debate within disability studies and then proceed to considerations drawn in from different frameworks.

Although disabled people's movements and social model theorists alike share the critical rejection of any ideal concept of normality, the debate within disability studies sees different positions on the sameness/difference binary and on the materialist/postmodernist approach. Analyses of the question of social difference by feminist disability scholars have played a central role in criticizing and reconsidering the social model's original rejection of normality and in reintroducing issues of difference into the debate. Criticisms have pointed out how the social model excludes or marginalizes differences associated with particular groups of disabled people, for instance women and ethnic minorities, and how the model itself does not represent the interests of people who have particular forms of impairments, for example learning difficulties or mental illnesses (Thomas, 1999: 101).

Some positions, however, expand this point further and aim at reconsidering the biological differences which have provided the basis for the discrimination between disabled and non-disabled people. Disability feminist scholars like Wendell (1996) and Morris (1991), for instance, while being well aware of the cultural and social meanings associated with 'normality' and 'abnormality' and their parallel postmodernist deconstructions, nevertheless reintroduce in their analysis elements related to the biological domain. Let us consider them briefly.

Wendell's approach to bodily differences 'appears to accept that there are biological differences which really do set some bodies apart from others' (Thomas, 1999: 105) and that there are specific experience and knowledge arising from these differences. According to Wendell, moreover,

> it would be cruel, as well as a distortion of people's lives, to erase or
> ignore the everyday, practical, experienced limitations of people's

disabilities [restrictions of activity] simply because we recognise that
human bodies and their varied conditions are both changeable and
highly interpreted.

(Wendell, quoted in Thomas, 1999: 106)

Wendell points to the valuable addition to knowledge and experience that
these differences bring about and suggests how, while setting some people
apart from others, these elements enrich and expand our culture. Similarly, Morris argues that what prevents a value-free use of the word
'normal', in terms of 'that which is common', is the high prejudice associated with the recognition of difference in terms of all that is undesirable,
wrong, not admirable, in general negative (Morris, 1991: 15). This has led
to the denial of difference in an attempt to overcome discrimination.
Nevertheless, Morris argues further that

we *are* different. We reject the meanings that the non-disabled world
attaches to disability but we do not reject the differences which are
such an important part of our identities.

(Morris, 1991: 17)

Morris mentions physical and intellectual characteristics that distinguish
disabled people's experience from that of the majority of the population
and the different needs arising from these differences. Moreover, she
claims that assumptions of disabled people's desire to be or become
normal are not only utterly wrong, but also one of the main sources of
oppression for disabled people themselves. Finally, in asserting the importance of disability and illness as part of human experience, as in Wendell's
position, Morris reclaims the value of disability and the celebration of
differences (Morris, 1991: 38).

Despite its important internal articulation, the debate within disability
studies on issues of normality and difference can be subsumed in the advocated 'celebration of differences' as the guiding value for an inclusive
society. However, even if at a prima facie moral level, accepting the
celebration of differences appears highly valuable, within a more critical
analysis this position shows its difficulties.

In dealing with the issue of normality, the social theory of disability faces
two main limits. First, it seems to perfectly deconstruct the ideology of
normality and its social components, without being able, however, to
provide a model or a different scheme for the evaluation of functioning
and its implications. This guides us to the second problem, namely that, in
advocating the celebration of differences, disabled scholars appear to lose

sight theoretically of the implications of their own claims, when referred to their political aims, that is, for instance, their demands for independent living and personal allowances. Why is this?

The rejection of normality both as a normative and descriptive concept is certainly important in counteracting its negative and discriminatory connotations. However, this complete unspecified rejection of a guiding concept, if applied consistently, leads to some untenable conclusions, both theoretically and practically. If we deny any reference to average, thus typical human functioning, how would we evaluate impairment and disability? Would any functioning or non-functioning be considered equally in a social theory of disability? What could then constitute impairment/disability? What non-impairment? Paradoxically, the social model of disability could be brought to its knees by saying that if there is no average, typical functioning, there is not non-average or non-typical functioning, therefore impairment and disability do not exist.

Secondly, how can we celebrate differences and then distribute resources accordingly? Against which principle should resources be devoted to a wheelchair user as compared to a 'non-disabled' person? Should we then say that being different is the guiding principle? And is this a satisfactory principle? Finally, the rejection of descriptive meanings of average functioning could indeed end up creating another category, that of difference, which, ultimately, appears more problematic and less coherent with the very aims of disabled people's movements. To illustrate this point through an example, consider the claims of independent living and the demand for personal assistance provided and supplied to disabled people as a matter of right. How could we sustain those claims while at the same time negating a departure from typical functioning in the case of some impairment and disability? True, each person experiences some need of assistance in different forms and at different points in their lives, but there are impairment effects that lead some people to a more significant and continued use of personal assistance or mobility aids than others. Ultimately, in my opinion, the total rejection of any descriptive idea of typical or average, and either the lack of a reference concept or its substitution with an unspecified notion of difference, show not only theoretical and political limitations, but perhaps also a mismatch between the theoretical basis of the social model and some of its practical, political aims.

Recent perspectives in bioethics and the philosophy of medicine have proposed more articulated and justified views of the rejection of normality as social construction in relation to disability. Anita Silvers (1998), for instance, has addressed the use of the concept of normal species functioning in matters of health care justice. In endorsing the social model of disability, Silvers critiques the concept of normal species functioning as a parameter for determining disease and disability as departure from it, and questions the related policies in health care that promote restoring predetermined 'normal' levels and modes of functioning. She rejects 'the assumption that normal functioning is natural and thereby neutral, and . . . the idea that the criteria for determining what functioning is normal are biological rather than social' (1998: 99). Silvers maintains that concepts of normality are meaningless in the light of the vast differences among people and argues that 'the idea, rather than the reality, of non-normal functioning has become the signifier of whether someone is equally well off, or is advantaged in comparison to others' (1998: 115). 'It is far from clear', she insists, 'that deviations from normal functioning mean either lowered productivity or decreased quality of life' (1998: 118) and she argues that alternative and atypical modes of functioning should be considered equivalent and as effective as the so-called normal species functioning in evaluating people's relative positions. This critique of the concept of normal species functioning is interrelated to a rejection of the 'normalization' assumptions underpinning perspectives in health care based on liberal political theory.

Silvers' discussion of the idea of normality and normal species functioning presents a carefully articulated view that accounts both for those disabilities that are the result of unjust social structures, and those disabling conditions that are neither caused nor addressed by changes in social arrangements. Silvers points in the direction of understanding disability in terms of atypical modes of functioning, some of which can achieve exactly the same level of functionality as typical ones. She also identifies a group of disabled people with needs that are not socially constructed, thus responding to more complex forms of impairments and disabilities.[7] Further, this view seems also to leave open the possibility of considering impairment, at least descriptively, as departure from an average condition, without encountering the problems that beset less articulated views of the social model of disability. However, despite these significant insights, more needs to be said in order to provide a theoretically unified understanding of the relation between impairment and disability and the design of social and institutional schemes, while identifying what kind of difference is disability and what is its weight in designing just social arrangements.

Concluding Comments

The social model is a fundamental contribution to our knowledge and understanding of impairment and disability as provided by disabled scholars, disabled people and their movements. Trying to engage with the complex debate in disability studies, in this chapter I have presented a philosophical critique of the social model, articulated in an internal critique of the materialist framework underpinning it, and in an external critique addressing issues of definition, causality and responsibility as well as normality and difference. My analysis has outlined three main limits of the social model, related to its over-socialization of aspects of impairments and disability, the overlooking of effects of impairment and the rejection of the concept of normality in the sense of average, typical human functioning, which, although understandable and justified in deconstructing oppression, can theoretically lead to unintended consequences. As a concluding note I suggest that, despite its internal limits, the social model of disability nevertheless acts as a powerful and important corrective to our understanding of disability, to simplistic views on the experience of disability and, more importantly, to the oppressive nature of some social arrangements. This is the actual powerful core value of the model, its constant reminder to face issues of inclusion as fundamental moral issues.

In the next chapter, I address some educational perspectives on inclusion based upon, or influenced by, the social model of disability. While highlighting the essential contribution of the social model to educational theory and policy, the chapter critically examines some of the tensions and problems that beset educational perspectives unilaterally based on the model.

Chapter 3

The Social Model of Disability and Inclusive Education

The notion of inclusion is currently shaping the educational debate, and specifically in relation to students with disabilities and special educational needs. Complex and contentious at the same time, the concept of inclusion is underpinned by different educational and political perspectives. Its connection to the idea of an inclusive society, which demands the full participation and equal recognition of all people and groups in society, has informed the more political orientation of perspectives of inclusive education. However, at the same time it has formed the basis for 'bold moral and political rhetoric' used by politicians and bureaucrats to different purposes in different countries (Clough and Corbett, 2000: 6).

The idea of inclusion in education has developed alongside changes in special education, but also, and more fundamentally, in opposition to the theory and practice of special education itself. As I have outlined in more detail in Chapter 1, in the last fifty years special education in Western countries has changed considerably. This change has taken place in three main phases: from initial perspectives that sought to educate children with disabilities and special educational needs in segregated institutions, through an integrationist phase, which supported the education of these children in mainstream schools, until the more recent emergence of policies of inclusive education. This development in the provision of special education has been accompanied by a theoretical shift, from positions based entirely on medical definitions of disability and learning difficulties, thus centred on the individual child seen as having some 'deficiencies', to positions analysing the limitations of school contexts and educational practices, through to the more recent understanding of disability and special educational needs as wholly socially constructed.

The theoretical underpinnings of ideas of inclusive education reflect their developments by professionals working in special education, as well as the variety of approaches and different disciplines that have contributed to their conceptualization. Psycho-medical disciplines, sociology of education, curricular approaches and school improvement strategies and, lately, the area of disability studies have all provided different theoretical insights into the field of inclusive education. More recently, as Armstrong and Barton notice, disciplines like linguistic and discourse analysis, as well as media studies, have provided new and interesting perspectives (2007: 12). While all these perspectives represent fundamental aspects of the debate, my analysis in this chapter will intentionally focus only on the contribution from positions informed by disability studies. More specifically, it will focus on the theoretical convergence of the social model of disability with sociological perspectives on inclusive education, and on some of their common theoretical and political claims. The aim of my analysis is to show how the same theoretical limits identified in the social model of disability constitute fundamental limits to a coherent theory of inclusive education, too.

This chapter is organized in three sections. The first concerns the conception of inclusive education presented by sociological perspectives. The second section briefly outlines the political claims underpinning this conception of inclusion, while the third and final part presents elements of a philosophical critique of sociological perspectives in inclusive education. My critique highlights how these perspectives operate in the absence of a coherent theoretical and normative framework, and are consequently unable to sustain the force of their claim for equal consideration and equal provision for children with disabilities and special educational needs.

1. Inclusive Education: A Process Towards an Inclusive Society

According to perspectives in sociology of education, inclusion in education represents a fundamental challenge to existing theories and practices, from special needs education to the broader context of general education. Inclusive education is directly linked to the idea of an inclusive society and the role of education is seen as fundamental to that achievement. Barton maintains that

> Inclusive education is not an end in itself, it is a means to an end, that of establishing an inclusive society. Thus, the notion of inclusivity is a radical one in that it places the welfare of *all* citizens at the centre of consideration.
>
> (Barton, 1998: 84)

And furthermore,

> [I]nclusion is a process. Inclusive education is not merely about pro-
> viding access into mainstream school for pupils who have previously
> been excluded. It is not about closing down an unacceptable system of
> segregated provision and dumping those pupils in an unchanged
> mainstream system. Existing school systems in terms of physical
> factors, curriculum aspects, teaching expectations and styles, leader-
> ship roles, will have to change. This is because inclusive education is
> about the participation of *all* children and young people and the
> removal of *all* forms of exclusionary practice.
>
> (Barton, 1998: 84–5)

This conception of inclusive education directly and immediately relates it
to perspectives in disability studies and, specifically, to the social model of
disability. The adoption of the social model framework, with its emphasis
on disablement as primarily caused by social structures and institutions, is
evident in the definition of 'inclusivity' as the process of removal of all
exclusionary and disabling barriers in education, and in the fundamental
role accorded to the latter in the achievement of an inclusive society.

Two further positions, moreover, are theoretically related to the framework of the social model of disability. The first is the shift from a perspective that individualizes the problem of disability and special educational
needs to a view that locates the difficulty or deficit within social institutions,
therefore within individual schools and education systems more generally.
The second position, related to the first one, conceptualizes the social construction of special educational needs operated by education and schooling structures. Some sociologists of education claim that policies and
school settings, in imposing the implementation of specific structures, curricula and standards of achievements, act as disabling barriers, excluding
de facto a wide number of children from its supposed mainstream. According to these positions, therefore, the question to be asked is why schools fail
to teach so many pupils successfully. Furthermore, it is through these positions that issues of inclusive education widen from considerations referred
primarily to children with disabilities and special educational needs to a
more general perspective that encompasses a response to pupils' diversity
in an inclusionary way.[1] Finally, these positions also situate inclusive education in a larger political movement, which, while considering technical
issues as marginal, primarily questions the organization of society and
declares the celebration of differences as its fundamental political aim. But
let us analyse these two positions in more detail.

The first concept relates inclusive education to the social models'
critique of the psycho-medical approach. According to sociological views

special education originated precisely from the development of the 'pathology of difference' within medical and psychological disciplines (Clough and Corbett, 2000: 11). Thus, medical and psychological views applied to education locate the supposed deficit related to a difficulty within the individual child, and suggest a compensatory model based on medical and clinical intervention. Reflected in educational theories, this position implies the essentialist view that individuals possess inherent characteristics, thus leading to definitions in terms of the grade of intelligence, or ability or skills and general capacity proper to the individual child, without any further consideration for methods of assessments, let alone elements of the wider social and educational context. Although this medical approach has pervasively informed special education and its effects are still currently relevant, a clear example of it relates to the segregationist phase of special education. During that phase children were assessed by clinically based procedures and medically categorized. This process of categorization, while 'pathologizing' pupils' responses, introduced also the discriminatory categories of normality and abnormality. Pupils identified as abnormal were therefore placed in segregated institutions and provided with a special education.

Tomlinson (1982: 21) has pointed out how medical and psychological perspectives in special education can actually become deterministic, especially if the emphasis is placed on individual causation. Moreover, the same author has addressed the problems posed by medical and psychological definitions used to special education purposes, in the 'conflation' between normative and non-normative conditions. Tomlinson adopts here a 'positivistic' account of the concepts of normative and non-normative situations. Thus, normative conditions are seen as related to some clearly identifiable physical and biological states. Non-normative conditions refer instead to those situations that are not directly related to medical or biological factors. According to Tomlinson, if the application of medical definitions is generally unanimous in the case of physical disabilities, the situation is rather more complex and certainly socially constructed in the case of supposed learning disabilities. Thus, for instance, if deafness and cerebral palsy are categories normatively agreed upon by professionals and readily applied to educational settings, categories used to classify learning difficulties do not have a normative status, in that they do not relate clearly to biological or medical conditions (as, for instance, categories like maladjustment or educational subnormality), and are therefore subject to the structural and cultural factors proper to social interpretation. This, in turn, is due to the fact that '[T]here are no adequate measuring instruments or agreed criteria in the social world to decide upon these particular categories, whether descriptive or statutory' (1982: 65.) Moreover, this social interpretation of non-normative conditions is reflected in the historical changes both in the descriptors and the use of these categories.

Tomlinson claims that psychological and mental testing and, later on, the complex and contentious debate on IQ[2] are significant examples of the social element of categories used to classify learning disabilities. When first established at the beginning of the last century, mental testing procedures, while labelling some children as abnormal or educationally subnormal, had the main purpose of separating and removing large numbers of children from normal schooling and of placing them in special educational settings. Data from that period show, however, that in England the vast majority of children identified as abnormal or uneducable were mainly from very poor social and economic backgrounds, if not entirely from the working classes. Later on, the sets of criteria applied became more complex. A child could be defined as educationally 'backward' but with a high or low IQ; 'he or she could be ESN (*educationally subnormal*) without requiring special schooling, or could be of above average ability and still require special schooling' (Tomlinson, 1982: 63). Still further on, in the early 1970s, psychologists started to rely less on IQ testing and to apply instead specific sub-tests in order to provide educational programmes that could reinforce the defined cognitive disability and compensate for the assessed deficit.

Some sociologists of education provide these examples to show the individualization and 'pathologization' of disability as consequences of medical models applied to education. Moreover, these examples are used to illustrate the social construction of the presumed deficit and disability, thus relating the idea of inclusive education to the social model of disability. These sociologists of education critically address the exclusion and marginalization of children from mainstream schooling through their categorization as educationally abnormal and, therefore, uneducable. They further link this process, both historically and sociologically, to the emergence of industrial societies with their requirements in terms of mass schooling and educated workforce. Furthermore, according to these perspectives, this process is also related to the empowerment of medical and educational professionals. On the one hand, therefore, special institutions were created to accommodate the children categorized as different and difficult to educate in mainstream schooling, while, on the other hand, powerful groups in society determined, through classifications and institutionalization, the abnormal child as opposed to the normally able one. Thus, according to Tomlinson,

[S]ociologically, the history of special education must be viewed in terms of the benefits it brought for a developing industrial society, the benefits for the normal mass education system of a 'special' sub-system of education, and the benefits that medical, psychological, educational and other personnel derived from encouraging new areas of professional expertise.

(Tomlinson, 1982: 29)

These themes relate consistently to the critical analysis of the medical model provided by the social model of disability, in that they see the relation of power between social groups and the dominant, hegemonic imposition of some groups on others, in this case medical and educational professionals on parents and their children. In Corbett and Slee's words, 'the traditional special education discourse is one in which the voices of the profession dominate' (Corbett and Slee, 2000: 135).

These perspectives, however, have emphasized how the social construction of special educational needs operates not only through medical classifications, but also by specific educational structures, in terms of policy, curricular approaches and cultural and relational aspects proper to the learning process and the school environment. Thus, curricular perspectives in inclusive education, for instance, can help illustrate the claim of the social construction of special needs more concretely. Clough and Corbett (2000), as well as Armstrong (1998), have pointed out how the curriculum as a 'cultural scheme' (Clough and Corbett, 2000: 18) and as 'concerned with the ways in which different kinds of knowledge and the values which underpin them are transmitted by schools' (Armstrong, 1998: 56) can actually either sustain and promote differences between pupils or, instead, produce students who fail. According to some curricular perspectives, therefore, the elevation of particular kinds of knowledge as the main aspect of a curriculum ends up producing unsuccessful students, and therefore students with different or special needs. Clough argues, for instance, that the elevation of the cognitive-intellectual domain above all the others, in 'valuing and rewarding a particular form of thinking, typically provides the basis for defining the students with learning difficulties' (Clough, 1998: 7). This perspective aims at showing how a curriculum based uniquely on abstract forms of knowledge would discriminate between students in a different way and to a different degree from that associated to a broader curriculum, one including, for instance, aesthetic-creative or physical-motor domains as well.

Consequently, by contrast to psycho-medical positions and in agreement with social model proponents, social perspectives on inclusive education see the category of special educational needs as the product of educational processes implying exclusionary practices and oppressive structures. The key concept at play here is not the difference in individual ability, but the ability of the school system and of the single school to respond to individual differences. More specifically, the key concept is the 'celebration of difference' since, according to Barton,

> [I]nclusive education is thus about responding to diversity, it is about listening to unfamiliar voices, being open and empowering all members. It is about learning to live with one another. The question of listening is a particularly important issue when applied to individuals and groups who have had their voice marginalised . . . Thus, the importance of listening to disabled pupils is crucial.
>
> (Barton, 1998: 85)

This last point refers in turn to the importance of creating inclusive learning, based on listening to the voices and the requirements of the individuals while adapting educational institutions to the demands posed by different learners. Cole endorses this position and suggests the importance of listening to mothers' voices and of positive and dialogical relationships between professionals, children and their families (Cole, 2005).

Thus, the principles informing inclusive education give way to a certain 'educational culture' of inclusive schooling (Corbett and Slee, 2000: 143), which is expressed through curriculum, pedagogy and through the organizational structures and the ethos of the institution. Inclusive schooling, consequently, demands the reconstruction of schooling in terms of

> different approaches to classroom organisation, [. . .] the way teaching occurs, to the development of curriculum content and materials, to assessment and reporting to the processes of school and community interaction and decision making.
>
> (Corbett and Slee, 2000: 144)

The educational culture enacting inclusive education, moreover, does not take place in a policy vacuum. Inclusive education begins from the context of policy, in that it does imply addressing the whole educational and schooling culture through the policy underlying it. Inclusive education is about a change in the ethos informing educational policies and, therefore, the schools' culture (Oliver, 1996: 87).

This very last point relates to the more political aim of sociological perspectives in inclusive education, that of contributing to the realization of an inclusive society, which values differences. As Armstrong *et al.* say,

> Our own starting point is that inclusive education is inextricably linked to a political critique of social values and practices and the structures and institutions which they support. The analysis of 'value' must explicate the role of education in the production and reproduction of different values . . . In struggling for the implementation of inclusive practice we are engaging in a political process of transformation.
>
> (Armstrong *et al.*, 2000: 11)

And it is to the political dimension of these perspectives that I shall now turn my analysis.

2. Inclusive Education: Rights, Entitlements and Opportunities

Inclusive education is primarily political as it is concerned with the inclusion of all citizens in a participatory democracy (Armstrong *et al.*, 2000; Barton in Clough and Corbett, 2000: 53). Its political dimension stems both from its commitment against exclusionary policies and practices and from its theoretical convergence with the social model of disability and the political struggles of disabled people's movements.

The first, important element of this political aspect consists in the challenge to the social and educational conditions that shape difference as disadvantage and abnormality, and combine to generate policies and practices of exclusion. It also consists in understanding and overcoming oppressive power relations, which, through the categorization by professionals, act to relegate disabled people's identities to the ideology of needs and care. Furthermore, it consists in critically engaging current practices and perspectives with the awareness that their institutional settings are neither neutral nor a-historical. Finally, this political dimension acts against any form of individualization of disability or special educational needs, while challenging the alleged expertise of professionals. In so doing, the political struggle of inclusive education aims at reinstating the voices of disabled people and disabled children into territories where they have been historically excluded (see Clough and Corbett, 2000; and Armstrong *et al.*, 2000.

These elements of a politics of inclusive education connect issues of inclusion in education to the political struggle of disabled people's movements, identified as part of the new social movements, whose political aim is that differences should be respected and promoted. These elements, furthermore, contribute to the outlining of inclusion in terms of entitlements of disabled people and disabled children to the benefits and opportunities entailed by rights of citizenship.

Inclusive education as a matter of rights, and, specifically, human rights, is central to the debate on inclusion. Barton, for instance, starts his challenging questions for a project of inclusive education by asking precisely: 'In what ways is inclusive education a human rights issue?' (Barton, 1998: 86). Subsumed in this question is a complex political view characterized principally by theoretical positions that link human rights issues to a project of social justice understood in terms of celebration of differences, thus in the participation of all groups in the process of democracy. In other words, this view assumes the politics of difference as central to its project, while seeing difference in terms of group differences.

Moreover, the political dimension advocated by sociological views of inclusive education, in embracing the stand of disabled people's movements, identifies the struggle for inclusion in terms of the critique and the removal of the exclusionary barriers experienced by disabled people in society, as well as by disabled pupils in schools. Here is where the alternative understanding of disability and of special educational needs comes in, in the uncovering of the social origins of disability operated by disabling structures: a process, which, in turn, acts as a starting point for the struggle for the recognition of disabled people's and children's human rights.

These positions in inclusive education insist on the fundamental importance of understanding human rights in their precise political dimension, thus related to the specific historical and social situation experienced by disabled people and children. In highlighting the concrete 'situatedness' of human rights issues, these sociological perspectives express their rejection of an obscure rhetoric of rights, voided of political content and, therefore, unable in itself to bring about the essential changes required by inclusion. They maintain that these changes should concern specifically the social structure causing disability, but also 'the relations of power and control that underpin the construction of the interests of some as the "needs" of others' (Armstrong *et al.*, 2000: 9). As the same authors claim, finally,

> It is important therefore to understand demands for 'human rights' in terms of specific historically located objectives. In other words, to organise around demands that contest the embodiment of dominant social interests as the 'needs' of those who experience discrimination.
> (Armstrong and Barton, 2000: 9–10)

The political dimension of human rights, according to this view, relates to the politics of difference, in that the rights of disabled people are enacted in the recognition of their difference as a value and, therefore, in its celebration. This is the main alternative understanding of disability as proposed by the social model, together with the struggle against all forms of discrimination. Furthermore, difference in this context means groups' differences, rather than individual, specific differences, but it also means all groups in society rather than groups identified on the basis of official and institutionalised categorizations (Armstrong *et al.*, 2000: 8). Thus, 'inclusive education begins from the context of policy and the recognition of the complexity of identity and difference' (Corbett and Slee, in Armstrong, *et al.*, 2000: 137).

This perspective is theoretically outlined against liberalism and the principle of equality of opportunity, seen as an empty rhetorical stance, which limits the possibility of inclusion.

> [W]here calls for 'inclusive' schools and practices are limited by a framework which appeals for 'equal opportunities', or understands the 'rights' of disabled people in universalistic rather than political terms, no serious challenge is made to the conditions under which discriminatory and exclusionary social practices operate.
>
> (Armstrong *et al.*, 2000: 11)

Moreover, according to the same authors,

> The apparently high profile which has been given to 'equal opportunities' in many European countries, both at the level of government policy and at the level of institutions over the past 25 years, has masked the real inequalities which exist in between different groups in terms of access to experience, opportunity and power. This is particularly true of equal opportunities in the context of education.
>
> (Armstrong *et al.*, 2000: 5)

Furthermore, policies for equal opportunities are seen as ineffective in changing the power structures in society, as they have been concerned mainly with improving opportunities for some groups within certain contexts, rather than promoting opportunities for all groups in an inclusive project. This has resulted in dividing policies, which have ameliorated opportunities for some while neglecting others. Examples of this situation are easily found, according to these scholars, in the case of priorities accorded to some groups on the basis of certain features, like race or gender, or, within the same group, in instances where tax benefits have been conceded to blind people but not to deaf people, thus producing divisive results.

Consequently, while rejecting a liberal concept of equality of opportunities as 'a bogus discourse' (Armstrong *et al.*, 2000: 5), at least in the way government policies, legislations and institutions have concretized it, the political framework of inclusive education is based instead on the demands of the rights of disabled children as inscribed in the critique of what constitutes normality. As Armstrong *et al.* have pointed out,

> [I]n the absence of such a critique, notions of 'opportunities' and 'rights' rest upon an understanding of 'normality' that reflects the partial self-interest of dominant social groups in our society.
>
> (Armstrong *et al.*, 2000: 11)

Is this really the case? In the next section I shall outline my critique of these positions and provide some arguments showing the difficulties that an inclusive political project understood in terms of politics of difference will have to address.

3. A Philosophical Critique of Social Perspectives in Inclusive Education

Inclusion as outlined in the previous section is a powerful moral and political position, difficult to reject but equally problematic to articulate in its precise content, both politically and educationally. Fundamentally, my intention is not to reject a defensible conception of inclusive education, but rather to endorse a specific understanding of it in relation to the wider political perspective of a more just society. An inclusive society appears intuitively more just than an exclusionary one. However, specifying the precise morality of inclusion, in terms of concepts and political elements, is fundamental not only for a coherent theoretical position, but also for an effective political action. My overall critique of social accounts of inclusive education argues that its unspecified and often confused use of theoretical and political concepts leads not only to a limited theory, but to a very questionable political position, too.

My critique of the concept of inclusion as outlined by sociologists of education will focus on some elements of the theoretical framework underpinning inclusive education and will be conducted along the lines of my analysis of the social model of disability outlined in the last chapter. My aim is to show that, while rightly addressing its moral dimension, current conceptions of inclusive education based on the social model of disability are hampered, both theoretically and politically, by the same limits addressed as problematic in the social model of disability. Consequently, my critique of this conception of inclusive education will address two main points:

i) The social construction of disability and special educational needs;
ii) The adoption of a politics of difference as opposed to, and as rejection of, a liberal framework and, within it, the confinement of the problem of resource distribution, seen as a mere technicality, to what are considered marginal aspects of the process of inclusion in education.

3.1. The Social Construction of Special Educational Needs

In my critique of the social model of disability I have extensively addressed the theoretical difficulties resulting from defining disability as unilaterally socially caused and from rejecting any idea of normality, while adopting the celebration of difference as main political aim. As I will show through a specific example, my critical framework is indeed sustained also when applied to issues of inclusive education. My analysis, therefore, will focus only briefly on some limits of the social model of disability applied in the context of education.

According to a specific sociological perspective in inclusive education (Tomlinson, 1982), definitions of special needs provided by the medical model see special needs as arising from children's own characteristics and the use of medical categories as a means to the implementation of special educational structures and practices. Different professional vested interests converged on the social creation of special education and special needs, which arose in a specific historical, social and economic setting. Moreover, categories, as Tomlinson says, are socially determined as they 'appear, change and disappear because of the goals pursued and the decisions made by people who control the special educational process' (1982: 22). Therefore, 'the terminology employed to categorise children is complex and ever changing' (1982: 58). Sociological positions see special needs as the results of social practices and endorse Oliver's view that 'The development of a pedagogic practice based upon the definition of special educational needs as a social creation is . . . an urgent and essential task over the next few years' (Oliver, 1988: 29). This should be part, furthermore, 'of a critique of what constitutes itself as "normal"' (Armstrong *et al.*, 2000: 11).

The nature of categorization is certainly problematic, especially when referred to education and when concerning those categories identified by

Tomlinson as non-normative, or non-directly arising from medical states, and thus connected to the vast and controversial area of learning difficulties. Nevertheless, I argue that the position endorsed by sociological perspectives in relation to inclusive education shows the two main limits that beset the social model of disability. First, insisting upon the social construction of special educational needs presents an obvious element of over-socialization and, second, the rejection of any concept of normality and the assertion of the celebration of difference as main educational aim is in itself problematic. An example will help in illustrating these points.

> Beth B. . . . expresses interest in people, especially in their faces. She smiles and laughs, responds positively to music, and has definite likes and dislikes concerning food, which she expresses through eye gaze, bodily movements and facial expressions. This is because Beth cannot speak, but instead communicates primarily through eye gaze. Beth is a child with Rett Syndrome, a form of . . . disorder involving multiple severe disabilities in the area of cognition, communication, and motor functioning. Beth's parents, her private therapists, and the staff of professional educators who work with her at school estimate her motor abilities lie within the range of five to seven months.
>
> (Ladenson, 2003: 525)

Beth has received her education in regular classroom placement until second grade, and her further education has been a legal case in the US Federal District Court. Beth, like many other children, is 'classified' as having Profound and Multiple Learning Difficulties, and in her education she receives the support not only of her classroom teacher and assistant, but also of some professional therapists.

If we apply the understanding of disability proposed by the social model to Beth's situation, we should define her disability as the result of social and educational barriers that act as constraints on her development. We should furthermore recognize the oppressive nature of her medical 'classification' and the ideology of needs that it promotes. Beth's needs, therefore, would be determined by the professional intervention defined as necessary in her situation. Finally, we should identify the oppressive relation that powerful professionals may exercise on those, like Beth, defined as impaired by Rett Syndrome, or on her parents, influenced by the configuration of disability as a personal tragedy.

Beth's educational needs certainly depend largely also upon the school's structure and culture, and how the school responds to Beth may create the space for her thriving or not as an individual. But it seems to me difficult to apply the understanding of special needs as external to the individual child and *tout court* located in educational barriers that categorize her. Moreover, Beth's experience in school, her communication and her socialization depend to a great extent also on the level of care and, indeed, of professional expertise that she receives. True, following social theorists we could argue that every child needs support and care in order to thrive in educational settings, and that what differentiates Beth in this situation is not that specific need, but indeed only the fact the she may need a different kind and level of care from that of other second graders. However, it seems equally difficult not to argue here that the level of care and expertise provided is associated to Beth's situation as departing from the average functioning of a child in second grade, thus, in a way, to her not being included in 'what constitutes itself as normal'. My claim here is that social perspectives in inclusive education appear at least inadequate to a complete understanding of the experience of impairment in the context of education.

What I argue, ultimately, is that Beth's story illustrates how views theorizing the social creation of special educational needs, in overlooking the experience of impairment, and in deconstructing and rejecting definitions and references to average functioning, present an over-socialization of the experience of impairment itself. Moreover, in identifying the oppressive nature of professional intervention in the area of impairment, as in the social model of disability, social perspectives in education may lead to the underestimation of the important contribution of professional expertise in children's development. Further, the education of Beth certainly requires an inclusive culture and ethos, and adequate curriculum and assessment methods, but it equally requires additional resources in terms of both logistical structures and specific technology aids (a point that I shall address further on). Finally, my critique here endorses positions within disability studies that have addressed the limits of the social model in explaining the experience of children with severe disabilities. Some researchers have pointed out how the social model is inadequate to express the experience of children with impairment 'with its strong emphasis upon self-advocacy and collective action, and given that children with profound impairment may be largely reliant upon others' (Brett, 2002: 830). And it seems to me that this critique holds especially when applied to education. The first line of my critique as now complete; let us now analyse its second aspect, namely the political level of social perspectives on inclusion.

3.2. The Politics of Inclusion: Difference, Equal Opportunities and Resource Distribution

According to the perspectives under discussion, inclusive education is about a positive self-definition of difference. It asks for the celebration of difference in opposition to the individualization and pathologization of it perpetuated by the oppressive ideology of normality. Moreover, it defines difference as providing the basis on which to establish equal entitlements for all groups in society as a matter of human rights. Finally, inclusion is defined against the rejection of concepts of equal opportunities as void and rhetorical; therefore, ultimately, against the broad liberal framework informing equality in terms of equal opportunities.

My critique of this politics of inclusion articulates three main points: first, it addresses some problems both within the politics and the celebration of difference and, second, it argues against the understanding of equality of opportunities provided by sociological positions in inclusive education. Finally, it addresses the problem of resource distribution as intrinsic to the first two positions and as fundamental to the political aims of inclusion.

Let us first address the celebration of difference as proposed by sociological perspectives in inclusive education. The celebration of difference assumes here mainly two meanings: on the one hand, it is a partial endorsement of the politics of group difference as theorized principally by Iris Marion Young,[3] while, on the other hand, being the celebration of the way people are, as opposed to abstract and ideological views of normality. These two facets of the meaning of difference are then related to issues of equal entitlement as human rights. In reclaiming the meaning of the positive sense of group difference and the necessity of respecting difference in politics, Young promotes the understanding of the primary goal of social justice as social equality. In her opinion a fair distribution of goods is not paramount in issues of justice. Social equality, she argues, entails a fair distribution of goods but refers primarily 'to the full participation and inclusion of everyone in a society's major institutions, and the socially supported substantive opportunity for all to develop and exercise their capacities and realize their choices' (Young, 1990: 173). According to Young,

> justice in a group differentiated society demands social equality of groups, and mutual recognition and affirmation of group differences. Attending to group-specific needs and providing for group representation both promotes that social equality and provides the recognition that undermines cultural imperialism.
>
> (Young, 1990: 191)

Sociological views in inclusive education are based on a partial endorsement of these claims accompanied by the recognition of the fundamental priority of the political and economical struggle against every form of discrimination, oppression and exclusion in general (Armstrong *et al.*, 2000: 7). What these views are mainly concerned with, ultimately, is to eradicate the social and economic structures that provide the basis for exclusion in the domination of some groups of people over others. This, they claim, is precisely enacted by the singling out of difference in terms of needs, either individual or group needs, and by the subsequent domination of the powerful defining groups over those who are defined. Moreover, priority resides in the social and historical context in which discrimination and exclusion take place as, in this view, 'it is only within this general perspective that discrimination as it affects different groups can be understood and confronted' (Armstrong *et al.*, 2000: 7). Finally, the struggle against discrimination implies a cultural change in the understanding of notions of normality and difference and a firm rejection of the individualization of difference as pathology.

This political position gives rise to some significant difficulties. The first relates to its emphasis on group differences alongside its parallel celebration of disability, and leads to possible disparities among sub-groups within groups. As recognized by disabled theorists, 'because of the division within the disabled population in terms of age, social class, impairments . . . the emergence of a coherent political movement is unlikely' (Barnes, 1990: 128). This, in turn, is reflected in the different groups within the same disabled people's movements, where, for instance, deaf people see themselves as a distinct group. Consequently, the unspecified theoretical position that sociological perspectives on inclusion adopt in questions of difference and group difference appears theoretically problematic, and specifically so when applied to the realm of policy. As I noticed earlier, for instance, governments have enacted divisive policies in terms of tax benefits accorded to some groups rather than others. This, however, instead of being only a consequence of some bogus understanding of notions of equal opportunities, can indeed be seen as related to unspecified and rather confused political positions that are not substantially underpinned by coherent normative frameworks. Moreover, the lack of a precise articulation of differences in relation to groups gives rise to problems of identity and difference. For instance, certain sectors of the deaf community do not agree on deafness being considered a disability, and promote instead an understanding of it as cultural difference. Finally, in promoting the celebration of difference, the politics of inclusive education falls back on the 'dilemma of difference', where difficulties arise both in acknowledging individual differences, but with the risk of stigmatizing, and in ignoring differences, with the corresponding risk of not providing what is required by the individual. In this sense, if we ignore the difference of disabled children with reference to education, we are short of reasons on which to provide them with an adequate education, whatever that may mean. On the other hand, the risk entailed by acknowledging the difference resides in a possible singling out of needs, which may be defined by others (I am here thinking of Beth, for instance), thus we are falling back to the possible ground of discrimination and exclusion.

Equal opportunities have been highly criticized by these proponents of inclusive education. In their view, equal opportunities have not only provided the basis for the substantial undermining of the real inequalities faced by many groups in society, but also for divisive policies whereby, for instance, disability has not received the same attention as race or gender issues. Moreover, disabled people, as Armstrong *et al.* suggest,

> have begun to challenge the representation of disability within an 'opportunities' discourse on the grounds that it discourages a critical stance towards the social conditions underpinning the experience of disabled people.
>
> (Armstrong *et al.*, 2000: 9)

These authors maintain that it is in the absence of such a critique that 'the discourse of opportunities is disempowering in that it does little more than reconstitute earlier discourse of "care"' (Armstrong *et al.*, 2000: 9), which have prevented the political and social recognition of disabled people.

Furthermore, when applied to the specific education context, the equal opportunity framework has been mainly associated with the latest changes in some countries toward neo-liberal economics and more general libertarian positions. In talking about school in England and Wales, for instance, Corbett notices that

> The current emphasis in schools in England and Wales is upon academic achievement, high standards of behaviour and consistency of curricular approach. Whilst this can be praised as an equal opportunity model, it reinforces an individualised, competitive attitude which rests uneasily with the emphasis on community values, cooperation and social learning which form integral elements of inclusive education.
>
> (Corbett and Slee, 2000: 137)

Slee reinforces this position by maintaining that Australia, too, 'is entrapped within a compensatory model of distributive justice (Corbett and Slee, 2000: 138).

In addressing this critical stance against equal opportunities, some specifications and clarifications are necessary. First, it is important to notice that these criticisms of the idea and the politics of equal opportunity are provided perhaps within a limited understanding of the meaning of 'equal opportunities' and without a significant operationalization of it. Second, it is necessary to explicate the difference between equality of opportunity as enacted by governmental policies and the principle of fair equality of opportunity as theoretically informing liberal egalitarianism. It appears that equal opportunities as declared in political manifestos have actually promoted the enactment of a very minimal understanding, if any, of the concept of equality. Thus, this minimal level implies equal opportunities as the absence of legal impediment to participate, the absence of preclusion to choice. This minimal level of opportunities has consequently shifted the debate from the complexity of the liberal meaning of equality to a very neutral and, therefore, bland conception. The first distinction, therefore, needs to acknowledge the difference between normative theory level and political enactment. At the level of ideal theory, the concept of equality of opportunities has a normative meaning, in that it provides us with a specification of it in terms of a set of principles and norms to inform and guide the design of social institutions. Moreover, in ideal theory, the meaning of equality of opportunity is certainly far more demanding and more complex than the simple removal of impediments to participation, since it may be taken to mean, for instance, the equal life-prospects that individuals with the same level of talent and the same willingness to exert efforts should have. Not only this, but also a further analysis may be needed in order to ascertain whether the political level has indeed proceeded on the basis of a clear liberal framework, as many liberal egalitarians actually claim that there has been a complete abandonment of egalitarian concerns by politicians and policy-makers, or a recent re-appropriation of it but at a very minimal level.[4]

Second, the importance of addressing principles of resource distribution is reinstated by the same considerations expressed previously. The bland and ineffectual politics of equal opportunities in terms of vague legal notions of absence of impediment to participate has masked not only the real inequalities in society, but also the real issue behind them. In other words, it has neglected the fundamental question of a principle of fair distribution of resources informing theories and policies. This, I argue, is the major limit of sociological perspectives in inclusive education, the fact they have not only identified policies with liberal positions, thus somehow mixing normative with policy level, but have also misrepresented the importance of distributing opportunities and resources according to a principled framework. And this is precisely what is missing in government policies.

Ultimately, against sociological positions on inclusion that confine the issue of resource distribution to the secondary aspects and the minor technicalities of inclusion, as opposed to the importance of values and ethos informing both education and schools, I suggest that resource distribution is among the primary concerns for a project of inclusion.

Finally, the identification of liberal positions and ideals of equality of opportunities with recent education trends in terms of standards of achievements and competitive policies represents a common misunderstanding among educationalists.[5] This is in part due to the complexities of the debate within liberalism and to the fact that the same debate has not addressed specific educational questions. However, it is also due to the lack of attention to normative theories characterizing the sociological debate in education and in inclusive education more specifically. Ultimately, these aspects highlight the importance of normative structures and, in particular, liberal egalitarian principles in informing the debate in inclusive and special education. What emerges from my analysis of the social model of disability and its application to concepts and ideas of inclusive education highlights the critical need and importance of a principled framework, conceptualizing impairment, disability and special educational needs and educational equality within a broader concern for social justice. This is my task for the next chapters, 4, 5, 6 and 7.

Concluding Comments

My critical analysis has presented perspectives in inclusive education that are mainly related, both theoretically and politically, to the social model of disability. In this chapter I have maintained that social perspectives on inclusive education fail to provide appropriate grounding for thinking of inclusion, not only when referred to children with disabilities and special educational needs, but also as a general framework for education. Moreover, I have addressed the limits shown by concepts of social constructions of impairment and disability, as well as tensions inherent to the political positions informed by these views within inclusive education.

My main contention is that the social model of disability presents theoretical limits, which make the model itself problematic to the achievement of its aim of an inclusive society and equally problematic in its application to the context of education. This, I maintain, is due both to its failure to recognize the importance of the question of justice as distributive justice and to its theoretical limits in providing a definition of impairment and disability that could inform a principled framework for just distributions.

The result of my analysis of current models underpinning inclusive and special education points in the direction of the need for a different framework, both at the theoretical and the normative level of analysis. The next chapters are a step in that direction.

Chapter 4

The Capability Approach:
Re-Examining Impairment and Disability

What disability is and how it can be defined in relation to human diversity and personal heterogeneities more generally is a theme common to several disciplines. In particular, recent perspectives in socio-medicine, disability studies and political philosophy have all engaged the topic of disability, outlining some of its dimensions with reference to their own internal debates. As we have seen in Chapter 2, socio-medical approaches and disability studies have mainly concentrated their analyses on the definition of disability and on its causal factors, and have provided contrasting understandings of what disability is and how it relates to human diversity and social and political matters. In their political struggle for equal consideration and equal entitlements, and against any reduction of disability to a biological notion of abnormality, disabled people's movements advocate the 'celebration of difference', or a positive recognition of disability as part of the inescapable human diversity that so enriches our life experience and our society (see Corker, 1999; Morris, 1991; Shakespeare, 1997; Thomas, 1999; Wendell, 1996). In this context, the concept of disability is articulated in terms of differences to be positively recognized, rather than stigmatized and discriminated against.

Conversely, the concept of human diversity plays a crucial role in contemporary theories of social justice. These theories engage with the questions of what traits constitute personal advantages or disadvantages, whether these are naturally or socially determined, and how and why diverse personal traits do or do not have to be taken into account in determining what is just. A disability is usually referred to as an individual disadvantage and considered as a further 'complexity' in the already complex framework of a just distribution of benefits and burdens, however defined. Aspects of this debate have also addressed the causal factors of disability, whether natural or social, mainly in connection with interpersonal comparisons of disadvantage and a concern for social justice (see Dworkin, 2000; Nagel, 2002; Rawls, 1971, 2001; Sen, 1992). What is a cause of celebration for disability scholars and disabled people's movements has therefore become an object of inquiry for political philosophers, particularly liberal egalitarians.

Notwithstanding this diversity of approaches, the debate raises three interrelated questions that are important both to disability studies and to political theories of social justice: 'What is disability and how can we think of it within a concept of human diversity?' 'What relevance do the causal factors of disability have for a theory of justice?' and 'How ought disability to be evaluated and considered in the design of equitable and inclusive social and political arrangements?' In addressing these questions, the debate operates on two distinct but interlocking levels: a theoretical level, concerned with definitional and causal issues, and a political level, where theoretical understandings of disability and ideals of social inclusion are translated into matters of equal rights and entitlements for disabled people. The three questions, and their respective answers, form a fundamental framework for addressing impairment, disability, and special needs in education.

The capability approach, developed in different ways by Amartya Sen and Martha Nussbaum, is well suited to providing justified answers to those questions. In this chapter, I argue that the capability approach advances the theorization of impairment and disability both at the theoretical and political level of analysis, and allows a comprehensive evaluation of disability in the just design of social and institutional arrangements. In the first section that follows, I shall discuss the main concepts of the capability approach and their relevance for understanding disability. I shall then, in subsequent sections, outline a capability perspective on impairment and disability, and discuss the relational and multidimensional conception of disability it suggests. Finally, in the last section of the chapter I shall consider some potential problems faced by the capability approach.

1. Sen's Capability Approach, Disability and Justice

1.1 Normative insights

Sen's priority in developing the capability approach has been to provide a more adequate framework for the conceptualization of human development and for the analysis and assessment of poverty. The frameworks commonly used in welfare economics are too narrowly based on income generation or income distribution, he contends. In examining poverty, inequality, and their relation to social arrangements, Sen's work also critically engages with the philosophical debate on equality and distributive justice, and develops a complex and compelling form of egalitarianism (Sen, 1992). I shall argue that Sen's capability approach offers new and important resources for redefining impairment and disability, and designing inclusive social policies. I begin with some key concepts: the space of capability, the informational basis of the metric used in interpersonal comparisons of equality, and the democratic decision process entailed by the approach.

The Space of Capability: Functionings and Capabilities

Sen maintains that closely linked to the central question of what it is that social arrangements should aim to equalize are two fundamental issues: first, the choice of the 'evaluative space' in which to assess equality, and second, the metric that should be used in comparing people's relative advantages and disadvantages. He identifies the evaluative space for the assessment of inequality and, conversely, for determining what equality we should seek, in the space of the freedoms to achieve valuable objectives that people have, that is, in the space of capability. Rather than aiming to equalize resources or welfare, Sen argues that equality should be defined and aimed at in terms of the capability each individual has to pursue and to achieve well-being, i.e. to pursue and enjoy states and objectives constitutive of her or his well-being. Thus, the capability approach delimits a space for the assessment of individual well-being and the freedom to achieve it.

Within this space, Sen distinguishes functionings and capabilities. Functionings are defined as 'beings and doings constitutive of a person's being', such as being adequately nourished, being in good health, being happy and having self-respect, or taking part in the life of the community (Sen, 1992: 39). Achieved functionings are the specific functionings that a person has accomplished and realized at any given time (Alkire, 2002: 6). Since functionings are constitutive of a person's being, according to Sen, 'an evaluation of a person's well-being has to take the form of an assessment of these constitutive elements' (Sen, 1992: 39).

Capabilities, on the other hand, are capabilities to function, and they represent a person's freedoms to achieve valuable functionings. In other words they represent 'various combinations of functionings (beings and doings) that the person can achieve. Capability is, thus, a set of vectors of functionings, reflecting the person's freedom to lead one type of life or another' (Sen, 1992: 40). Capabilities amount to the substantive freedoms a person has, or the 'real alternatives' available to the person herself to achieve well-being. In that respect, capability is related to well-being both instrumentally, as a basis for judgements about the relative advantage a person has and her place in society, and intrinsically, since achieved well-being itself depends on the capability to function, and the exercise of choice has value of its own as part of our living (Sen, 1992: 41, 62). The capability approach endorses equality of capabilities as a policy objective and asserts the fundamental importance of capabilities and functionings as value-objects for the assessment of individual well-being (Sen, 1992: 46). With this in mind, it is important to address the basis for interpersonal comparisons implied by the space of capability.

Interpersonal Comparisons and Human Diversity
The 'evaluative space' of capability encompasses the use of a 'metric' (Pogge, 2004) to evaluate people's relative advantages and disadvantages. In other words, the capability approach theorizes a space where consideration of the 'basic heterogeneities of human beings' or 'empirical fact' of human diversity is crucial in assessing the demands of equality (Sen, 1992: 1). In Sen's words, '[H]uman diversity is no secondary complication (to be ignored, or to be introduced "later on"); it is a fundamental aspect of our interest in equality' (Sen, 1992: xi). According to his view, human beings are diverse in four fundamental ways.[1] First, they are different with respect to their personal, internal characteristics, such as gender, age, physical and mental abilities, talents, proneness to illness, and so forth. Second, different individuals are different with respect to external circumstances, such as inherited wealth and assets, environmental factors, including climatic differences and social and cultural arrangements (Sen, 1992: 1, 20, 27–8). Third, a further and important form of diversity, defined as inter-individual variation, pertains to differences in the conversion of resources into freedoms, i.e. to different individual abilities to convert commodities and resources in order to achieve valued objectives (Sen, 1992: 85). To illustrate this last point, Sen provides the example of a lactating woman, who, due to her specific condition, needs a higher intake of food for her functionings than a similar but non-lactating woman. A fourth, fundamental way in which human beings are diverse is that they have different conceptions of the good, and therefore aim at different ends or objectives. Sen calls this inter-end variation, and the recognition of it leads him to envisage capabilities as the overall freedoms that people have to achieve actual livings that one can have a reason to value (Sen, 1992: 85; 1999: 18), without specifying what ends there is reason to value or (hence) specifying a definitive list of capabilities.

Within this view of human diversity as central, the capability approach holds that it makes a difference whether someone is a man or a woman, has physical and mental prowess or weaknesses, lives in a temperate physical environment or in a more adverse climatic zone, and lives in certain social and cultural arrangements rather than in others. The differences entailed by these variations have to be accounted for when addressing the demands of equality. The actual differences in conversion factors and conceptions of valuable ends and objectives that people have must be considered too. Thus, ultimately, the metric used to make interpersonal comparisons includes the four central aspects of human diversity pertaining to personal characteristics, external circumstances, inter-individual variations in conversion factors, and inter-end variations related to the plurality of conceptions of the good.

An example taken directly from Sen's work may help to illustrate the use of this metric, and to introduce considerations pertaining to disability that will be expanded later on.

> [C]onsider two persons 1 and 2, with 2 disadvantaged in some respect (e.g. physical disability, mental handicap, greater disease proneness). They do *not* have the same ends or objectives, or the same conception of the good. Person 1 values A more than B, while 2 has the opposite valuation. Each values 2A more than A and 2B more than B . . . With the given set of primary goods person 1 can achieve 2A or 2B, also – though there may be no great merit in this – A or B. On the other hand, given 2's disadvantage . . . she can achieve only A or B.
>
> (Sen, 1992: 83)

It is evident here that person 2 finds herself in a situation of inequality owing to her personal characteristics and how she converts resources into functionings, despite having the same amount of resources or opportunities. Her disability, which is regarded for the purposes of this example as an inherent disadvantage, must be taken into account in evaluating equality.[2]

Democratic processes and public reasoning

It is this set of considerations regarding human diversity and its centrality in the metric used to compare individual advantage or disadvantage that has ultimately led Sen to conceptualize the space of capabilities and functionings as the relevant space for equality. He identifies the capability approach as a framework of thought, a general approach to the assessment of social schemes, while declining, in light of the variability of human ends, to specify a definitive list of capabilities or functionings. He leaves these details to the processes of public choice, reasoning and democratic procedure that are themselves the most freedom-preserving means by which social policy can be determined. Hence the deliberately under-specified character of the capability approach (Sen, 1999: 78; Robeyns, 2003a: 6). Capabilities are context-sensitive, or sensitive to social and cultural arrangements, and their selection should be the result of a demo-cratic process involving public consultation, Sen argues. This implies that, in considering a person's capability set, attention should be given to individual conceptions of well-being, and to their interplay with political, social and cultural settings, thus, ultimately, with conditions that may influ-ence choice and reasoning. Some authors (Alkire, 2002 and 2006; Crocker, 2006 and Robeyns, 2003a) have expanded this aspect of the capability approach, envisaging different perspectives on what forms this process of social deliberation and democratic participation may take with regard to such areas as the operationalizing of capability in poverty reduction, delib-erative democratic procedures, and the analysis of gender inequality.

It is within this normative framework that important insights for a perspective to disability can be developed. I now turn to that perspective.

1.2 Sen's capability approach and disability

What does Sen's capability approach contribute to our understanding of impairment and disability and to our moral quest for an inclusive society?

A superficial reading of Sen's work suggests that it treats the identifica-tion of disability with personal disadvantage as non-problematic. For instance, in addressing personal heterogeneities, Sen maintains,

> People have disparate physical characteristics connected with disabil-ity, illness, age or gender, and these make their needs diverse. For example, [A] disabled person may need some prosthesis, an older person more support and help, a pregnant woman more nutritional intake, and so on. The 'compensation' needed for disadvantages will vary, and furthermore some disadvantages may not be fully 'cor-rectable' even with income transfer.
>
> (Sen, 1999: 70)

Similarly:

> [E]qual incomes can still leave much inequality in our ability to do what we would value doing. A disabled person cannot function in the way an able-bodied person can, even if both have exactly the same income.
>
> (Sen, 1992: 20)

And finally:

> [T]he extent of comparative deprivation of a physically handicapped
> person vis-à-vis others cannot be adequately judged by looking at his or
> her income, since the person may be greatly disadvantaged in con-
> verting income into the achievements he or she would value.
>
> (Sen, 1992: 28)

These examples suggest how disability, defined as an individual condition,
influences individual functionings, as these are correlated with various
personal characteristics and diverse individual conversion factors. Disability is equated with an individual disadvantage, an asymmetry that should
be taken into consideration in interpersonal comparisons. However, it
would be an oversimplification of Sen's approach to read this as an
endorsement of the medical model and its definition of disability as an
individual limitation causally linked to biological impairment.

A more sensitive reading yields two important contributions that Sen's
capability approach makes to our understanding of impairment and disability and their assessment in interpersonal comparisons. The first insight
relates to how we can think of impairment and disability as aspects of
human diversity, and more specifically to Sen's understanding of personal
heterogeneities and their role in the metric for assessing equality. The
second insight concerns democratic deliberation and the active participation of disabled people and their political movements in the process of
identifying relevant capabilities and evaluating how social policies should
be designed when aiming at inclusion. Both require some explanation.

The first reason for considering the capability approach innovative with
respect to current understandings and models of impairment and disability relates both to the centrality of human diversity in assessing equality in
the space of capability, and to the specific understanding of human diversity proposed by Sen. First, in repositioning human diversity as central to
the evaluation of individual advantages and disadvantages, Sen's capability
approach promotes an egalitarian perspective that differs from others in
dealing at its core with the complexities of disability. Second, Sen's
concept of human diversity, in encompassing personal and external
factors as well as an individual conversion factor, implies an interrelation
between individual and circumstantial aspects of human diversity. This
enables disability theory to overcome current understandings of impairment and disability as unilaterally biologically or socially determined,[3]
because disability can be regarded as one of the aspects of individuals
emerging from this interlocking of personal and external factors.

Moreover, the capability approach provides an egalitarian framework in which entitlement does not entirely depend upon the causal origin of disability. In determining entitlement, the approach shifts attention from identifying whether a disability is biologically or socially caused as such, to the full set of capabilities a person can choose from and the role impairment plays in this set of freedoms. Furthermore, the capability framework opens the way to considerations of disability as multidimensional and relational, a conception that will be discussed further on, in that it sees disability as one aspect of the complexity of human heterogeneities, and therefore as one aspect of the complexity of individuals in their interaction with their physical, economic, social and cultural environment. In this respect, the approach goes also in the direction of promoting a conception of disability as one aspect of human diversity, comparable to age and gender, without suggesting monolithic and direct notions of diversity as abnormality. This appears to be fundamental in overcoming the discrimination and oppression denounced by disabled people's movements as inherent in current notions of normality, abnormality and diversity.

An example can help in illustrating these insights. Walking is a functioning, and so is moving about from one space to another, and it is a functioning that enables other functionings, such as taking one's children to school, or going to work, or serving as a politician. In this sense moving about may be seen as a basic functioning enabling more complex functionings to take place. Now consider an impaired person who uses a wheelchair. In determining the full set of capabilities that a wheelchair user has to achieve her valued ends, the capability approach looks at how this specific physical activity (moving about by wheelchair) interacts with circumstantial factors, such as the physical environment where the person lives and the presence of wheelchair accesses to buildings, and how it interacts with personal conversion factors, such as general strength, health, and aspects of attitude. The approach also considers the interplay between wheelchair use and the person's most valuable ends, one of which could be, for example, having an interest in politics and aspiring to serve as a politician. The capability approach suggests that being a wheelchair user may be considered a disadvantage when the wheelchair is not provided or the physical environment is not designed appropriately. In the same way many people would be disadvantaged should stairs or lift not be fitted between storeys in buildings, since very few individuals would be able to move from floor to floor (Perry *et al.*, 1999: 2). The provision of a wheelchair and wheelchair accessibility is a matter of justice on the capability approach, because these contribute to the equalization of the capability to pursue and achieve well-being.

Let us continue with this example and consider the achievement of more complex functionings, such as serving as a politician. Let us suppose that acting in her political capacity is fundamental to the achievement of well-being for the physically impaired person considered in this example. And let us also assume that the physical environment is designed so as to prevent her from moving about, thus ultimately preventing her from the achievement of some basic functionings. This person, although potentially able to exercise her political role, is prevented from achieving her valued end by the interaction of some of her personal features with some of the characteristics of her physical environment. In this case, well-being freedom appears to be restricted in some fundamental ways, and hence the full set of capabilities available to this person is diminished. As we shall see later on, this insight has fundamental implications for justice for disabled people.

The second contribution of the capability approach to disability theory pertains to democratic participation in determining relevant capabilities. Here the approach is compatible with the demands of disabled people's movements on the one hand, and with questions of the design of social schemes and policies on the other. Disabled people's organizations have long denounced their de facto exclusion from active participation in society and have reclaimed their role in society as a matter of right. The capability approach seems to provide a substantive framework to fulfil disabled people's demands. In promoting some forms of public consultations on the choice of relevant capabilities, it commends a participatory democratic process that avoids exclusion and discrimination as a matter of principle. Moreover, in his explicit commitment to forms of participatory and deliberative democratic procedures, Sen endorses the view that people who are most affected by a decision should be part of the decision-making process as well as sharing in its results. This suggests a positive and active role for disabled people in the selection of relevant and valuable capabilities in consultation with non-disabled people. More specifically, this process is envisaged as a form of 'open public reasoning' both for deciding equality of democratically selected capabilities, and equality of agency freedoms (Crocker, 2006: 190–1). The role accorded to democratic decision, however, if extremely relevant to the agency of disabled people, is problematic in failing to provide sufficient normative guidance for adjudicating the demands of disabled people in relation to the demands of others (more on this later on). Furthermore, choices concerning which capabilities to protect are to be made through democratic processes, but the capabilities essential to democratic participation would themselves need to be protected as a matter of prior constitutional principle, in order to ensure just outcomes.[4]

These insights provide the basis for a multidimensional and relational concept of impairment and disability that will be outlined in a subsequent section of this chapter. In what follows, I consider instead Martha Nussbaum's approach to capabilities, which goes beyond Sen's in its understanding of justice as a fundamental dimension of the issues surrounding impairment and disability.

2. Nussbaum's Capabilities Approach, Disability and Justice

2.1. Normative insights

Nussbaum has presented her own account of the capabilities approach through a philosophical perspective on issues of international development aimed specifically at reconsidering and addressing the unjust conditions of women in developing countries (Nussbaum, 2000). In her book *Frontiers of Justice: Disability, Nationality, Species Membership* (2006), she extends her account of the capabilities approach in connection with previously unexplored issues of justice, including justice for mentally impaired citizens. She endorses Sen's concept of capability as the space for comparisons of freedom and quality of life, but refines the approach in some important ways. In particular, she gives it a universal and normative dimension by stipulating a list of central human capabilities and a threshold of adequacy in the universal possession of these capabilities. These elements form the basis for constitutional principles to be adopted by all nations (Nussbaum, 2000: 12).

The central human capabilities listed and endorsed by Nussbaum include 'life', 'bodily health', 'bodily integrity', 'senses, imagination and thought', 'emotions', 'practical reason' and 'affiliation', as well as 'play' and 'other species', and 'control over the environment', understood as both political and material control (Nussbaum, 2000: 78–80). She identifies these and the other items listed as 'combined capabilities', or 'internal capabilities *combined with* suitable external conditions for the exercise of functioning' (Nussbaum, 2000: 84). Further, she distinguishes basic capabilities, generally intended as the basic innate equipment of individuals, from internal capabilities, seen as 'developed states of the person herself that are . . . sufficient conditions for the exercise of the requisite function' (Nussbaum, 2000: 84). Each capability on the list is therefore some combination of innate and internal capabilities and external conditions. Among these, Practical Reason and Affiliation are particularly important capabilities, because they make it possible for other capabilities to be pursued in ways that are genuinely human. Practical Reason, intended in its Aristotelian sense of being able to form one's conception of the good and to engage in the planning of one's life, and Affiliation, or being able to engage in meaningful relationships and having the social bases of self-respect and dignity, are fundamental capabilities without which a life loses its characteristically human features (Nussbaum, 2000: 82).

Nussbaum's focus on central human capabilities subsumes and is related to the intuitive idea of the moral worth and the dignity of each and every human being (Nussbaum, 2000: 5, and 2006a: 160). She maintains that when we ask the question central to the capabilities approach, 'What is this person actually able to do and to be?', we imply a set of considerations related to evaluating the position of the person in interpersonal comparisons while, at the same time, referring to some core human capabilities, the absence of which would preclude the possibility of leading a truly human life (Nussbaum, 2000: 71, and 2006a: 182, 190–1). In posing that central question, we are evaluating what this individual person, considered as an end in herself, is actually in a position to be and to do, what her liberties and opportunities are, and how the resources she can use allow her to function in a human way (Nussbaum, 2000: 71, 74). Nussbaum thus defines a universal set of capabilities, which should be secured for every person at least up to the threshold below which any life loses its dignity or humanness.

Nussbaum maintains that the universality of the list of capabilities provided is justified not only by the idea of respect for human dignity, but through a political concept of overlapping consensus. She claims that the political justification is grounded on the recognition that the items on the list can be considered crucial to human functioning by people who otherwise endorse very different conceptions of the good. Nussbaum does not support her claim with further articulations, but maintains that the normative universality of central human capabilities could be politically endorsed – as the 'underpinnings of basic political principles that can be embodied in constitutional guarantees' (Nussbaum, 2000: 74) – through an overlapping consensus, by people of different religions, beliefs, cultures and understandings of what constitutes a good life (Nussbaum, 2006a: 174). Nussbaum's political justification intersects here with her appeal to the moral worth and dignity of persons, through the idea that the central human capabilities 'can be convincingly argued to be of central importance in any human life, whatever else the person pursues or chooses' (Nussbaum, 2000: 74). She maintains that by providing a list of central human capabilities and by setting a threshold level below which a life cannot be deemed truly human, the capabilities approach sets the basis for a decent social minimum that governments have to deliver

(Nussbaum, 2000: 71). Capabilities cannot be directly distributed, but governments are to provide the social bases for central human capabilities. Governments 'cannot make all women emotionally healthy', for instance, but they 'can do quite a lot to influence emotional health through suitable policies' (Nussbaum, 2000: 82).

Nussbaum further articulates her position on the normative aspect of capabilities by relating them to human rights, understood both as political and civil liberties and as economic and social rights (Nussbaum, 2000: 97). She maintains that the political dimension of capabilities provides the philosophical underpinning for basic constitutional principles, and in that way plays a role similar to that of human rights. But she argues, furthermore, that the capabilities approach goes further than the language of rights (Nussbaum, 2006b: 48–51), and for two reasons. First, 'thinking in terms of capability gives us a benchmark as we think about what it is to secure a right to someone' (Nussbaum, 2000: 98). Second, as a capabilities analysis considers what people are actually able to be and to do, how they are enabled to live,

> Analyzing economic and material rights in terms of capabilities thus enables us to set forth clearly a rationale we have for spending unequal amounts of money on the disadvantaged, or creating special programs to assist their transition to full capability.
>
> (Nussbaum, 2000: 99)

For these reasons, the political dimension of the capabilities approach has ramifications for equality with respect to both political liberties and resource distribution. For instance, from a capabilities perspective, acts of (invidious) discrimination entail a 'failure of associational capability, a type of indignity or humiliation' (Nussbaum, 2000: 86), and the demands associated with the delivery of the threshold level of capabilities imply policies entailing redistribution of resources.

2.2 Nussbaum's capabilities approach and disability

Nussbaum's version of the capability approach advances the analysis of the political and normative dimensions of impairment and disability in three main ways. First, the universality of its conception of human capabilities makes it applicable to all individuals, irrespective of differences due to impairments. Second, it can precisely inform and guide interpersonal comparisons involving impairment and disability, pursuant to evaluating the respective positions of individuals in social arrangements. Finally, it allows us to frame matters of justice for disabled people in the language of basic constitutional guarantees, or inescapable demands on governments for their intervention in securing the social bases of capabilities. These claims require some elaboration.

First, the universality of central human capabilities and their being sought for each and every person implies not only including all individuals under this framework, irrespective of their differences and the causes of their differences, but entails also a regard for the dignity of each person as an underlying principle. This makes the capabilities approach developed by Nussbaum an appealing basis for a principled political project of inclusion. The definition of a threshold of adequate capability to be aimed at leaves open the question of what is mandated when the health and bodily integrity of impaired people does not allow them to reach the threshold level (see, for instance, Kittay, 2003; Silvers and Francis, 2005; and Wasserman, 2006), but Nussbaum evidently does not intend that their condition would disqualify them from moral concern. In her articulation of the capabilities approach in relation to justice for mentally disabled people (Nussbaum, 2006a), she introduces as a fundamental dimension of justice the care, compassion and love of others that are the response of a decent society to our condition of humanity. A decent society would provide care and respect for our needs in times of dependency, and it would provide this care and respect to mentally impaired people on the basis of our 'claim to support in the dignity of our human need itself' (Nussbaum, 2006a: 160).

Second, the merit of considering each person's capabilities in the evaluation of their respective positions in social arrangements seems intuitively evident, and the application of this to impairment and disability is clear. Asking 'What is this person able to be and to do?' and thinking of the person as physically or mentally impaired implies a reconsideration of the actual condition of impairment and disability and their effects and consequences. The approach thereby allows these factors to be fully recognized and assessed in evaluating each person's capabilities.

Finally, the third contribution that Nussbaum's capabilities approach makes to the analysis of disability is a normative and political framework that is fully compatible with disabled people's movements' efforts to overcome their discrimination and oppression in society and secure the recognition of their entitlements as citizens. Nussbaum's approach, in identifying the central human capabilities as having a role broader to the language of (bare) human rights (2006a: 7), and grounding government policy standards in the resulting normative concepts, provides a framework that accords the legitimate demands of disabled people full constitutional recognition.[5]

3. A Capability Perspective on Impairment and Disability

3.1 A relational understanding of disability

Having summarized the aspects of Sen's and Nussbaum's versions of capability theory that seem most useful for the construction of a relational and multidimensional view of disability, a view concerned with issues of definition as well as justice, I shall now on this foundation attempt to construct such a view. In doing this, I shall mainly, although not exclusively, adopt Sen's insights. I shall also draw on accounts of the relational aspect of disability developed by Allen Buchanan (Buchanan *et al.*, 2000), John Perry (Perry *et al.*, 1996, 1999) and others.

Let us begin with matters of definition. Here the concepts of functionings and capability are particularly significant, as they can be related in turn to the restriction in functionings and to the consequent limitations of capability experienced by disabled people. Thus, it is important to distinguish impairment from disability, and to see how and why disability is inherently relational and circumstantial, or, in other words, a phenomenon of the interface between personal characteristics of the individual and the specific design of the social and physical environment that the individual inhabits. Impairment, either physical or mental, relates to the loss of some aspect of functioning. For instance, a lesion of the spinal cord that results in restricted movements – whether caused by a genetic condition or trauma – is an impairment of average movement functioning (see Buchanan *et al.*, 2000: 285). Perry defines impairment in this sense as 'a physiological disorder or injury' (Perry *et al.*, 1996: 3). Disability, on the other hand, is the inability to perform some significant functionings that individuals are on average and typically able to do under favourable conditions, or 'where the inability is not due to simple and easily corrigible ignorance or to a lack of the tools or means ordinarily available for performing such tasks' (Buchanan *et al.*, 2000: 286). Buchanan's definition suggests that disabilities are inabilities that cannot be overcome by simply supplying relevant information or tools. For instance, if one is unable to play Monopoly because one does not know the rules of the game or because one lacks the game board and pieces, one's inability does not constitute a disability. On the other hand, if someone cannot perform certain functionings that, typically, average people in equivalent circumstances are able to, and if this is connected to an identifiable impairment, then the person is disabled with respect to that specific functioning. So, for example, if a blind adult person is unable to drive, whereas on average and under favourable conditions an adult is able to do so, then the blind person is disabled with respect to driving.

Disability, so defined, is distinct from impairment, and impairment does not always result in disability. Buchanan provides a very convincing example to illustrate this. He suggests the case of a hearing-impaired person who has lost the hearing function with regard to a range of sound frequencies that is detected on average by persons. If the range of sounds undetectable by the impaired person is irrelevant to the functionings in her social environment, then she is not disabled (Buchanan *et al.*, 2000: 287). Consequently, whether impairment does or does not result in disability depends on the design of the physical and social setting and on whether or not it is possible to 'overcome' the restrictions in functionings relating to impairment. For example, if the means existed to provide cars whose operation did not require sight – the functions associated with sight being played by computerized monitoring devices, say – then a blind adult might be able to overcome her inability to drive, and hence, her disability with respect to that functioning. Thus, disability can be seen as inherently relational, or arising from the interplay between impairment and social arrangements. The relation between impairment and disability does not appear to be one of straightforward causality.

Disability involves impairment, but a full understanding of it requires recognition of its other dimensions. Disability can involve impairment of multiple functionings, arising from different impairment effects. Certain traumas, illnesses, or the pain and fatigue associated with back injuries and arthritis, may impair not only physical functionings, such as walking, for instance, but also aspects of health or other functioning. Disability also has a temporal dimension, as the inability to function in a certain way can be temporary, such as after an eye operation, or more permanent, such as in the event of blindness resulting from a permanent loss of optic nerve function, occurring in conditions that do not allow the inability to be overcome. There is, finally, a dimension of dependency, either on tools or on other people, to help with carrying out functions that, on average, are done more or less independently by non-disabled people. So, for instance, a quadriplegic person or a severely cognitively impaired child may require a personal assistant or support not needed by an average or typically functioning individual in order to achieve certain basic functionings.

As we have seen, the design of physical infrastructures and social schemes plays a substantial role in the relation between impairment and disability. Circumstantial elements such as wheelchair accessible buildings and public transportation, as well as the provision of different tools, all provide interfacing between the individual and her environment, and the greater the interfacing is, the less possibility there is that impairment will result in disability. So, for instance, blindness becomes a disability with

respect to reading text messages on computer screens to obtain information, when, and if, no use of Braille displays and speech-output screen
readers is provided (Perry *et al.*, 1996: 4). Moreover, society's attitude and
dispositions towards severely cognitively impaired people, although more
difficult to assess, have a considerable influence on the extent to which
their impairments result in disability. An illustration of this is provided
by Eva Feder Kittay's description of how people's indifference to her
daughter Sesha's attempts to communicate narrowed the range of interactions she could enjoy and amplified her disability (Kittay, 2003).

Ultimately, impairment is a personal feature, which relates to functionings, both in terms of possible restrictions of average functionings, and/or
in terms of atypical modes of functionings. When impairment interacts
with circumstantial elements to determine functionings restrictions, it
results in a disability. Disability, therefore, emerges from the interaction of
personal and circumstantial factors, and relates to a limitation of capabilities, or a capability failure.

The definitional aspect of the capability perspective seems to have some
similarity with the revised WHO *Classification of Functioning, Disability and
Health* (WHO, 2001) and with its circumstantial elements. This classification, as we have seen in Chapter 2,[6] substantially revises the previous ones
based primarily on medical views of disability, and shifts the focus onto the
'impact' of disability, rather than its causes, while taking into account the
contextual factors and the social elements that may determine disability.
However, beyond these possible convergences, two main elements make the
capability perspective a richer and more promising framework. These
elements, as we have seen, consist both in the specific meanings of functionings and capability analysed so far, and in their relevance within a framework primarily informed by considerations of justice and equal entitlements
for disabled people. I shall now say more about the latter aspect.

3.2 Disability, capability and justice

The capability framework, as we have seen, suggests a conception of
disability as inherently relational, as one aspect of human diversity that has
to be considered when evaluating the reciprocal positions of individuals
and the distribution of benefits and burdens in social arrangements. In a
capability perspective, impairment may restrict functionings, and thus
yield a disability, through the complex interrelation between the individual's characteristics, her conversion factors, and her environment. When
the whole capability of the person in achieving her valued ends is thereby
compromised, impairment and disability become matters of justice. It is in

this way that disability and justice are related to one another in the capability approach. In identifying disability as an aspect of individuals emerging from the interlocking of personal and external factors, as mentioned above, the approach sets aside the debate over the causes of disability, and promotes a direct concern with functionings and with providing the social bases of adequate capability to pursue valued ends. The capability approach thereby provides a criterion of justice that is sensitive to disabled people's interests. Two elements appear crucial in positioning a capability perspective on disability with respect to dimensions of justice: the place of disability in the metric chosen in evaluating people's reciprocal positions in social arrangements, and the choice of design of the social framework. I now turn my attention to each of these dimensions.

The capability perspective provides a metric of interpersonal comparison in which the personal characteristics that regulate the conversion of resources and goods into valuable ends should define individual shares. Thus, according to capability theorists, physical and mental impairments should receive attention under a just institutional order and the distribution of resources and goods should be correlated with the distribution of natural features. In this sense, disability is evaluated as a 'vertical inequality', or as a kind of difference that, in affecting the individual set of valuable capabilities, and unlike a 'horizontal inequality' such as the colour of one's eyes (Pogge, 2004), has to be addressed as a matter of justice. For instance, as we have seen, the interest of a wheelchair user has to be accounted for in comparisons made in the space of capabilities and, consequently, a wheelchair provided as a matter of justice. Moreover, consideration should be given to the full set of capabilities available to the person using the wheelchair, and when environmental or social barriers hinder her capabilities these should be removed as a matter of justice too. Seeking equality in the space of capability implies using a metric in which disability, considered as one aspect of human diversity and as a limitation on relevant capability, has to be addressed within the distributive pattern of functionings and capabilities. This implies extra provision for disabled people as a matter of justice, and such provision to a large extent does not appear to be a straightforward 'compensation' for some natural individual deficits, since social frameworks are as fundamental to the relational nature of disability as individual traits are.

The second fundamental element of a capability perspective on disability pertains to the criterion of social justice and the design of social arrangements. If we agree that the design of the dominant social framework substantially determines who is competent and who is incompetent (Buchanan *et al.*, 2000: 290), who is included and who is excluded, and whether impairment becomes disability, and hence a limitation of capability, then the burdens of justice must be discharged largely through the choice of appropriate social arrangements. Buchanan defines the dominant co-operative framework as the 'institutional infrastructure of social interaction' (Buchanan *et al.*, 2000: 288) and describes the framework of most advanced industrialized societies as extremely complex, and involving institutional structures as well as economic ones, highly specified symbolic languages, and the dominance of competitive markets in the private sectors. The demands on individuals in this society are very high and determine a correspondingly high threshold of competence, involving complex arrays of skills and abilities. In placing these demands on individuals, this dominant social framework already implies who is excluded and who is included. The choice of dominant social framework is, according to Buchanan, like choosing which game a group of people is going to play. If the game chosen is, say, bridge, then for instance young children will be necessarily excluded from the game. Conversely, if the game chosen is 'family', then participation by children is certainly possible. The point is that the choice of the framework determines the level of inclusion, and involves possibly competing interests,[7] namely the interest of those able to efficiently participate in the scheme and those potentially excluded from it. The design and choice of a dominant co-operative social framework is consequently a matter of justice, and one that should be guided by a criterion of social justice that balances the interests of impaired people with those of 'normal' people. Thus, the slogan of the disabled people's movement, 'change society, not the individual', needs to be evaluated with respect to these considerations, too.

However, the balancing of interests between disabled and non-disabled people and the claim that the burdens of justice should be discharged largely through the adjustment of social and institutional arrangements need further specification. Here the problem consists in determining the demands of justice when provision aimed at 'intervention' on the impaired individual proves not only more efficient, but also enables a broader range of opportunities for functionings than the actual possible changes to social and institutional arrangements.[8] The contentious case of cochlear implants for hearing-impaired children is a clear example of the complexity of the issues at stake. Cochlear implants are technological means which overcome deafness through electrical stimulation of the auditory nerve (Sparrow, 2005: 135). These implants, available both to adults who have lost their hearing and to children born deaf or deafened during early childhood, facilitate the child's learning of spoken language, but significantly curtail the ability to learn Sign Language. What are the implications of the funding for, and the availability of, this treatment? While providing cochlear implants to deaf children certainly complies with the liberal principle of ensuring broader opportunities for effectively functioning in the individuals' dominant social framework, and hence broader capability, such provision is conversely regarded by many within the Deaf Community as a restriction of opportunities for participating in the 'natural' Deaf Community to which these children belong. As noted above,[9] the capability criterion of justice presented in my account remains unspecified on the decision of whether to adjust the social and environmental design, say by generalizing the use of Sign Language, or instead support cochlear implants. A complex evaluation of the interests of disabled and non-disabled people compounds this question, as well as similar ones, and a more precise, comprehensive and unified capability criterion of justice than that presented here is therefore needed for adjudicating these cases. Such a criterion would presumably include considerations of respect as well as fairness, and could be envisaged as the result of the processes of open public reasoning advocated by Sen.

Despite these contentious and still open questions, however, there are two compelling reasons for inclusion, and hence for a criterion of social justice that aims at promoting full capability with respect to disability. The first relates to the devastating consequences of exclusion on the lives and well-being of those excluded, not to mention the disrespect that such exclusion shows, and the second relates to the balancing of interests that such a criterion can aspire to. The capability perspective on disability provides important insights towards such a criterion for social justice in evaluating the demands of disability within the space of capability, in considering disability as having a specific place in the metric used to assess individual shares, and in reinstating the importance of the social framework both in influencing disability and in determining inclusion.

Notwithstanding these positive and promising insights, however, the capability approach faces some problems and challenges. To some of these I shall now turn my attention in the final section of this chapter.

4. Problems with the Capability Approach

There are several problems with the normative framework of the capability approach. The first, and probably most significant one, relates to the unspecified character of the approach, particularly in Sen's version, and the related problems of listing relevant capabilities and indexing them. Connected to this first difficulty is a second one, namely the vagueness of the concept of capability and, consequently, the necessity of providing further and more precise articulations of its meaning. Let us consider these difficulties in turn.

As we have seen, Sen does not specify a list of relevant capabilities, but maintains that this should be the result of processes of public reasoning and discussion, both in relation to the selection of relevant capabilities and their indexing, i.e. their weighting against each other, and their evaluation in each context. However, there are countless capabilities that people may have reason to value, some important to well-being, such as participating in public without shame, and others relatively more trivial, such as choosing a washing powder (Williams, 1985). Furthermore, not all individuals can achieve all valued functionings. The difficulty here resides in deciding which capabilities are relevant and how they can be evaluated, both independently and in relation to each other.[10] Consider for instance the capability set of a hearing-impaired individual and that of a person suffering from arthritis. How can we compare these very different sets of capabilities? And, moreover, how can we decide which person is disadvantaged, and, consequently, less well-off than the other? Further, the problem becomes even more complex when comparing the set of capabilities of the people in the example with that of many others, who may have – and value – certain capabilities and not others. Given the unspecified character of the approach, this evaluation appears to be at least problematic. In this sense, therefore, Sen's approach is vulnerable to the charge that either it needs an objective view of what kinds of human functionings are valuable – which could potentially violate the liberal principle of neutrality and perhaps require discounting the actual valuation of some individuals – or must distribute resources to equalize capabilities which are patently not of the same worth.[11]

Sen replies to this critique with two considerations. First, he highlights how his approach entails the selection of some basic, fundamental capabilities, which would figure in every list of relevant capabilities, and in every social context (Sen, 2004: 79). Second, he emphasizes the 'reach of democracy' in articulating important and valued capabilities in specific contexts, while pointing out the limits of pure theoretical accounts in relation to the variables of each context. More specifically, with reference to selecting capabilities, Sen outlines a specific 'list' of basic capabilities which, as he explains, 'demand attention in any theory of justice and more generally in social assessment' (Sen, 2004: 78). In his understanding, basic capabilities are a subset of all capabilities, and refer to the possibility of satisfying 'certain crucially important functionings up to certain minimally adequate levels' (Sen, 1980: 41; 1992: 45 n.19). They include the capability to be sheltered, nourished, to be educated and to appear in public without shame (Sen, 1999: 20; 1992: 69). Sen maintains that the discussion of these relevant capabilities is central to his approach, specifically in contrast to commodities (Sen, 2004: 78; 1985), but argues against determining a fixed and complete list of capabilities, valuable in all cases and contexts, and not open to public reasoning. He claims that such a list would deny the importance of 'what the citizens come to understand and value' (Sen, 2004: 78) through democratic discussion, and would be divorced from the particular reality of any society. Further, he maintains that even within a given list, the problem of indexing capabilities cannot be avoided, and moreover, that ordering capabilities cannot be determined *a priori* from the circumstances of each specific context. In his words,

> For example, the ability to be well nourished cannot in general be put invariably *above* or *below* the ability to be well sheltered, so that the tiniest improvement of one will always count as more important than a large change in the other. We may have to give priority to the ability to be well nourished when people are dying of hunger in their homes, whereas the freedom to be sheltered may rightly receive more weight when people are in general well fed, but lack shelter.
>
> (Sen, 2004: 78)

Hence the fundamental importance accorded to public reasoning and democratic discussion in his approach. Further, the focus on capabilities, rather than on functionings, is precisely aimed at ensuring individual choice among valued functionings and the formation of different individual life plans, in line with the liberal tradition underlying Sen's perspective. However, this position still leaves open some difficulties in adjudicating between different sets of non-basic, more complex capabilities, as illustrated for instance in the case of the hearing-impaired person and the person suffering from arthritis. Moreover, as noticed above, the capabilities essential to democratic participation should be the object of prior constitutional guarantee in order to allow the process of public discussion to take place.

Nussbaum's articulation of the capabilities approach, as we have seen, provides a list of functional capabilities, which, in her view, would be universally accepted as essential to human flourishing. She maintains that these capabilities 'exert a moral claim that they should be developed' (Nussbaum, 2000: 83) and specifies a threshold level that should be guaranteed to all citizens as a matter of justice. Nussbaum further maintains that, below the threshold, capabilities are not fungible, as each of them is crucial for a truly human life. Her account is therefore more directly concerned with addressing the problem of selecting and indexing capabilities than Sen's. However, albeit providing an answer to the problem, some maintain that Nussbaum provides only a partial response to it (Brighouse, 2004: 73–5; Wolff and De-Shalit, 2007: 89–94). More specifically, Brighouse notices that specifying a threshold level of capabilities allows the identification of the least advantaged as those individuals who do not have all the functional capabilities, and up to the required level. This provides some guidance, both normatively and for public policy, and helps in partially addressing the indexing problem by directing attention to the achievement of the established threshold level for all citizens. More critical is the position of Wolff and De-Shalit, who not only maintain that setting thresholds necessarily entails levels of arbitrariness, thus somehow undermining their validity, but also highlight the possible implausibility of a view that gives priority to the achievement of a threshold, without due attention to contextual factors, or the possible inefficiency pertaining to the achievement of the threshold itself (Wolff and De-Shalit, 2007: 93). This view, they notice, may legitimate enormous expenses devoted to the achievement of the required threshold, thus leading to inefficiency, while discounting the possibility of different and less inefficient distributions of resources. These latter comments seem to point more towards the direction suggested by Sen for addressing the problem of selecting and indexing capabilities through processes of open public reasoning, rather than predetermining certain thresholds of capabilities deemed basically necessary to functionings as a human being.

A second difficulty faced by the approach, and specifically by Sen's version, consists in the vagueness of the concept of capability. While acknowledging the value of Sen's view, Wolff (2007) highlights the vagueness of the concept of capability, and therefore of the capability approach in general. Wolff points out that Sen's understanding of capability in terms of opportunities for functionings is inscribed in a framework that rightly seeks to provide people with the opportunities to achieve certain functionings, namely those they have reason to value, rather than supplying achieved functionings. This is aimed at ensuring that people can exercise degrees of choice and responsibility, thus enacting their specific conception of what constitutes a worthwhile life. However, Wolff maintains that this appealing aim conceals a lack of clarity in the approach, since, generally speaking, opportunities are the only kind of goods that governments can legitimately offer (Wolff, 2007: 7). Furthermore, Wolff connects the unspecified character of the approach to the vagueness of the idea of a capability. An opportunity for functioning, he claims, can become an achieved functioning only upon exercising some actions on the part of the agent, that is, only if this action falls within the agent's power. Consequently, in his view the real issue at stake consists in specifying what kind of actions to expect of people in order for them to achieve and enjoy a certain functioning, i.e. to have a capability in the relevant sense (Wolff, 2007: 8). Wolff suggests a notion of reasonableness that justifies acting in some ways rather than others, not only at an individual but also at an interpersonal level. Thus, a person is expected to act on opportunities, and achieve the related functionings, only insofar as this is interpersonally reasonable to expect. This constitutes, in his view, a 'genuine' opportunity for functioning, as distinct from, and more specific than, a 'formal' opportunity (Wolff, 2007: 8).

Wolff's critique and further specification of the concept of capability presents a careful and plausible account, which is generally compatible with Sen's endorsement of democratic processes and open public reasoning for selecting capabilities. Moreover, in specifying a notion of interpersonal reasonableness in relation to the achievement of functionings, Wolff provides a much-needed account of the kind of reason required for a capability to count as relevant. Perhaps Wolff's concept of reasonableness, in order to be theoretically and politically fully justified, should be further determined in relation to more explicit criteria of what constitutes reasonableness. As he aptly notices, his account is likely to be contentious, given the different notions of reasonableness that people may have (Wolff, 2007: 9). However, Wolff's is an important clarification and addition to the idea of capability and to the capability framework more generally.

Concluding Comments

Conceptualizing impairment and disability within the capability approach takes their understandings beyond the divide between individual and social elements characterizing current 'models' of disability, and towards a relational and multidimensional perspective. In capability terms, disability is seen as a specific aspect of human diversity emerging from the interlocking of individual with social, environmental and circumstantial factors. It is therefore seen as a disadvantage interrelated both to impairment and to the design of social arrangements. This disadvantage, which corresponds to an effective capability limitation, thus to a restriction in freedom, has to be addressed as a matter of justice. It is in this sense that the capability metric is sensitive to disabled people's interests. Moreover, the democratic process advocated by Sen's version of the approach is responsive also to one of the more pressing demands for participation by disabled people's movements. Despite the internal problems faced by the capability approach, the perspective on impairment and disability it suggests positively advances the understanding and the evaluation of disability as a specific human difference.

This perspective, as we shall see, has important implications both for addressing the problems of current understandings of disabilities and special educational needs, and for determining what constitutes a just educational provision for students identified as having disabilities and special educational needs. I consider some of these implications in the next chapter.

Chapter 5

Beyond the Dilemma of Difference: The Capability Perspective on Disability and Special Educational Needs

The current framework in special and inclusive education is hindered by a tension between the aim to treat all learners as the same, and the intention to treat them as different, with due attention to their individual needs. This tension between 'sameness' and 'difference' – the dilemma of difference analysed in Chapter 1 – subsumes two fundamental and inter-related questions. The first concerns the problem of identifying and defining disabilities and special educational needs, while the second consists in determining how best to respond to these 'differences' in order to meet the equal entitlement of *all* children to education. The debate on these issues largely reflects the opposing perspectives in socio-medicine and disability studies explored in previous chapters. It is therefore characterized, on the one hand, by positions that see disabilities and special educational needs as individual or 'within-child' limitations (the 'medical model'), and on the other, by positions that see them as limitations and deficits of school systems, a failure to accommodate the diversity of children (the 'social model').

This opposition between individual and social elements, as we have seen, is not only artificial, but leads also to limited and unsatisfactory conceptions of both disability and special educational needs. As Norwich notices,

> [I]ndividual difficulty versus the organizational inflexibility is a false causal opposition. The social and the individual are not exclusive alternatives between which causal accounts are chosen. We need accounts which can accommodate the individual personal with the social organizational.
>
> (Norwich, 1996: 20)

This absence of normative frameworks encompassing the complex relational dimension of disability, and its evaluation with respect to notions of justice or fair educational entitlements, is also evident at the level of schooling systems, where inequalities in provision are widespread and pervasive. As we have seen in Chapter 1, the educational provision, and specifically the funding for students with disabilities and special educational needs, is characterized by substantial inequalities, both in England and in the USA (the countries directly analysed in this work. See Evans *et al.*, 2001; Marsh, 2003: 74, 81; and Parrish, 2000: 433). Moreover, evidence suggests that differences and inequalities in provision are a common feature of many Western industrialized countries as well (OECD, 2000, 2005, 2007).

In this chapter, I argue that the capability perspective on impairment and disability helps in resolving the tensions at the core of the dilemma of difference. The approach provides a framework that allows the interplay between the theoretical dimension of conceptualizing disability and special educational needs as aspects of human diversity (the difference), and the political level of responding to the equal entitlement of all children to education (the sameness). As I hope to demonstrate, the concepts of functionings (people's beings and doings) and capabilities (people's real opportunities for functionings) are key in advancing the educational thinking on these issues.

I also address two important objections to the capability perspective on disability thus outlined. These argue against the feasibility of the approach in representing the interests of disabled people on grounds of its stigmatization of disability and its overstated emphasis on functional capabilities. In the course of the discussion, I provide counter-arguments that reassert the validity of the approach in responding to the demands of justice for disabled people. This clears the path for examining, in the following chapters of the book, what constitutes educational equality for students with disabilities and special educational needs.

1. Beyond the Dilemma of Difference

The concepts of functionings and capability and the centrality of human diversity in the assessment of individuals' relative advantages are among the capability approach's theoretical strengths and innovative insights. They prove particularly important in informing a perspective able to express the complex nature of disability and its relevance for theories of justice. As we have seen in Chapter 4, reconceptualizing impairment and disability within the capability approach implies reframing these concepts in terms of functionings and capabilities, and it is perhaps worth restating here the main elements of this perspective. Impairment is a personal feature that may affect certain functionings and, therefore, become a disability. Consequently, disability is a restriction of functionings. This is the result of the interlocking of personal with social and circumstantial features. Since functionings are constitutive of a person's being, and capability represents the various combinations of functionings that a person can achieve, and hence her freedom to choose one type of life or another (Sen, 1992: 39–40), a restriction in functionings results in a restriction of the set of functionings available to the person. Consequently, it results in a narrower range of capability. Thus, within this framework, disability is conceptualized as a limitation on relevant capabilities and is seen in its relational aspect, both with respect to impairment and to the design of environmental and social arrangements. Disability is therefore evaluated as a 'vertical inequality', and hence as a kind of difference that has to be addressed as a matter of justice.

1.1. Beyond the dilemma of difference

What is the relevance of this conception of disability as 'capability limitation' for education? And, more specifically, how can this approach resolve the tensions of the dilemma of difference? My argument is that reframing the questions of the dilemma through the capability approach allows the overcoming of the theoretical and political tensions at its core. This position requires some explanation.

The theoretical level of the dilemma concerns the identification and definition of what constitutes disability and special needs in education. Within the capability approach disability and special educational needs are considered aspects of human diversity, and are seen as inherently relational, thus accounting for the interaction between children's individual characteristics and the features of schooling systems. Furthermore, in capability terms, disability and special educational needs are conceptualized in relation to individuals' full sets of functionings and capabilities. These include alternative ways of functionings as well as more typical ones, all part of a comprehensive view that does not rely on predetermined assumptions of normality, thus responding positively to some of the concerns expressed with regard to current understandings of disability and special educational needs.

Some examples can help in illustrating these aspects. Consider, for instance, dyslexia. Resulting from specific neurological conditions,[1] dyslexia may considerably affect the achievement of basic functionings such as reading and writing, and hence it may result in a consistent limitation of immediate functioning achievements and of future capabilities. Dyslexia is therefore an individual disadvantage in certain aspects of education – namely, all those related to literacy where the individual may experience 'learning difficulties'. Yet when the educational environment is appropriately designed to address the learning modalities of an individual with dyslexia, and the individual is receptive to it, this potential restriction in functionings may not become a disability; that is, it may not become a realized functioning restriction. The capability framework looks precisely at the relational aspect of how the individual child interacts with her schooling environment and how she converts resources into functionings, while at the same time considering the design of the environment. No emphasis is placed on within-child factors over educational factors, or vice versa, since the focus of the framework is on the interaction between the two elements. Moreover, no unilateral causal relation is established between individual or indeed circumstantial features and disability or special educational needs. Furthermore, this approach takes into account not only the interaction but also the complexity of both dimensions, individual and circumstantial, as these elements are part of the metric proposed by the approach.

Consider now hearing impairment. Understanding hearing impairment involves looking at how this has an impact on related functionings and capabilities sets within education. Hearing enables other basic functionings such as, for instance, listening and communicating. The latter, while being fundamental to all dimensions of learning, play a specific role, for example, in language acquisition. Hence, prima facie, a complete hearing loss, as in the case of deafness, significantly restricts basic functionings and relevant capabilities. However, there may be a second way of considering hearing impairment and of looking at its specific implications for education. We need to refer here to concepts of alternative or atypical functionings. It is widely recognized that deaf people can effectively 'listen' to vocal messages by way of 'lip-reading' and that they can communicate through Sign Language. For example, in the community of Martha's Vineyard, the wider population commonly and effectively adopted both English and Sign Language, learning them from infancy and thus virtually allowing the communicative functionings of the deaf group of the community to be exercised (Rèe, 1999: 201). It is important to notice that there was a relatively large congenitally deaf population on Martha's Vineyard, and that this was probably a determinant factor in the adoption of both languages. Yet our social arrangements are not designed like Martha's Vineyard, and are instead based almost exclusively on vocal languages. Without exploring here the reasons for and the implications of the design of such arrangements, it is worth considering how education can enhance (or hinder) the achievement of alternative or atypical functionings. Education can play a significant role in expanding capabilities for deaf children while providing for the functionings, including the alternative or atypical functionings that they can achieve. Many hearing impaired people can become effectively competent in the understanding of two languages, albeit not completely in their production, through the adoption of specific learning and teaching strategies (Jarvis, 2007; Gregory, 2005).

Conceptualizing disability and special needs in education in terms of functionings limitations and related restrictions in capabilities, therefore, provides fruitful answers to the theoretical tension of the dilemma of difference. Before addressing the second level of the dilemma, i.e. its political dimension, it is worth touching upon the possible implications of the capability perspective for classificatory systems in education. Recall here that, related to the theoretical level of the dilemma of difference, a crucial aspect of the educational debate concerns the use of so-called 'labels'. As for the causal relation between impairment and disability, the debate about the use of definitions of disability and special educational needs, and related classifications, sees also polarized views. On one side are perspectives that endorse the use of categories and classification systems in the belief that these underlie differential and appropriate educational provision. On the other side are perspectives that critically highlight the possible discriminatory and oppressive use of these systems. The capability perspective I propose does not necessarily presuppose any specific system of classification of disability, or indeed special educational needs, nor does it encourage the use of particular forms of categorization. However, it does not imply the uselessness of medical or psychological understandings of certain disabilities or special educational needs either.[2] Rather, the approach outlines the variety of possible functionings, and the restrictions that may occur in relation to specific impairments, in their interaction with particular social and educational arrangements. Thus, although differences pertaining to disability and special educational needs are specifically conceptualized and accounted for in the capability approach, they do not appear to be used in stigmatizing or discriminatory ways. However, the wavering reader may, at this point, raise questions about the worth of the approach to 'settling' issues of educational needs. After all, it may be claimed, how can we determine educational 'needs' that are different from typical and average ones? This, in my view, need not be the case. The concept of functionings, and its application to education in relation, for instance, to reading and writing, or mathematical reasoning functionings, is useful in identifying important enabling competencies, as well as possible restrictions, or atypical forms of functionings, which may require specific adjustments. While the contribution of the capability perspective outlined is primarily a theoretical and ethical one, the centrality of functionings and capabilities in the perspective is also important in providing guidance for the design of curricula and particular forms of pedagogy aimed at expanding freedoms. Thus, the reach of the approach goes beyond the fundamental aspect of definitions and of entitlement. The more practice-oriented elements of the approach, however, are beyond the scope of my analysis. I now turn to the 'political' level of the dilemma of difference, which considers more directly issues of provision.

The second level of the dilemma of difference entails considerations about the just entitlement of all children to education. In short, it is the problem of treating all children as equals, thus accentuating their 'sameness'. Reconsidering differences and diversity relating to disability and special educational needs in terms of functionings and capabilities implies seeing these as central in the evaluation of individuals' capabilities, i.e. of their effective opportunities for educational functionings. This, in turn, relates to issues of justice and equalization of people's opportunities to achieve well-being. In view of these considerations, let us now analyse how the capability metric evaluates, for example, dyslexia and hearing impairment in relation to education. Dyslexia, as we have seen, impairs reading and writing functionings, and hence a child with dyslexia is disadvantaged in certain aspects of her education when compared to a 'non-dyslexic' child. Since being literate has intrinsically and instrumentally important values, dyslexia limits not only the achievement of reading and writing functionings, but also the achievement of prospective relevant capabilities yielded by education. In short, it limits contingent and future freedoms. Consequently, dyslexia is considered a difference that, in affecting functionings, constitutes an identifiable disadvantage. This is not an absolute disadvantage, but a relative one, depending on the design of educational systems. Suppose, for example, that there is an educational system completely based on visual arts curricula. In such education, dyslexia would certainly have a very different impact from the one it has on literacy-based systems. Ultimately, in capability terms dyslexia constitutes a vertical inequality, and, as such, addressing it in terms of additional resources in literacy-based systems is a matter of justice. Likewise, the capability metric considers functioning in alternative ways – such as that of hearing-impaired children – a personal feature, which stands as a vertical inequality with respect to the functional demands of dominant educational arrangements.

The capability framework outlined, however, is not applicable only to 'mild' notions of special educational needs, but seems justified also in relation to more complex ones. Consider the case of autistic spectrum disorders. As in previous examples, the two dimensions highlighted by the capability approach, i.e. considering autism in terms of functionings and capabilities and evaluating it through a capability metric, not only capture the complexity of autism both in itself and with respect to the design of educational systems, but also fundamentally show how it stands as a vertical inequality with respect to the 'absence of autism'. Let us see how. Although 'experts differ on the range and the severity of behaviours identified with autism' (Alderson and Goodey, 2003: 73), and despite the fact that autism has a vast array of different manifestations – and hence the more appropriate definition of autistic spectrum disorders[3] – the condition is generally defined in terms of a disorder in the development of mental and psychological functionings. It is characterized as a qualitative impairment, which affects functionings of social interactions and social integration, the acquisition of language, and verbal and non-verbal communication (Frith, 2003: 9–10). This impairment may be accompanied by strengths in other functionings, like 'a style of information processing that is focussed on detail' or excellent selective memorizing functionings, and fluent and articulate language related to specific individual interests. However, none of these possible functionings seem to act as alternative functionings, thus somehow 'counteracting' the qualitative impairment itself. Moreover, the level and significance of the impairment vary from severe to mild in relation to the child's development, and differ at different ages (Frith, 2003: 206–7). A child with autism, therefore, may present significant limitations in functionings such as talking, understanding ordinary communication, understanding verbal and non-verbal cues, attributing thoughts to others and intentions to their actions and, more generally, understanding and participating in ordinary social interactions. Moreover, reading functionings, especially those related to reading for meaning and to processing content, may be significantly limited, as is the capacity to relate meanings to contexts. Notwithstanding the complexity of the condition, in the case of autism too, education can play a crucial role in expanding functionings, and hence present and future capabilities. Explicit learning activities such as promoting the knowledge of own and others' thoughts or the emphasis on conscious rules to reach the ability of understanding non-literal remarks in social utterances, have all proven to be effective ways, among others, of enhancing communicative functionings in children with autism (Frith, 2003: 218). Although more difficult to highlight in its relation to the design of educational systems, given its foundational and consistent limitation in functionings, autism presents some relational aspects to the choice of educational arrangements.[4] Let us imagine, for instance, an educational system characterized by uniquely promoting and strengthening the child's specific individual ability and interests, irrespective of a wide array of activities and of the achievements of broader educational aims. Suppose, moreover, that the school environment were designed so as to limit or even nullify social interactions by focusing on the assignment of specific individual tasks only. In this educational system the impact of autism would certainly be less significant than the one it has on a system characterized by a wide range of learning activities and by the substantial promotion of forms of social interactions. This 'understanding' of autism in terms of capability leads us once again to the fundamental evaluation implied by the capability metric with respect to the functioning restrictions of the disorders. The limitations experienced by children with autism may starkly restrict their functionings achievements and their future choice among sets of valuable beings and doings, and hence of valuable capabilities. In this sense, autism is a vertical inequality, and a child with autism is at a considerable and, in some cases, pervasive disadvantage when compared to a non-disabled child.

In conclusion, in light of the specific role of education in expanding capabilities,[5] a child's functionings limitations result in limitations of the child's future capabilities. The capability metric highlights disability and special educational needs as vertical inequalities when compared to the absence of disability or special needs, or as kinds of differences that, in limiting functionings, have to be addressed as a matter of justice, since this contributes to the equalization of the individual's capability to achieve well-being. The capability approach highlights the equalization of people's effective freedoms, their capabilities, as the main goal of social, and therefore educational, institutions, and suggests that within their design, the inequality related to disability and special educational needs has to be addressed through the deployment of additional resources as part of a just educational provision (I address this aspect in more detail in the next two chapters).

These, I maintain, are important and fundamental insights provided by the capability approach to disability and special educational needs. Before proceeding to analyse the implications of the approach for equality, however, some objections to the framework outlined so far need addressing. These will be the focus of the next section.

2. Defending the Capability Perspective on Disability and Special Educational Needs

My analysis so far has attempted to highlight how the capability approach provides an important normative framework for a conception of disability and special educational needs that goes beyond current unilateral perspectives, while providing a metric for interpersonal comparisons that make progress towards formulating a just distributive response to disability and special educational needs. However, the capability perspective has been critiqued in relation to its feasibility of offering a positive account and treatment of disability. As David Wasserman points out, the approach still 'faces formidable challenges in developing a realistic and plausible account of political justice that incorporates people with disabilities' (Wasserman, 2006: 215). In this section, I analyse and address two of these challenges. The first, raised by Thomas Pogge (2004), concerns the alleged stigmatization of disability as an inferior natural endowment entailed by the capability metric. Pogge maintains that the capability approach, in considering disabilities in terms of vertical inequalities, evaluates them as negative characteristics. This leads to a view of disabled people as less well-endowed than non-disabled people, and thus to their stigmatization as 'less valuable' than others. The second objection, raised by David Wasserman (1998), is directed specifically to Nussbaum's earlier version of her capabilities approach, and concerns the 'rigid and dogmatic account of human flourishing' she proposes (Wasserman, 1998: 196). This account, Wasserman argues, tends to emphasize not only the value of functional capabilities, but also the actual range of opportunities for functionings, thus presupposing that a wider set of functionings and capabilities is preferable and intrinsically more valuable than a different and more restricted one. This, according to Wasserman, leads to questionable comparisons of otherwise incommensurable and different ways of flourishing, such as that of a disabled person as different from that of an able-bodied person, and to the wrong evaluation of the former as inferior to the latter.

My purpose in this section is to argue in defence of the insights of the capability approach and to reassert the value of its positive account of impairment and disability (and, consequently, of special educational needs, too). In particular, I argue that Pogge's view underestimates the theoretical reach of the approach and perhaps overstates its alleged stigmatizing connotations. Further, I contend that Wasserman's critique may reflect a partial understanding of the capability approach. It presents also a questionable position with respect to the possibility of establishing comparisons between people's states, and more so since these comparisons are fundamental to issues of justice. Wasserman (2006) has recently revised his critique, and has conceded that later theoretical developments of the approach, proposed by Nussbaum in her *Frontiers of Justice* (2006), provide a framework sensitive to disabled people's demands and more apt to encompassing their flourishing. However, it seems interesting and important to respond to his initial criticism, as this helps in exemplifying the debate on the theoretical reach of the capability approach. Let us start by addressing the more radical of the two objections, Pogge's critique, and then proceed to analyse Wasserman's concern.

2.1 Pogge's critique

Thomas Pogge's objection to the capability approach, and specifically to its evaluation of disability, is potentially problematic for the perspective I outline and defend in this book. However, it is perhaps less justified than it claims to be. Pogge's critique is based on John Rawls's egalitarian position, and is inscribed in the debate between Rawlsians (or resourcists, as Pogge refers to them) and capability 'theorists'. Without engaging in lengthy expositions of Rawls's complex egalitarianism,[6] or indeed in the debate between the two perspectives, it is worth recalling here some elements of both. According to Rawls, social arrangements should be designed to give people equal holdings of social primary goods, specified as those features of institutions and resources that free and equal citizens need in order to live a complete life.[7] Notably, both Sen and Nussbaum point out how a focus on primary goods, and hence ultimately on resources, overlooks fundamental dimensions of inequality, given people's different conversions of resources into valuable functionings. Thus, they contend that what is important in evaluating individuals' relative positions is not their shares of primary goods or resources, but what people can actually do with them, and hence their focus on capability. A key difference between the two approaches lies precisely in the element of sensitivity to personal differences in interpersonal comparisons. While the resourcist approach does not take into account personal heterogeneities as relevant factors in determining people's advantages or disadvantages, the capability approach argues instead that these variations are fundamental to the evaluation of relative positions.

Pogge's critique is inscribed in this debate. He maintains that the capability approach is an important and helpful heuristic device, but argues that it does not provide a criterion of social justice that could in any way be considered a valid alternative to the resourcist perspective (Pogge, 2004: 176). The capability approach, in his view, overstates its contribution to the egalitarian debate, and cannot ultimately be justified. In order to substantiate his claims, Pogge challenges the capability approach on several counts, but primarily and powerfully on what he maintains are its serious problems in dealing with natural inequalities. More specifically, he claims, the capability approach, in including individual natural differences among the elements of moral concerns, ends up identifying disability as 'vertical inequalities', and hence in stigmatizing disabled people as overall worse endowed than other people. Conversely, Pogge claims, the resourcist view considers personal endowments irrelevant to moral concerns, thus equating disability to any other natural feature, like the colour of one's eyes, or one's height. These features are considered overall 'horizontal inequalities', and as such do not constitute grounds for additional resources. The resourcist view, Pogge concludes, avoids stigmatizing people on the basis of their natural characteristics, and it is therefore better positioned to respond to disability than the capability approach. In Pogge's words,

> While the resourcist approach is supported by this conception of natural inequality as horizontal, the capability approach requires that natural inequality be conceived as vertical. When a capability theorist affirms that institutional schemes ought to be biased in favor of certain persons on account of their natural endowments, she thereby advocates that these endowments should be characterized as deficient and inferior, and those persons as naturally disfavoured and worse endowed – not just in this or that respect, but overall . . .
>
> (Pogge, 2004: 221)

And furthermore,

> The capability approach seeks to give such a person [*disabled person*] a claim in justice, so she need not ask for extra resources as a special favor, but can come forward proudly, with her head held high, insisting on additional resources as her due. (. . .) To have a valid claim that she is owed compensation as a matter of justice, she must present her special limitation, need, or handicap as one that outweighs all other particular vertical inequalities and entitles her to count as worse endowed all things considered.
>
> (Pogge, 2004: 222)

Can the capability approach respond to this objection? A first consideration refers to a possible agreement between the two approaches in evaluating the impact of the design of social and institutional arrangements on disability. As we have seen, the extent to which impairment becomes a disability relates to the design of social and institutional arrangements. For instance, a mobility impairment becomes a disability when wheelchair accessibility and facilities are unavailable. In this case, both the resourcist and the capability approach would convene on the necessary environmental and institutional adjustments for the elimination of inequalities. However, how can the resourcist explain the necessary adjustment in the institutional design in relation to disability? As Unterhalter and Brighouse point out, the difference between a visually impaired person and a sighted one does not consist in unequal shares of resources, but in their possibility to function in relation to the design of certain arrangements. More specifically, they note,

> The blind person does not have an expensive taste, as, for example, we might think of someone who is sighted but prefers reading Braille to reading print, because she enjoys the tactile experience. But why not? It's hard to explain why not without appealing to the fact that she (unlike the sighted Braille reader) lacks a valuable capability absent but for the provision of Braille. It is hard to see how the primary goods approach can determine whether social institutions are set up to the disadvantage of the disabled without appealing to some notion of functioning.
>
> (Unterhalter and Brighouse, 2007: 76)

It seems, therefore, that the capability approach introduces considerations relating to functionings that are essential to the just evaluation of disability in interpersonal comparisons. Perhaps the differences between the two perspectives emerge even more starkly when considering cases when inequalities in functionings cannot be addressed with social and environmental changes. Consider, for instance, the restrictions related to visual impairments with respect to the possibilities of recognizing people, or reading social and non-verbal cues in social interactions.[8] Clearly, no environmental or institutional reform could currently be conceived to the extent of addressing the limitations in social functionings experienced and expressed by visually disabled people in these cases. How does the resourcist evaluate this situation? In order to avoid considering the limitation a vertical inequality, the resourcist needs to think of the disadvantage either as entirely socially determined or as overall irrelevant. However, both positions appear evidently problematic. First, the specific limitation of the visually disabled person in the situation mentioned above cannot be considered entirely socially determined and cannot be addressed by a related institutional change. Second, and consequently, the resourcist, in maintaining that differences associated with impairments and disability are irrelevant to questions of justice, ends up seriously overlooking substantive inequalities related to certain restrictions in functionings. A further example can confirm this position. Consider the case of special educational needs, and specifically the case of dyslexia analysed above. Why should we devote additional resources or adopt specific learning techniques in teaching children with dyslexia, if dyslexia is indeed a horizontal inequality, comparable, for instance, to being medium build? A child with dyslexia and a medium build child attending the same class do not have inequality of resources as such. Both can presumably enjoy the same facilities when the same levels of resources are available to them. However, the child with dyslexia is evidently at a disadvantage in reading and writing functionings with respect to the other child, and this disadvantage seems better addressed by a notion of functionings. Thus, the capability approach captures a fundamental dimension of justice in drawing attention to whether the child with dyslexia has the same opportunities for functioning as the medium build child. This is, contra Pogge, the valuable insight of the approach.

However, this defence of the capability approach does not entirely address the stigmatization that Pogge ascribes to it, and a further argument is therefore needed. I start by noting that recognizing, as the capability approach does, that certain personal characteristics, in interacting with circumstantial factors, may lead to a vertical inequality, does not establish a relation between such inequality and any stigmatizing effect. Nevertheless, disabled people's movements, as we have seen, have long denounced the discrimination and oppression embedded in any evaluation of disadvantage. Pogge's critique of the capability perspective presents some similarities with that view, in that it appears to argue against establishing any correlation between impairment, disability and disadvantage. But does the evaluation of disability and special educational needs in terms of capability limitation really correlate to a stigmatizing view? I maintain that this need not be the case, since the recognition of the kind of difference entailed by impairment and disability is inscribed in a view of human heterogeneity that encompasses all aspects of diversity. The capability approach does not necessarily stigmatize disability in as much as it does not stigmatize pregnant or lactating women. Recognizing, as the capability approach does, that certain personal characteristics, in interacting with environmental and social factors, may lead to a disability, and that the latter has to be considered in interpersonal comparisons, does not necessarily lead to discriminating positions. Instead, it reconsiders these differences in their specificity and with a view on the person's well-being and her choice over the kind of life she has reason to lead. And undeniably such a choice would be compromised, should disability be addressed in terms of equality of resources only, since in the latter case the person's specific difference and its related possible disadvantage would remain not addressed. Ultimately, in aiming at equality in opportunities for well-being, and in allowing in considerations on valuable different sets of capabilities, not exclusively related to an average person but instead encompassing human heterogeneity, the capability approach is sensitive to issues of positive recognition of differences.[9] Although this represents only a partial response to Pogge's critique, it nevertheless suggests themes for further exploration of issues of respect as fundamentally interrelated to issues of distributive justice, and of how the capability approach may encompass both dimensions.[10]

2.2 Wasserman's critique

In light of these considerations, let us now turn our attention to Wasserman's initial critique of the capability perspective on disability. Although Wasserman refers primarily to Nussbaum's position, his critique questions the foundation of the approach by raising two important issues. The first relates to the excessive emphasis the approach places on standard sensory and motor functionings for human flourishing, while presenting questionable comparisons between different ways of flourishing in life. Being sighted and being blind lead to rather incommensurable ways of flourishing, and it is unclear why a larger set of functionings should determine a better flourishing, Wasserman claims. His second argument, interrelated to the first, refers to the rather fixed version of human flourishing presented by the approach, whereby a restricted set of capabilities for functionings is seen as less valuable than a broader one. Ultimately, according to Wasserman, the capability approach is difficult to translate into a usable metric for comparative well-being and is therefore inadequate to consider issues of disability (1998: 199).

Can the capability approach address these problems in significant ways? I maintain that the arguments discussed with reference to Pogge's critique can effectively be used to counter-argue Wasserman's concerns. Consequently, here I will only add some considerations to those already outlined above. I start by discussing the incommensurability of human flourishing based on comparing sets of functionings. It seems that Wasserman tends not only to overstate the importance accorded to sensor and motor functionings by the approach, but also, and more importantly, to overlook how capabilities – opportunities for functionings – relate to questions of justice. The capability approach considers the individuals' opportunities for functionings and the element of choice among valuable sets, while evaluating individuals' advantage with respect to them. Recall here the example of the visually disabled person experiencing restrictions in her

functionings of reading non-verbal cues in social interactions. While it is
perfectly acceptable to maintain that a person can flourish in the absence
of these functionings, it is conversely rather evident that reading non-
verbal languages enhances people's social interactions, which, in turn,
may contribute to personal well-being. Here the capability approach does
not impose a set of functionings as intrinsically more valuable than
another, but acknowledges the possible disadvantage associated with
certain restrictions in capabilities. After all, while the visually disabled
person cannot, at least under present circumstances,[11] achieve the functioning of reading non-verbal messages, an able-bodied person could
always choose not to read these cues. The acknowledgment of this restriction is relevant for issues of justice. Furthermore, and interrelated to the
previous point, the capability approach does not deny the flourishing of
the lives of disabled people per se, but outlines how certain functioning
restrictions may need additional or appropriate resources exactly when
aiming at human well-being and flourishing. And the importance of this
last point is recognized by Wasserman when he states,

> A society in which people with atypical functions enjoyed roughly the
> same standard of living as the general population, in terms of food,
> clothing, housing, work, security, and leisure, would clearly be more
> just than our own society.
>
> (1998: 200)

This kind of society is really one of the core aims of the capability
approach and hence Wasserman's first concern is actually appropriately
addressed within the approach itself.

But Wasserman's critique goes further, and questions the understanding
of human flourishing in terms of well-being, since he maintains,

> But that society could still be faulted if its impaired citizens, despite
> their comfort, security and leisure, had little opportunity for friend-
> ships, adventure, or cultural enrichment. It is unclear, though, how we
> could assess their comparative disadvantage without recourse to a
> more comprehensive account of human flourishing.
>
> (1998: 200)

Here again, Wasserman's position reflects perhaps an under-specified
account of the capability approach, and, in particular, of its conceptualization of people's well-being. While Wasserman does not express what a
more comprehensive account of human flourishing would involve, thus

somehow eluding his own challenge, he also seems to present a partial account of the concept of well-being as conceptualized within the capability approach, and of how it relates to people's freedom. Recall here that, according to Sen, '[T]he well-being of a person can be seen in terms of the quality (the well-ness, as it were) of the person's being' (Sen, 1992: 39) and consists in functionings and related capabilities. Further, fundamental to the approach is the well-being freedom enjoyed by individuals, thus the possibility of choosing among valuable beings and doings, and hence the actual and effective opportunities to choose one's valued way of flourishing. All the capability approach maintains is that people should be given equal and effective access to these opportunities. Moreover, inequalities should be assessed in terms of these effective and real opportunities for functionings, and any inequality in this space be considered a matter of justice. Ultimately, the capability approach in no way excludes considerations of 'opportunities for friendships, adventure and cultural activities' for disabled people, but, while providing equal and effective access to these functionings, leaves choosing them to the individual. In this sense, it appears that the capability approach can, and indeed does, find appropriate answers to Wasserman's concerns. Furthermore, within the variables that may determine individuals' different conversion factors, the approach requires necessary attention to the social and cultural, and, at least in Sen's version of it, endorses processes of public open reasoning for the choice of valuable capabilities, envisaging the equal participation of disabled citizens. These factors suggest a perspective sensitive to disabled people's demands of equal participation and recognition in determining valuable capabilities and thus effective opportunities for flourishing.

In conclusion, the capability perspective on disability and special educational needs presents a theoretically and morally justified account of the kinds of differences entailed by these dimensions of human heterogeneity. As I have tried to show in this section, the perspective does not necessarily present a stigmatizing view of disability as inferior natural endowments, or an exclusionary understanding of individual flourishing which undervalues disabled people. Rather, the approach seeks to provide the institutional conditions for the well-being of all individuals, in the light of their individual different features.

Concluding Comments

The capability approach usefully advances the theoretical and practical understanding of disability and special educational needs. I believe that it *resolves* the dilemma of difference in the way that Norwich says it needs to be resolved, when he writes: 'Dilemmas call for resolutions rather than solutions. They require the balancing of tensions, accepting less than ideal ways forward, and working positively with uncertainties and complexities' (Norwich, 2007, quoted in Terzi, 2007a: 100). Conceptualizing disability and special educational needs in capability terms involves, on the one hand, seeing them as inherently relational, thus as emerging from the interlocking of personal features and schooling factors, and, on the other hand, reconsidering questions concerning the definition of differences among children within a normative framework aimed at justice and equality. This overrides unilateral understandings relating to artificial individual/social duality, and helps in avoiding the negative 'labelling' associated with current definitions of special educational needs.

The capability perspective on disability and special educational needs seems also theoretically and morally justified against the objections of stigmatization and excessive emphasis on functional capabilities raised by current critiques.

Furthermore, this perspective on disability is inscribed in a normative framework for equality that is responsive to the demands of disability and its positive recognition. The capability approach, as we have seen, is fundamentally concerned with the egalitarian ideal of equal consideration for individuals and aims at providing a wider and more appropriate per-spective for the enactment of this value than current competing accounts. The important egalitarian dimension of the approach is the focus of the next chapter, where I begin to address how the approach positively contributes to the liberal egalitarian debate.

Chapter 6

Capability Equality and the Egalitarian Debate

Theories of distributive justice are fundamentally concerned with the fair distribution of benefits and burdens among individuals. Egalitarians maintain that social and institutional arrangements should be designed to give equal consideration to all in some substantial aspects. This concern with equality subsumes two distinct but interconnected dimensions. The first relates to the kind of equality that we should seek, or, in short, is the 'distribution of what?' question (Sen, 1980; 1992). The second refers instead to the form that such distribution should take, i.e. it refers to the distributive implications proposed. Amartya Sen, as we have seen, defends capability, or opportunity for functionings, as the variable that should be equalized among individuals. Capability, in his view, is the appropriate currency of egalitarian justice and the right alternative to competing perspectives, based respectively on equalizing resources or welfare. According to Sen, these perspectives fail to enact the egalitarian principle of equal concern by focusing either on commodities, rather than on what people can actually do with them, or by evaluating inequalities on the basis of subjective accounts of welfare, such as preference satisfaction or levels of happiness. In contrast, Sen maintains that the capability approach fruitfully expands the range of egalitarian thought in relation to the 'equality of what' question, by evaluating inequalities in people's actual freedoms to be and to do what they value being and doing, thus in their capability. However, since the approach is a normative framework, rather than a complete theory of justice, it does not specify, as least in Sen's version of it, any distributive implication.

This chapter presents an analysis of the main questions informing the egalitarian debate. It aims to show how Sen's capability approach helps in giving coherent expression to the egalitarian concern for equal consideration, and in particular with reference to the evaluation of disability and special educational needs. Furthermore, as we shall see more thoroughly in Chapter 7, the approach provides theoretical foundations fruitful for conceptualizing educational equality.

The chapter is organized in four sections. The first addresses the egalitarian reasons for valuing equality, both intrinsically and instrumentally. The second and third sections focus instead on the two main egalitarian perspectives on equality – equality of resources and equality of welfare, respectively – and try to evaluate to what extent their views treat all individuals as equals. Finally, the last part re-examines elements of the capability approach and focuses specifically, and in more detail than in other chapters, on how they respond to fundamental egalitarian concerns. Throughout the chapter, attention is devoted to the potential insights that each perspective may offer to a view of educational equality.

1. The Debate on Equality

Theories of social justice are concerned with how the design of social and institutional arrangements determines the distribution of benefits and burdens among individuals (Swift, 2001: 19). Egalitarians maintain that equality is the correct distributive principle and argue that social and institutional arrangements should be designed to give equal consideration to all.[1] Subsumed in this position are two interrelated questions. The first concerns why we should treat people as equals, and hence relates to the reasons for valuing equality in itself. I shall refer to this as the 'Why equality' question (Sen, 1992: 12). The second issue concerns how we should treat people as equals, namely what form of equality would best enact the equal consideration due to individuals. As we have seen, Sen (1980; 1992) notably refers to this as the 'equality of what' question. These two issues can be considered interdependent, since knowing the reasons for caring about equality may help in understanding what form of equality we should care about. Thus the fundamental reasons that support equality as a valuable ideal are related to the form of equality that should be sought through social and institutional schemes. Both these questions deserve further attention, and I begin with the 'why equality' question.

Why, then, should we care about equality? According to egalitarians, for two interdependent reasons, which relate respectively to the intrinsic and the instrumental value of equality. There is primarily only one truly intrinsic reason for equality: equality is good in itself, is the correct principle to respond to conflicting demands, and, as such, is a fundamental element of justice.[2] All notions of justice or fairness seem to be underpinned by an elementary understanding of equality, even if only in the formal sense of 'treating like cases alike' or in requiring that inequalities be justified by relevant reasons (White, 2006: 16). Thus equality can be regarded as intrinsically valuable because intrinsically just or fair. Several instrumental reasons support equality as a distributive ideal and complement this intrinsic one. First, there is a theoretical reason: equality is instrumentally valuable because it provides plausibility to theories of justice. In order to be theoretically plausible, these theories have to justify any distribution of benefits and burdens showing that it meets a stipulated ideal of equality. This is important, as Sen argues, since a lack of theoretical plausibility would result in the theory being arbitrarily discriminating and, therefore, difficult to defend (Sen, 1992: 18–19). Second, equality is instrumentally valuable because it is a necessary precondition of political legitimacy. In order to be legitimate in their exercise of power, governments have to provide evidence that their decisions, regulations and actions show and enact the equal concern due to individuals. For instance, any scheme of taxation, to be legitimate, has to be designed in accordance with a certain criterion of equality, and governments have to provide reasons for the aggravations in some people's circumstances, or the added constraint any tax scheme may cause (Dworkin, 2000: 1). Linked to this, a further instrumental reason for equality is that it defends the costs likely to be associated with any particular enforcement of regulations, tax schemes, or law. When such costs are justified on grounds of equal concern, they are made acceptable to those who may otherwise find them unjust. For instance, the regulation to wear seat belts has the added cost of installing such a device. Its implementation, however, enacts equal concern for citizens, albeit of a mildly paternalistic kind, and hence it may be shown to be a just and justified cost. These intrinsic and instrumental reasons provide important answers to the 'why equality' question and confirm the egalitarian position that seeking equality as a political and distributive ideal is a fundamental matter. However, the importance of equality is also interconnected with the specific kind of equality valued, and hence it relates to the second crucial question: what kind of equality would best represent the equal concern due to individuals?

If egalitarians agree to a considerable extent on the value of equality, they disagree rather substantially on this second fundamental issue: the 'equality of what' question. There are different important views on the kind of equality that would best enact the equal consideration due to individuals, and each view focuses on the equalization of rather different variables or currencies. These variables constitute, at the same time, the metrics for the evaluation of people's relative advantages and disadvantages. In what follows, I shall discuss three main positions in the debate on equality: equality of resources, equality of welfare and equality of capabilities.[3] I shall try to illustrate in what form and to what extent these positions give equal consideration to citizens. It is important to state at the outset that all three views appeal to a notion of equality of opportunity, where equality is broadly defined in terms of the equal chances that people have to get, for instance, either resources or welfare. As Richard Arneson puts it, 'The argument for equality of opportunity rather than straight equality is simply that it is morally fitting to hold individuals responsible for the foreseeable consequences of their voluntary choices' (Arneson, 1989: 88). In contrast to a view of equality of outcomes, equality of opportunity thus conceived introduces in the debate not only the dimension of possibilities, but also the important elements of personal responsibility and choice-sensitivity. Thus, people are held responsible, in different degrees, for their voluntary choices and the possible consequences these might entail on how well their lives are going.

Generally, theories supporting equality of resources – also referred to as the resourcist views, as we have seen in the last chapter – maintain that equal consideration to individuals obtains when people have equal shares of resources.[4] Conversely, those advocating equality of welfare – the welfarist perspectives – support the view that equal concern obtains when people are equal in their welfare, seen for instance as happiness or preference satisfaction. While these are only the main abstract ideas underpinning each currency of equality, their more precise specification entails different understandings of resources, as well as the nature of welfare. Finally, as we have seen in previous chapters, equality in capabilities requires equality in the effective opportunities that people have to choose the life they value. In the following sections I shall analyse each of these perspectives in more detail. I shall focus on their metrics for interpersonal comparison and highlight specifically how they respond to issues of differences in 'natural' endowments. At the same time, I shall focus on the possible conceptions of educational equality they suggest, and on the extent to which they might inform a just educational provision, particularly in relation to students with disabilities and special educational needs.

2. The 'Resourcist' Approach

2.1. Equality of primary goods

An important position relating to equality of resources of some kind is the conception of equality as equal shares of primary goods. This position was addressed in previous sections, but it is perhaps worth recalling here some of its main elements in relation to the issue at stake. As we have seen, on this view primary goods are social conditions, features of institutions and resources that free and equal citizens need in order to live a complete life (Rawls, 2001: 58; 1982: 166). These conditions include basic rights and liberties, freedom of movement and choice of occupations against a background of fair equality of opportunity, power and prerogatives of offices and positions of responsibility, income and wealth, and the social bases of self-respect (Rawls, 2001: 58–9). This index is inscribed in a theory of justice that ensures that citizens are equal in their basic liberties, including political ones, and in fair opportunities. Inequalities are permissible only if they are to the advantage of the least well-off people in society, who are identified as those with the lowest holdings of primary goods. The index of primary goods constitutes, therefore, not only a way of evaluating whether people have these lifelong necessary means to lead a complete life, but also of assessing inequalities among individuals (Daniels, 2003: 242).

Both Sen (1980 and 1992) and Nussbaum (2000 and 2006a) critique this view and point out how, by measuring people's relative position with reference to resources, the index of social primary goods neglects the fundamental aspect of human heterogeneity and its implications in terms of advantages or disadvantages. Further, it neglects the fundamental fact that people vary in their efficiency to convert resources into well-being. This was discussed in the last two chapters with specific reference to disability and special educational needs, but it is perhaps worth re-emphasizing the point here. Let us therefore compare the position of two people: Bob, a visually impaired man, and Sally, an able-bodied woman. According to the primary goods approach, if their holdings of primary goods are equal, Bob and Sally are equally well-off, and hence they have equal all-purpose means to live complete lives. Yet it seems plausible to argue that, notwithstanding equality in their social primary goods, Bob might be at a disadvantage with respect to Sally, due to some of his personal characteristics and how they interact with the social and physical environment he inhabits. For instance, his opportunities for independent mobility, say using a car, or for choice of occupations, are presumably not the same as Sally's. Furthermore, reconsider the example I have applied elsewhere in this book, concerning the aspects of communication relating to non-verbal behaviours and their relevance in social interactions. Suppose Bob and Sally are both university lecturers: in this instance, Bob cannot detect non-verbal language in communicating with his students, and hence this important dimension of social interaction is unavailable to him. Sally does not experience this restriction and enjoys students' non-verbal feedback, which may prove helpful in her job. Even with an equal share of primary goods, Bob's relative position is not equal to Sally's. What this example ultimately aims to re-emphasize is that an exclusive focus on resources, rather than on what people can do with them owing to their personal differences, leads to limitations in comparing individuals' relative positions. This appears to question, at least to a certain extent,[5] an equal share of primary goods as a correct and comprehensive answer to the 'equality of what' question.

These limitations are further reflected on how this perspective informs a possible conception of educational equality, and in particular the case of equality for students with disabilities and special educational needs. Here the discussion centres on the feasibility of social primary goods as the appropriate metric for establishing valuable comparisons for an equal educational provision. The difficulties of the primary goods approach in accounting for individuals' personal characteristics apply perhaps rather distinctively to the case of education, thus entailing a possible neglect of relevant differences leading to morally arbitrary inequalities. Let us see why. Recall here again, for instance, the possible functioning restrictions experienced by a student designated as having dyslexia. These do not seem to be identified and well-served by an index that focuses essentially on resources. What should concern egalitarians in this case, as we have seen in the last chapter, is not whether this student has fair opportunities for educational resources, but whether the student with dyslexia is actually given the conditions *to be able to function* in school as we think he or she should be functioning,[6] i.e. in ways not fundamentally hindered by dyslexia. In other words, a student with dyslexia is at a disadvantage because of a restriction in functioning, but his or her index of primary goods does not necessarily account for this situation, since it focuses primarily on the educational resources available. The distribution of educational resources should therefore be geared at that level of functioning, an aspect that is not acknowledged by equality in primary goods, but is instead central to the capability approach, as we have seen in Chapter 5. This appears to be a consistent limitation of the primary goods position in informing educational equality for students with disabilities and special educational needs.

I now turn to a different understanding of resources, with the aim of ascertaining whether it provides a more appropriate egalitarian currency.

2.2. Equality of resources

A first and simplistic understanding of resources as equal goods informs a view of equality as the distribution of identical bundles of resources to individuals. It is immediately evident, however, that this view runs into a major problem in relation to people's differences. If we reconsider our previous example, providing Bob and Sally with an identical share of resources would presumably leave Bob at a disadvantage, due to his possible requirement for specific and atypical resources, say for example voice synthesizers for his computer. Similarly, identical bundles of generic educational resources distributed to both Bob and Sally would again obtain the result of disadvantaging Bob, given his likely need for specific Braille resources. This initial understanding proves therefore inadequate to respond both to the demands of equal consideration to individuals, and to those of educational equality.

In his sophisticated and complex view of equality of resources, collected and comprehensively presented in *Sovereign Virtue*, Ronald Dworkin (2000) proposes a view of resources as distinct in impersonal and personal ones. On his view, impersonal resources include material goods, inherited wealth and assets, whereas personal ones amount to talents, health, and general strengths and weaknesses. Dworkin sees resources as means for leading fulfilling and worthwhile lives according to individuals' different conceptions of what makes a life good.[7] He supports an equal distribution of these privately owned means (2000: 65–6), and a consequent equalization of morally arbitrary inequalities deriving from different levels of wealth and assets, or indeed from lack of talent. Inequalities resulting from different personal ambitions, choices or preferences, including personal tastes, are not to be equalized on this view, since they are the results of people's responsibilities, and are therefore considered morally legitimate. Thus Dworkin defends an egalitarian distribution of resources that is at the same time ambition sensitive, i.e. a distribution that allows individuals to retain, for instance, the benefits of choosing to invest rather than consume, and endowment insensitive, i.e. a distribution that is not adversely affected by lack of talents or skills, or the possible disabilities that people may have (Dworkin, 2000: 89). Consequently, under this metric people should receive additional resources as a result of their low levels of skills and indeed their disabilities, but not as a result of situations deriving from personal preferences, tastes or ambitions.

In order to equalize morally arbitrary inequalities Dworkin defends a compensatory redistribution mechanism, which resembles the scheme of a fair insurance market. The extent of the compensation due to individuals for their low natural endowments and for their disabilities is determined by the amount that people would be willing to pay to insure themselves against these circumstances in a hypothetical equal auction. This heuristic device plays a very important equalizing role in Dworkin's theory and, as we shall see, informs also a possible and quite compelling scheme for the distribution of educational resources to students with disabilities.

How does this conception fare in terms of the equal consideration due to individuals? Let us reconsider the case of personal differences through the example of Bob and Sally. Remember that Bob is a visually impaired person, whereas Sally is able-bodied. Clearly, under this understanding of equality of resources, Bob lacks an important personal resource, his sight, and is therefore disadvantaged when compared to Sally. Prima facie, equality of resources seems to include a wider range of variables in its evaluation of individuals' relative positions than the primary goods approach. Bob and Sally are not considered equally well off under the metric of equality of resources as they are in terms of primary goods. However, despite this attention to personal differences, equality of resources does not avoid two consistent objections. The first relates to the partial and rather fixed understanding of human diversity implied by considering talents and disabilities unilaterally as personal features, detached from any relation with social and environmental arrangements. Although Bob's visual impairment is acknowledged by the resource metric, it is evaluated as an inherent individual disadvantage, without any concern for its relation to the environmental design. This resembles the understanding of disability as entirely pertaining to the individual suggested by the medical model. As we have seen, however, the specific design of social and physical arrangements proves fundamental in determining the impact of certain impairments on functioning limitations. Thus, the resource metric misses out on an important determinant of people's relative advantage and seems to focus exclusively on compensating the individual, while neglecting the possibility of modifying the environment to equalize conditions. This does not mean, however, that the view could not be extended to encompass this latter possibility. Second, equality of resources, as does equality of primary goods, overlooks the fundamental facts that people differ enormously in their conversion of resources into well-being, and that this conversion varies also in relation to the design of the environment they inhabit. Providing people with an equal share of resources does not seem to account for this crucial variation and leaves some individuals in a disadvantaged position.

The limits of this view extend perhaps to its possible conception of educational equality, and specifically when considering children with disabilities and special educational needs. Here again, by understanding talents and disabilities as inherent personal characteristics, this view overlooks the important relational nature of certain disabilities and special educational needs with the schooling design, and ends up presenting a rather partial approach focused unilaterally on compensating 'less favoured' individuals, with no or little account of possible adjustments to the schooling system. Furthermore, the view does not account for individuals' different conversion of educational resources into valued functionings, thus somehow limiting the scope of its equalization process. This process, however, which takes the form of the hypothetical insurance market, provides potentially a very interesting framework for the distribution of resources to those considered less favoured by a 'natural' distribution of talents. As we have seen, the equal auction envisages a hypothetical amount that people, on average, would be willing to pay to insure themselves in the event of a prospective disability.[8] This amount could legitimately constitute the additional resources devoted to the education of children with disabilities and special educational needs. It would act as an equalizing device, which provided at the same time a just level of 'compensation' as the result of a fair process, and set a precise criterion for determining the additional distribution due to disabled students. Notwithstanding these very appealing features, however, this solution falls short of its own aims on at least two grounds. First, let us emphasize once again that the device is still beset by the limitations of the resourcist view in relation to the individuals' different conversion of resources into valuable beings and doings. It furthermore still overlooks the fundamental importance of social and environmental elements in this conversion. Second, there are certain procedural features that might limit the accuracy of the hypothetical auction in terms of prospective amounts of resources, and therefore undermine its overall fairness. As Robert Veatch notices (1986: 155–6), if the hypothetical amount resulting from the auction is achieved through a process similar to those applied by the 'willingness to pay' approaches in cost-benefit literature, then it might be argued that rare, and therefore less known forms of impairment and disability, will not be valued appropriately under this scheme. This is due to the presumed lack of information on less common forms of disability and special educational needs and their incidence in the population, with a consequent possible reduced willingness to pay of the interested parties (Veatch, 1986: 156). These limitations seem therefore to compromise rather substantially the proposal of a fair auction mechanism for determining an equal educational provision for students with disabilities and special educational needs. There is, however, a further element that might be considered problematic with the proposal of the insurance market. This relates to the possible devaluing of disability and special educational needs entailed by seeking both to insure against their incidence, and to 'compensate' for them in order to equalize resources.

Ultimately, equality of resources, like primary goods, provides a limited understanding of equal concern to all and does not lead to a satisfactory understanding of educational equality either. More specifically, the primary goods approach overlooks the fundamental fact of human diversity, whereas equality of resources presents a partial account of it. Both views furthermore focus on the means to leading worthwhile lives, rather than on the extent to which people are free to choose the kind of life they value. The latter, as we shall see, represents a richer and more extensive account of equality (Sen, 1992: 37). This leads us to conclude that social primary goods and resources do not fully constitute appropriate standards for interpersonal comparisons, and provide partial answers to the 'equality of what' question. Further, while both views suggest important elements towards a conception of equality in education, they are still unable to provide significant guidance in the important case of disability and special educational needs. I now turn my attention to theories of welfare in order to analyse their positions on this fundamental question, and to determine whether their answers are more complete.

3. The 'Welfarist' Approach: Equality of Welfare

Broadly speaking, equality of welfare holds that people should be equal in their levels of welfare. Intuitively, the concept of welfare has an immediate positive connotation that relates to people's success, happiness and overall satisfaction with their own lives. As Ronald Dworkin notices in his critique of these theories, economists introduced this idea precisely to mark a distinction between what is fundamental to people's life and what is merely instrumental, and to assign a proper value to resources. These, they maintain, are valuable only insofar as they produce welfare (Dworkin, 2000: 14). Although various conceptions of welfare inform the egalitarian debate, they fundamentally relate to two main understandings. On the one hand, welfare is seen as overall success in fulfilling preferences and desires, thus in achieving one's life plans. On the other hand, it is seen as the achievement of personal conscious states such as happiness, enjoyment and pleasure. Welfare equality, therefore, corresponds either to equal levels of preference satisfaction or to equal levels of personal happiness.

This focus on the fulfilment of personal preferences or the generation of happiness, however, runs into some distinctive difficulties. These have been the subjects of extensive critique by non-welfarist egalitarians such as Rawls, Dworkin and Scanlon,[9] and of further comments by Sen. The first and major difficulty with welfarist metrics concerns the subjective and possibly 'distorted' formation of personal preferences and tastes, leading to the necessity of providing an adequate account of preference-authenticity in order to justify welfare as the variable for interpersonal comparison

(Clayton and Williams, 1999: 448). The second relates instead to the subjective, and therefore questionable nature of welfare proposed. Let us analyse each of these difficulties in turn.

The first problem arises because equality of welfare does not acknowledge any compensation due to people whose preferences have been deformed by morally arbitrary factors and influences (Kaufman, 2006: 3). Thus, for example, the situation of a destitute person who expresses contentment in living a bleak and deprived existence is not a matter of concern for welfare egalitarianism, since this person's preferences appear to be satisfied. This judgement, however, shows the limitations of a metric based on the subjective account entailed by preference satisfaction. As Sen aptly notices,

[I]n situations of persistent adversity and deprivation, the victims do not go on grieving and grumbling all the time, and may even lack the motivation to desire a radical change of circumstances . . . The extent of a person's deprivation may be substantially muffled in the utility metric.

(Sen, 1992: 6–7)

This furthermore shows that the problem of discerning whether preferences are authentic or have been adapted is central to a welfarist metric of interpersonal comparison. In order to defend the evaluation of people's relative positions on the basis of how their preferences are met, the welfarist should therefore provide a principle of preference-authenticity (Clayton and Williams, 1999: 448). But the problem with a metric based on preference satisfaction becomes even more serious when considering the case of people with expensive tastes, or conversely, but equally problematically, with cheap ones. Here the problem is to determine whether the person who has, or has acquired, a taste for a very expensive lifestyle should be compensated in order to avoid a welfare deficit.[10] Consider the case of Laura and Ryan, who have equal resources at their disposal and are otherwise roughly similar in many respects. Suppose however that Laura, unlike Ryan, has very expensive tastes in matters of living accommodation, and claims that her welfare is badly compromised if she is unable to live in a centrally located penthouse. Ryan, on the other hand, has cheap tastes and would be satisfied with rather modest accommodation in a much less expensive area. Should Laura receive additional resources in order to achieve the same level of welfare as Ryan's? Insisting on equality of welfare in this case appears intuitively wrong, and shows the flaws of a standard of interpersonal comparison based on preference satisfaction. Clayton and

Williams notice (1999: 449), however, that here the convinced welfarist
can provide a counter-argument by introducing the element of responsibility for one's tastes. Thus, the welfarist could suggest that it is evidently
unjust to provide Laura with additional resources, were her expensive
tastes voluntarily cultivated, since in this instance she could be rightly
considered responsible for them. This does not hold, however, had Laura
not set out to develop her expensive preferences, as in this case she would
not be accountable for her situation. Let us assume that this distinction is
satisfactory, but what about the case in which Ryan – who initially has cheap
tastes – then sets out to choose a more expensive lifestyle? Here it would
seem appropriate to give Ryan additional resources to equalize his initial
low demand. However, since Ryan subsequently chooses his new tastes and
is therefore considered responsible for them, by the same token used in
Laura's case, the welfarist egalitarian must deny him an additional distribution of resources. This, however, seems objectionable to many. Without
further proceeding into the discussion of the issues exemplified by these
cases, all still debated, it is important to notice that they nevertheless show
the questionable value of the welfarist metric of preference satisfaction in
providing a guiding criterion for interpersonal comparisons, and consequently for informing what kind of equality should be achieved.

Among the different responses to these critiques, Richard Arneson
(1989) defends a conception of equality of opportunity for welfare, and
attempts to resolve the problem concerning responsibility for tastes by
determining a set of preferences that are free from morally arbitrary
influences (Kaufman, 2006: 5). Arneson's view stipulates that equality of
welfare holds when people face effective equivalent arrays of options for
preference satisfaction. He then proposes a precise and reasoned account
of preferences in terms of 'ideally considered preferences', which are
defined as those 'I would have if I were to engage in thorough-going deliberation about my preferences with full pertinent information, in a calm
mood . . . and making no reasoning errors' (Arneson, 1989: 83). Thus
preferences are defined as hypothetical, ideal and rationally deliberated
ones, against a background of full relevant information (Arneson, 1989:
86). Notwithstanding these important specifications, however, it is still
unclear how Arneson's view can effectively avoid the problems of tastes.
More specifically, even in the case of rationally deliberated preferences, it
is not clear how the process of deliberation could convince Laura to
abandon her taste for lavish penthouses, instead of confirming even
further her preference (Kaufman, 2006: 6). Likewise, it is still unclear how
the same process of deliberation could change the adapted preferences of
the destitute person. Presumably this modification could only be achieved

through substantive changes in her existing conditions. These changes would allow the destitute person to envisage different situations as both attainable and preferable, and consequently produce a different set of preferences. Thus, even in Arneson's position, the welfarist metric fails to respond adequately to the difficulties entailed by preferences and tastes, and consequently appears questionable as a criterion of egalitarian justice.

This seems to be further confirmed when analysing the second objection to an egalitarian account based on welfare, i.e. its subjective account of well-being. While the subjective nature of welfare has already emerged in discussing the problems of preference satisfaction, an overview of the difficulties arising in relation to both equality as overall satisfaction with one's life, and as equal levels of happiness, shows once more the limitations of this currency. Consider two people who have equal resources and are otherwise similar in many respects, including their personal achievements. Suppose that one person has a very simple view of what makes a life successful, while the other has high demands. If asked to assess their overall satisfaction, the second person would probably rate her level of welfare lower than the first one. Should she therefore receive additional resources? It is not really clear why this should be the case, since, as Dworkin notices, in this instance the differences between the two people are differences in beliefs about their welfare, rather than in their actual overall success with their lives (Dworkin, 2000: 38). It appears therefore evident that conceptualizing equality of welfare in terms of equality in overall success runs into the problem of how to adjudicate between people's conceptions of what makes a life successful. The same problem applies to equality of desirable states of pleasure and happiness, since the latter as well are based on subjective accounts of what constitutes a pleasant and happy life. In both these cases, the claims of success or happiness lack sufficient and reliable connection to what objectively makes a life successful or what is good for the person (Scanlon, 1991: 38). Ultimately, the welfarist metric seems to lack an acceptable and objective standard of well-being.

The difficulties presented so far should have already proved the limitations of a welfarist metric in giving coherent expression to the egalitarian convictions of equal concern for individuals. However, two more points need further analysis. The first concerns how equality of welfare would respond to the demands of disabled people, while the second concerns a possible conception of educational equality for students with disabilities and special educational needs. In considering the welfare of a disabled person, the metric based on preference satisfaction faces once more the problems encountered in relation to its subjectivity. As Dworkin argues

(2000: 59–60), although the welfarist metric seems to respond to the intuition that disabled people as a group enjoy lower levels of welfare, it is
unclear how such a metric would be at all helpful in determining why they
should sometimes receive more resources than non-disabled people as a
matter of justice. In particular, it is unclear how this metric would evaluate
the situation of a disabled person who expresses satisfaction with her
overall life, even if she had less material resources than an able-bodied
person, or in the case of having to deploy a much greater deal of resources
than other people to achieve the same levels of functioning in her
everyday life. It is not even clear, Dworkin continues (2000: 60), what
should be done when disabled people's specific preferences conflict with
our reflected judgements on how resources should be used. In order to
support this latter objection, Dworkin discusses the example of a disabled
violinist who is given a large amount of money to buy an expensive piece
of equipment that could improve his everyday life, but who chooses
instead to buy a Stradivarius, claiming that his welfare is considerably
enhanced by acquiring the precious violin, rather than the piece of equipment (Dworkin, 2000: 61–2). How should this preference be evaluated?
Should the violinist receive the additional distribution of resources?
Ultimately, these problems constitute powerful objections against welfare
as a defensible and valuable standard for comparisons, and as the kind of
equality that should be achieved.

Furthermore, these problems seem also to hamper a conception of
educational equality based on welfare accounts. How would such an
account consider the equal welfare of students? Should equal overall
success in education constitute the aim of an egalitarian system? And how
should this success be evaluated and by whom? Should the latter be
assessed in terms of the equal opportunities students have to pursue their
individual preferences? What role would education, both as formal schooling and informal upbringing, play in forming and influencing preferences
and tastes? And moreover, how would such accounts consider the welfare
of students with disabilities and special educational needs in the absence
of an objective account of what constitutes welfare and a clear understanding of how to adjudicate between competing preferences? These
questions serve the only purpose of highlighting the difficulties faced by
welfarist theories of equality, when confronted with the compelling
demands of disabilities and learning difficulties, and hence they highlight
the possible limitations of these approaches in informing a conception of
equality in education.

This long analysis of possible answers to the 'equality of what' question
has outlined how both resourcist and welfarist currencies of egalitarian

justice, with their internal variations and specifications, lead to limited conceptions of equality that do not appear to show equal consideration to all individuals in some substantial ways. I now turn to the perspective I have deployed throughout this book, namely the capability approach.

4. The Capability Approach: Equality of Capability

Sen argues for capability as the appropriate currency of egalitarian justice and the right alternative to resources and welfare metrics. As we have seen, in Sen's approach capabilities are people's effective freedoms to choose among valued beings and doings, i.e. among valued functionings. According to Sen, therefore, what a person is able to be (for example, being well or poorly educated) and to do (for instance, performing more or less rewarding work activities) determines a person's quality of life, and hence her well-being, seen as the quality or the 'wellness of the being' (Sen, 1992: 39). Thus, for Sen the object of egalitarian concern resides in evaluating people's freedoms to achieve the functionings that they have reason to value, which corresponds to their freedoms to achieve well-being.[11] This constitutes at the same time the metric for interpersonal comparison, and the kind of equality that social and institutional arrangements should seek to achieve.

Three important aspects of the capability metric make it a promising framework, which, as Kaufman notices, 'expands the descriptive and analytic range of egalitarian thought' (Kaufman, 2006: 128). The first is the chosen 'focal variable' for interpersonal comparisons: while encompassing both functionings and capabilities, the variable for equality is explicitly focused on capabilities, and hence on the freedoms to achieve rather than on achievement. This has important implications for the kind of equality that should be sought. Second, although functionings belong to the constitutive elements of well-being, a precise relation between capabilities and well-being is established, as the latter fundamentally depends on the capability to function (Sen, 1992: 40). In this sense, capabilities are equally constitutive of well-being, and seeking equality in their space corresponds to equalizing actual possibilities for well-being. Finally, in focusing on what people can do with resources and on their possibility to function, the capability metric is both distinct from, and more promising than, both resourcist and welfarist currencies. It therefore constitutes a perspective that seems to show equal consideration to all in some substantial ways. Let us analyse each of these features in some more detail.

Interpersonal comparisons should be based on people's overall freedoms to choose among sets of possible functionings, reflecting the person's freedom to lead different types of lives, Sen claims (Sen, 1992: 40). This focus on capabilities, rather than on achieved functionings, entails attention to people's opportunities to pursue their own objectives. Sen argues that equality in capabilities – or otherwise 'the elimination of unambiguous inequalities in capabilities' (Sen, 1992: 7) – does not correspond to the standard concept of equality of opportunities commonly used in policy literature, and seen as the equal availability of some particular means. Instead, he maintains that 'real' equality of opportunity amounts to the equal effective freedoms to achieve valued functionings, since these identify the real alternatives that people have (Sen, 1992: 49). As we have seen, the importance of addressing interpersonal comparisons in terms of individuals' freedoms relates to the fundamental and pervasive diversity of human beings. Central to the capability metric is the concept of human heterogeneity, entailing attention to the complex interrelations of personal and external variations, as well as people's different abilities to convert resources into valued objectives. This allows for the pursuit of people's individual well-being, and the making of their life-planning through individual choice (Robeyns, 2003b: 544). Sen further specifies that among the countless capabilities that people may have reasons to value, some are considered basic in the sense of being fundamental for well-being. As we have seen, these basic capabilities include, for instance, being well-nourished, being sheltered, being clothed, being educated, and being able to participate in society without shame (Sen, 1992: 44). It is within these basic constituents of well-being that equality, according to Sen, has to be primarily sought.

This leads us to the second point, namely the important relation of capabilities to well-being. Sen envisages this as two-fold: first, since achieved functionings are constitutive of well-being, so are the real opportunities, i.e. the capabilities for these functionings. Second, achieved well-being in itself depends on the capability to function, and 'the capability set gives us information on the various functioning vectors that are within reach of a person', and hence on the actual possibilities for achieving well-being (Sen, 1992: 41–2). Capabilities and well-being, therefore, are inherently connected, and this reinstates the importance of seeking equality in this space.

There is, however, a further element that enters the domain of egalitarian concerns and that might conflict with the freedom to achieve well-being thus characterized. This is the role of agency, in the wide terms both of actively choosing one's own broader goals, and of achieving them. While in Nussbaum's account of the capability approach agency and well-being interests converge in the idea of both valuable and chosen functionings (Crocker, 1995: 166), Sen maintains instead that well-being and agency interests are distinct. However, they are equally fundamental for egalitarian considerations, since they both provide important information on the actual quality of life of a person. Hence, in Sen's view, the dimensions of agency and well-being can, and indeed often do, take different directions. To illustrate this with an example, Sen reminds us of the case of a person who happens to be present at the scene of a crime that she would ideally like to prevent. While the well-being of this person might indeed decrease in taking some form of action to stop the crime, since she could be harmed, her agency – in this case her agency achievement – might instead increase considerably. Without getting any further into the analysis of the implications of this distinction, it is perhaps worth noticing here that according to Sen the acknowledgement of both agency and well-being, as important elements in furthering the individual's freedom to choose a valued form of life, does not detract from the emphasis on well-being freedom as the dimension constitutive of the capability set, and as the kind of concern that should inform egalitarian policy. It is in the dimension of well-being freedom, Sen argues, that inequalities are most pervasive, and it is therefore in this dimension, as we have seen, that equality should be primarily sought (Sen, 1992: 72). On the other hand, the importance of encompassing both agency and well-being relates to the plurality of the informational bases for interpersonal comparison proposed by the approach.

It is this rich and plural dimension that makes the capability currency a more appropriate standard of interpersonal comparisons than resourcist and welfarist metrics. On the one hand, the approach is distinct from equality of resources, since it focuses on the effects that resources have for people, and hence on the extent of people's freedoms rather than on the means to it. On the other hand, in specifying the space of equality in terms of capability for functionings that people have reason to value, the approach overcomes the problem associated with the subjectivity of both preference satisfaction and the pursuit of personal happiness. In this sense, as Kaufman notices (2006: 9), the approach is distinct from, and more rigorous than, equality of welfare, since it focuses on the ability to function rather than on subjective end-states measured in terms of welfare. Hence the approach provides an account of what is fundamental in people's life which, while respecting individual choices and including aspects of responsibility for one's choices, nevertheless gives a normatively justified account that is not focused on a single, objectionable element.

While, as we have seen in the previous two chapters, the capability approach is not immune to powerful critiques and problems, it appears, nevertheless, that it provides a rich and justified standard for interpersonal comparison. The richness of the standard is reflected in its internal plurality, while its justification resides in its objective view of well-being freedom. This framework, therefore, has the potential to inform a perspective that shows substantial equal consideration to all. As we shall see in the next chapter, this aspect has important implications for addressing some of the demands of equality in education.

Concluding Comments

The value of equality is expression of the ideal of equal consideration to all citizens. The current egalitarian debate is characterized by competing approaches to the enactment of that ideal. I have shown in this chapter how egalitarian perspectives based on equal distributions of resources, as well as those based on equality of welfare, provide standards of interpersonal comparisons that present some limitations, and specifically when evaluating the position of disabled people relative to that of others. They therefore fail to fully enact the principle of equal consideration to all. These perspectives seem also to lead to partial or unsatisfactory accounts of what constitutes educational equality, and in particular a just educational provision for students with disabilities and special educational needs. In contrast to these perspectives, and by placing people's effective freedoms to achieve well-being at the centre of the egalitarian concern, the capability approach provides an account of justice that offers a more comprehensive expression of the ideal of equal consideration to all. This is reflected in the kind of metric suggested by the approach, as I have discussed at some length in this chapter. Furthermore, combined with the relational understanding of disability and special educational needs outlined in the previous chapters, the approach offers an important framework for determining what constitutes educational equality for students with disabilities and special educational needs. The next chapter is devoted to the analysis of this complex issue.

Chapter 7

Justice and Equality in Education: Towards a Principled Framework

The ideal of educational equality is fundamentally grounded in the egalitarian principle that social and institutional arrangements should be designed to give equal consideration to all. Educational institutions should therefore enact the value of equal concern by ensuring that all students have a fair share of educational goods and fair access to the benefits these yield. However, beyond this broad and generally agreed stipulation, the precise content of the ideal of educational equality is difficult to determine. A conception of equality in education would need to articulate three interrelated normative dimensions, each entailing debated aspects. First, it would need to determine exactly the kind of equality that educational institutions should seek to achieve. While liberal perspectives generally conceive of educational equality in terms of equal opportunity,[1] the exact specification of the concept is debated, as are its implications. Second, such a conception would need to determine the principles that regulate the distribution of educational goods, and justify what inequalities, if any, are permissible. However, while there is general agreement on addressing the inequalities caused by society, and hence resulting from individuals' circumstances, such as socio-economic and cultural backgrounds as well as gender and ethnicity, the equalization of so-called 'natural' differences is instead more controversial. Here difficulties arise in determining whether, and how, to equalize inequalities in education caused by different levels of abilities and talents. In particular, the question of how to address differences relating to disabilities and special educational needs – the central focus of my analysis – constitutes a very problematic and difficult aspect of the debate on educational equality.[2] Finally, none of these dimensions of educational equality can be identified independently from the role of education and its functions for individuals and, more generally, for society. In short, a conception of educational equality cannot be fully conceived separately from an understanding of what kind of good is education.

A possible, justified way of addressing these issues consists in applying a principled perspective on equality to education, and hence in deriving a precise conception of educational equality from normative egalitarian positions. In particular, the question of educational equality for students with disabilities and special educational needs can be addressed by analysing how egalitarian positions evaluate disability and special needs within the kind of equality they propose, and by applying these insights to the specific case of education. As we have seen in the previous chapter, the capability approach provides positive answers to some fundamental egalitarian questions, and in particular to those relating to disability and special educational needs. The specific insights of the approach are applied here to the case of educational equality.

This chapter outlines, therefore, a capability perspective on educational equality, and aims at articulating an answer to the central question of my enquiry: what constitutes a just educational provision for students with disabilities and special educational needs, and, more specifically, what, and how much, educational resources should be distributed to these students? I shall claim that the specific capability currency for egalitarian justice, and the important role played by education within it, both in achieving well-being and in expanding individuals' freedoms, provide a justified theoretical framework for responding to this central question.

The chapter is organized in four parts. In the first section that follows, I analyse the important role of education in the achievement of well-being and in expanding capabilities, while aiming at equipping individuals with the transformational resources required for effectively participating in society as equals. In the second section, I outline elements of a fundamental educational entitlement. This implies addressing the implications of proposing a threshold level of capabilities. In the third part, I articulate some elements of such an entitlement for students with disabilities and special educational needs, while examining the problems of proposing a capability threshold for these students. Finally, drawing on Rawls's theory of justice, the last section outlines elements of a principled framework for a just distribution of resources to students with disabilities and special educational needs, and discusses some of its main implications.

While this framework aims at providing a justified answer to the specific demand of equality in education for students with disabilities and special educational needs, it does *not* constitute a full theory of educational equality. Such a theory would require an extensive formulation of the case for educational equality in relation to other values, like parental rights and liberties, as well as to broader principles of justice. However, some of the elements of the capability perspective presented here may suggest insights towards the formulation of a full theory of equality in education.

1. Education, Capability and Well-being

Education, both in terms of formal schooling and informal learning, is central to the capability approach.[3] The approach emphasizes specifically the contribution that the capability to be educated makes to the formation and expansion of other capabilities, and hence the contribution it makes to people's opportunities for leading worthwhile lives. As we have seen in previous sections, Sen identifies education among basic capabilities, i.e. among 'a relatively small number of centrally important beings and doings that are crucial to well-being' (1992: 44). In his account, equality has to be sought primarily in these basic capabilities, which constitute, therefore, areas of specific concern for egalitarians. Included among the basic capabilities, education is therefore of specific interest for egalitarians, too. But what are the implications of understanding education within the capability approach? And, furthermore, how would a conception of capability equality in education differ from other liberal egalitarian views?

I maintain that the distinctive contribution of the approach consists precisely in identifying education, in terms of the basic capability to be educated, both as essential to well-being and to the enhancement of freedom, as well as among the primary concerns of equality. Two fundamental considerations follow. First, this understanding implies asserting the importance of education both in the sense of meeting a basic need to be educated, and for the promotion and expansion of other capabilities. It also implies determining the role played by education both at the individual and the collective level. The second consideration relates to the role of education in promoting well-being and in enhancing freedom. Education promotes the achievement of those functionings that are constitutive of one's well-being and quality of life, while also providing the resources for the enactment of important aspects of agency, thus enhancing individuals' effective freedom. Given the complex interrelation of individuals with the society they inhabit, forms of civic and indeed economic participation play an important role in determining one's well-being, while providing the basic structure for the exercise of effective freedom. Consequently, among the countless capabilities that might be developed through education and schooling, the approach suggests the promotion and expansion of those capabilities necessary to participate as equals in society.[4] This responds, on the one hand, to the duty of institutional arrangements to show equal consideration to all, while, on the other hand, providing the constitutive elements for leading good lives, thus for the enactment of effective freedom. These considerations are foundational to a conception of capability equality in education. Each of them, however, requires further discussion, and I begin with the analysis of education as a basic capability.

1.1. The capability to be educated[5]

The question of determining basic capabilities relates to the possibility 'that some capabilities may be so basic to human welfare that they can be identified without any prior knowledge of the particular commitments that are held and expressed by an individual or group' (Alkire, 2002: 154). Sen has addressed issues of basic capabilities in his analysis of poverty. He maintains that basic capabilities are a subset of all capabilities and refer to the possibility to satisfy 'certain crucially important functionings up to certain minimally adequate levels' (Sen, 1980: 41; 1992: 45). Notably, Sen does not provide a definite list of basic capabilities, nor a fully justified account of how to identify them, but he mentions several elementary capabilities, which include the capability to be sheltered, nourished, educated and clothed, as well as that of appearing in public without shame (Sen, 1999: 20; 1992: 69). He furthermore specifies that the 'ambiguity of the concept of basicness' (1992: 45) leaves the idea of basic capability open to different interpretations.

One such possible interpretation, which has interesting implications for the understanding of the basic capability to be educated, is provided by Sabina Alkire's work (2002) on the operationalization of capability for poverty reduction. Alkire presents an account of basic capabilities that subsumes the idea of human needs. In her view, basic needs are described both with reference to the substantive functioning that is harmed if the basic need is unmet, and are expressed at a level of sufficient generality as to be independent of specific socio-cultural contexts. They are therefore valid to be applied to different situations (Alkire, 2002: 160). For example, not meeting the functionings of being well nourished or being clothed fundamentally harms the individual, and this applies beyond specific contexts and situations. Thus Alkire specifies that

A basic capability is a capability to enjoy a functioning that is defined at a general level and refers to a basic need, in other words a *capability to meet a basic need* (a capability to avoid malnourishment; a capability to be educated, and so on). The set of basic capabilities might be thought of as capabilities to meet basic human needs.

(2002: 163)

Alkire's conception of basic capability retains, therefore, the strong sense of needs as fundamental requirements while, at the same time, grounding it in the important concept of potential for intentional choice and agency implied in the idea of capability.[6]

A further understanding of basic capabilities, and one that seems also particularly relevant in thinking of education, is provided by Bernard Williams (1985). Williams understands basic as fundamental capabilities in the sense of some invariant, underlying capabilities, which are 'derived from some universal and fundamental fact about human beings' (Williams, 1985: 101). His reference to the capability to appear in public without shame is particularly useful in understanding the precise meaning of fundamental capabilities. Williams recalls Sen's use of Adam Smith's example of the man who cannot appear in public without shame, given the cultural and social arrangements he lives in, unless he can wear a linen shirt. In Williams' understanding, although the requirements in order to appear in public without shame depend on specific contexts, the invariant, fundamental capability at play here is the capability to 'command the materials of self-respect' (1985: 101). And it is in this sense, according to Williams, that certain capabilities are basic, in that they are absolutely fundamental to human well-being. Moreover, these capabilities are distinct from more trivial ones, like those associated with the commodities of choosing from an increased range of washing powders (1985: 98). Finally, these capabilities are also foundational to the exercise of other capabilities, since the freedom to appear in public without shame allows the achievement of other functionings, thus ultimately expanding individuals' effective freedom.

On the basis of these interpretations, the capability to be educated can be considered basic in two interrelated respects. The first relates to its crucial importance for people's well-being, since absence or lack of education would essentially harm or disadvantage the individual. This is specifically, albeit not solely, the case for children, as lack of education during childhood, both in terms of informal learning in social interactions and of formal schooling, determines a disadvantage that proves difficult, and in some cases truly impossible to compensate in later life. As Nussbaum (2000: 90) argues, the exercise of certain functionings, like that of play and imagination, is particularly important during childhood in order to form the future mature capability. In this first facet, therefore, the capability to be educated responds to some essential basic needs of human beings, which, if unmet, cause substantial harm. The second facet in which the capability to be educated is basic is in the sense of being a fundamental capability, and foundational to other capabilities as well as future ones, thus expanding individuals' freedoms. Consider, for instance, the case of learning mathematics. Formally learning mathematics not only expands the individual's various functionings related to reasoning and problem solving, but also widens the individual's sets of opportunities and capabilities with respect, on the one hand to more complex capabilities and, on the other, to better prospects for opportunities in life. The broadening of capabilities entailed by education extends to the advancement of complex capabilities, since while promoting reflection, understanding, information and awareness of one's capabilities, education promotes at the same time the possibility to formulate exactly the valued beings and doings that the individual has reason to value (Saito, 2003). On the other hand, the expansion of capabilities entailed by education extends to choices of occupations and levels of social and political participation. Learning mathematics may lead to choosing to become an economist or a teacher, for instance, as well as promote one's civic participation in different forms.

Both Sen (1999, 2002) and Nussbaum (1997, 2000, 2002, 2004, 2006b) explicitly emphasize the importance of education in itself and in expanding other capabilities. Sen (1999: 198) highlights, for instance, the benefits related to the education of women, both in broadening their freedom to exercise agency, and in its correlation to a reduction in infant mortality. Nussbaum (2004, 2006b) defends the value of education as crucial not only to human dignity, but also and specifically to the promotion of women's capabilities in many areas of their lives. Alkire's (2002: 255–71) study on a literacy project for women in Pakistan emphasizes the transformative effects of education on their lives, leading not only to the acquisition of skills and knowledge, but also to the enhancement of dignity and awareness of their rights.

Thus the approach emphasizes a view of education as a complex good, entailing both intrinsic and instrumental values. Drèze and Sen (2002), among others,[7] highlight the various roles that education can play, and focus on the intrinsically important value it yields for individuals, as well as the range of its instrumental functions, both for individuals and for society (Robeyns, 2006: 2–3). On this view, education is intrinsically good, is valuable in itself, in that being educated, other things being equal, enhances the possibility of appreciating and engaging in a wide range of activities, which are fulfilling for their own sake. For instance, being initiated through education into the appreciation of literature, or aspects of the wildlife in natural environments, or different kinds of music, relates to a personal fulfilment which is not simply instrumental in securing better jobs or positions in life, but brings about a more fulfilling life in itself. On the other hand, education serves several instrumental aims, since it is a means to other valuable goods, such as better life prospects, career opportunities, and forms of social and economic participation. This role of education is fundamental in ensuring people's standards of living, since education, and specifically schooling, promote the achievement of important levels of knowledge and skills acquisition, which play a vital role in one's well-being and in the further exercise of agency. Furthermore, as Robeyns notices (2006: 3), the roles played by education, both in itself and instrumentally, are valuable not just at the individual but also at the collective level. For instance, an educated population promotes economic growth, but it is also more likely to promote more tolerant social arrangements, characterized by different views of what constitutes a worthwhile life, thus indirectly contributing to the actual well-being of all individuals. Furthermore, this view is wider and richer than the unilateral emphasis on the economic instrumental role of education suggested by other current approaches, such as human capital theory, with its emphasis on skills and productivity (Robeyns, 2006: 3). This leads us to a further consideration, pertaining to the kind of education that would better promote levels of well-being and freedom, and hence that would be consistent with the main aims of the approach.

The centrality of well-being and freedom in the capability approach, and the parallel centrality of education in promoting them, suggests important considerations about the kind of education that should be provided to individuals (and, as it will be outlined later, how it should be distributed). Well-being can be seen as requiring forms of engagement in economic as well as civic participation in one's dominant social framework, but also forms of reflection on one's valued functionings. This constitutes the basis for the exercise of effective freedom. It follows that an education consistent with enabling people to achieve well-being, and to expand overall freedoms, entails the promotion of functionings and capabilities pertaining to abilities and knowledge that enable them to become participants in dominant social frameworks, while at the same time promoting reflection on valued goals.

But what functionings and capabilities would be constitutive of education thus conceived? Considering this aspect requires attention to those basic functionings and the related capabilities, which are at the same time crucial in avoiding disadvantage for the individual, and foundational to the enhancement of other capabilities. More precisely, we are looking here at certain basic enabling conditions[8] that form the resources necessary for individuals to become effective participants in society and to form their life plans. The precise content of education thus defined should be the result of processes of democratic deliberation, such as those advocated by Sen in relation to the choice of fundamental valued capabilities, and should also, to some extent, relate to specific contextual circumstances. In this sense, the process would resemble the democratic establishment, for instance, of school curricula. However, some functionings developed by education appear to be truly foundational and essential for other, more complex ones, and might be suggested as constitutive of a basic education. The latter, therefore, would plausibly include the cultivation and expansion of literacy and numeracy, as well as forms of scientific understanding, attitudes and dispositions to sociality and participation, and to learning functionings, such as being able to concentrate, to pay attention and to engage in activities, but also to exercise and to play.[9] Furthermore, the functionings entailed by basic forms of practical reasoning, such as relating means and ends and reflecting on one's own actions and their consequences, appear to have a central role in the kind of education promoted by the capability approach. This is consistent with the centrality that Nussbaum assigns – among the capabilities selected in her Central Human Functional Capabilities – to practical reason, seen as 'being able to form a conception of the good and to engage in critical reflection about the planning of one's life' (Nussbaum, 2000: 79). Moreover, the importance of practical reason, in enacting the individual's possibilities of choosing among valuable functionings, supports some forms of autonomy-promoting or autonomy-facilitating education.[10] In other words, it suggests a kind of education that allows children 'the opportunity to make and act on well-informed and well-thought out judgements about how to live their own lives' (Brighouse, 2006: 14). As Walker and Unterhalter notice,

> [T]he key issue here is that to count as *education*, processes and outcomes ought to enhance freedom, agency and well-being, by "making one's life richer with the opportunity of reflective choice" (Sen, 1992: 41) . . . and enhancing 'the ability of people to help themselves and to influence the world' (Sen, 1999: 18).
>
> (Walker and Unterhalter, 2007: 15)

Ultimately, the capability approach suggests a perspective based on selecting basic, fundamental functionings, whose achievement is specifically promoted by education. These, in furthering knowledge and skills, as well as the ability to deliberate about means and ends and conditions of autonomous agency, contribute to people's well-being, while forming also conditions for the expansion of their effective freedom. It is perhaps worth emphasizing here that the kind of education implied by this view is not aimed at promoting a specific conception of the good, or only at instrumentally educating for citizenship, but rather is aimed at equipping individuals with those transformational resources that will allow them to participate effectively as equals in society, while developing and enacting their own valued life-plans.

1.2. Education and effective participation as equals in society

The idea that education should equip individuals to become effective and equal participants in their social framework, and the precise meaning of effective and equal participation in society, needs further articulation. After all, it could be objected that education should instead promote all possible functionings and related capabilities, rather than certain specific ones.

Two fundamental reasons support the idea of an effective and equal participation as an appropriate goal of education, and provide a reply to the possible objections raised. First, as Elizabeth Anderson has rightly argued in defending her view of democratic equality, the basic duty of citizens, acting through social and institutional arrangements, is to secure the conditions of everyone's freedom (Anderson, 1999: 329). This implies that among the countless capabilities that can be chosen, institutional schemes have a duty to promote those that are significant and crucial for well-being, as foundational to freedom. In this sense, as Anderson notices, being an excellent card player is hardly significant towards that end, whereas being literate and able to participate in a system of production and in civic life is (1999: 317). Second, Sen insists on the importance of assessing social inequalities and public policy – and therefore in promoting equality – in the space of well-being freedom, since pervasive inequity and disparities emerge primarily in the actual opportunities that people have to enjoy well-being (Sen, 1992: 72). However, he also maintains that 'the person's actual use of her well-being freedom' will allow well-being agency to be pursued. Thus, well-being freedom provides the conditions for effective freedom. It follows that an education that provides individuals with the conditions for their equal effective participation in society provides also the conditions for the possibility to exercise agency, and therefore with wide opportunities for freedom. This, furthermore, supports and legitimates the inclusion of forms of practical reason and deliberation within the functionings promoted by education.

But what is the meaning of being an effective and equal participant in one's social framework? While an immediate understanding of this concept may conjure up images of success and adherence to a predefined, somehow 'normal' view of what effectively participating in one's framework entails, that need not be the case. An understanding in line with the capability approach endorses instead the view of an individual who has effective opportunities to lead a meaningful life, free from the constraint of deep inequalities in well-being, and able to choose, among a set of capabilities, those that she has reason to value. Here the effectiveness in participating in dominant social arrangements relates to the possible engagement in forms of economic, political and democratic activities, while exercising one's agency in bringing about the outcomes and changes, both in one's life and in society, that one has reason to value. This further relates to the element of participating as equals, and hence, as Anderson suggests (1999: 316), in relations of equality to other participants. In having effective opportunities to take part in social and political schemes, people are also enabled to 'stand as equals' in those schemes, since this contributes to the removal of relations of oppression or discrimination.

This view, however, entails the requirement of having equal opportunities for functionings in education. I now turn my attention to this aspect.

2. Capability Equality in Education: Elements of a Fundamental Educational Entitlement

The capability approach allows the identification of functionings and capabilities, developed by education, that are fundamental in providing individuals with the transformational resources necessary to function and to participate effectively in society. In this sense education and its equal provision is one of the concerns of egalitarians. In this section I analyse the demands of equality in relation to those fundamental functionings and capabilities.

I start by analysing the reasons in support of equality in the fundamental educational capabilities. There are three important interrelated reasons in support of equality in this space. The first concerns the equal consideration due to citizens. Recall here that according to Sen (1992), seeking equality in the space of capabilities constitutes the appropriate enactment of the equal consideration due to individuals. Education is crucial for people's well-being and plays a substantial role for the promotion of those achieved functionings necessary for individuals to participate effectively in society. Unequal provision in basic educational capabilities would lead to unequal freedom to develop effective functionings in society. While being an obvious inequality of consideration, this would at the same time undermine the legitimacy of social and institutional arrangements. Consequently, opportunities for educational functionings should be equally provided. Interrelated to this reason is the fundamental importance of education for people's freedoms. Within the space of capabilities, the variable we are trying to equalize is the effective freedom people have to choose the life they value. It therefore follows that the capability to be educated, as fundamentally constitutive of well-being and freedom, has to be part of the equalization, too. There is, finally, another aspect of education, which supports equality in the space of fundamental educational capabilities. Thinking of education, and especially the education of children, implies considering the future-oriented dimensions entailed by education. Education has a prospective value for the child in the future, while also entailing considerations of the present, contingent value it yields for the child as a child, now. It follows that unequal provision in educational capabilities would substantially put individuals at a disadvantage in a consistent and pervasive way, both contingently and for future prospects. These important reasons support seeking equality in the space of educational capabilities, and point in the direction of its possible meaning. Let us analyse it.

The capability approach suggests an understanding of educational equality in terms of equal opportunities to the achievement of fundamental educational functionings that are necessary for an effective and equal participation in society. This understanding, while drawing on the conceptualization of education as basic capability, relates substantially to the dimension of opportunity inscribed in the idea of capability. Capabilities represent the substantive freedoms that people have to choose among valuable functionings: they are capabilities to function. Inscribed in people's substantive freedom are the opportunities to enact this freedom in achieving functionings. Sen maintains that

> [F]reedom is concerned with *processes of decision making* as well as *opportunities to achieve valued outcomes* . . . we have to examine . . . the extent to which people have the opportunity to achieve outcomes.
>
> (1999: 291)

Applied to education, this view translates into considering the extent to which people have opportunities to achieve fundamental educational outcomes. The insight of the capability approach is that people should have the same extent, in terms of equal opportunities, to achieve fundamental educational functionings, like being able to read and to write, or to concentrate and accomplish tasks, or to reflect critically on one's own actions. Opportunities are here considered in a broad sense. They include: educational resources, both in terms of physical resources and human resources; settings, like school buildings and facilities; and external conditions, like policies and regulations that are necessary to promote educational achievement. Hence, the kind of freedom we are equalizing encompasses the opportunity to achieve a valued functioning and the conditions for that functioning to be achieved (Unterhalter and Brighouse, 2007: 83).

The aspect of opportunity within the idea of capability emphasizes furthermore that what we are equalizing is not actual achieved functionings, but the effective access to the achievement of these functionings. For instance, people should have equal effective opportunities to achieve reading, writing, and reasoning functionings. This allows considering the individuals' freedom to choose to achieve certain functionings by deploying means at their disposal and, furthermore, it leaves open the possibility of choosing whether to achieve certain educational functionings or not. An example may illustrate the important distinction between equal effective access to functionings and achieved functionings. Consider, for instance, Len and Josh, who have achieved different mathematical outcomes. Len has high numerical reasoning, whereas Josh has achieved basic counting functionings. Suppose they have similar personal characteristics and both have attended a very well-equipped school, with highly motivated and qualified teachers, and wide possibilities to learn in a stimulating environment. Suppose furthermore that Josh has achieved lower outcomes since he has decided to spend his time in leisure activities rather than in learning. Here the capability approach does not consider the different achieved functionings as a matter of equality, since difference in achievement in this case relates to the individual's choice. Suppose instead that Len and Josh have different achieved functionings due to the fact that Len's school could provide for additional courses aimed at improving levels of achievements. The differential outcomes in this instance relate to a substantial inequality of capabilities. The capability approach highlights this difference and insists on equality as equal effective opportunities for functionings. What matters in terms of equality of capabilities is the equal opportunity that people have to secure educational functionings, rather than equality in achieved functionings. This position allows the possibility of choosing whether or not to achieve certain functionings, providing the relevant opportunities are available.

There is, however, a tension in this position, which relates primarily to the possibility of choice when considering the education of children. There are levels of choice that, given their status, are unavailable to children. Children's status requires adults to protect their interests and meet their needs, and hence children's agency freedom or the exercise of autonomous choices are fundamentally limited. Hence, when operationalizing the capability approach in relation to the education of children, the emphasis is on providing a kind of education that, while considering the actual well-being of children during their childhood, can, at the same time, equip them with the fundamental capabilities that they will exercise in future. On the one hand, this endorses the importance of equal access to fundamental educational functionings, and therefore to a kind of education that will provide children with the means to function effectively in society. On the other hand, however, it raises the problem of justifying choices actually made for children and not by children. For instance, children cannot choose not to be educated and cannot choose among educational functionings and capabilities. In this case, the parent or guardian, as well as the state for certain capabilities, exercise the actual choice for the child. A possible way of solving this tension is to consider parents' choices and the enforcement of certain regulations by the state, for instance compulsory schooling requirements, as actually made in the child's best interest, and hence for the child's present and future well-being. These can therefore be seen as proxy-choices. In this sense, however, when referring to the education of young children, as Sen suggests (Saito, 2003: 27), it is perhaps more appropriate to consider actual functionings, rather than the related capability. Nevertheless, from the point of view of the design of social and institutional arrangements, what can be reasonably provided and distributed by democratic governance are ultimately opportunities and resources. This solution, albeit partial, allows considering equality in terms of equal opportunities to educational functionings, with the caveats illustrated above, valid and justified also in the case of children's education.

Drawing on these considerations, we can now outline a first, provisional understanding of what constitutes a fundamental educational entitlement. The capability approach suggest a conception of a fundamental educational entitlement in terms of the equal opportunities and access to levels of educational functionings necessary to function and to participate effectively in society. Basic educational functionings form the necessary enabling conditions that, once achieved, allow individuals to function effectively in their dominant framework. In so far as we can, ultimately, we should provide individuals with equal secure access to these educational functionings, which constitute the transformational resources necessary to function and participate effectively in society. While conceptualizing equality in terms of the equal opportunities for functionings, this view highlights the importance of the prospective educational achievements in terms of levels of functionings necessary to participate effectively in society. This implies therefore a threshold level of achieved functionings that educational institutions should promote and foster, set at the level necessary for effective participation in dominant social frameworks.

This position presents evident similarities with the threshold level of capabilities proposed by Martha Nussbaum in her version of the approach, addressed in Chapter 4. Recall here that according to Nussbaum her list of human capabilities 'gives us the basis for determining a decent social minimum in a variety of areas' (2000: 75), which constitutes at the same time the underpinnings of basic political principles informing constitutional guarantees. In her view, therefore, governments should provide a threshold level of capabilities, and this provision should be a constitutional requirement. The threshold of educational capabilities I suggest is more specific and circumscribed in scope, since it aims primarily at selecting levels which are essential for functioning in society, and hence it aims at outlining those educational capabilities that are of central egalitarian concern and, as such, that should be equally distributed. Furthermore, the educational entitlement proposed, as we shall see, aims also at addressing issues of equal educational entitlement for children with disabilities and special educational needs. Nevertheless, despite the more restricted scope of my proposal, its underlying idea draws on Nussbaum's conception.

Thinking of an educational entitlement in terms of equal capabilities for functioning at a level necessary to participate effectively in society, although already demanding a goal for social and institutional arrangements, may raise objections. Two, in particular, are significant. The first relates to the provision of a subset of basic capabilities rather than the full range of possible educational ones. Should individuals be equally entitled to achieve higher levels of educational functionings? Or to a broader range? This issue relates directly to the problem of indexing capabilities inherent to the approach, while also implying considerations about education. As we have seen in Chapter 4, the capability approach faces the problem of deciding which capabilities society should aim to equalize. At the same time, the presumptive dimension proper to education compounds this problem, since deciding in advance what capabilities and what level of achieved functionings will ultimately allow a person to flourish is a very difficult task. However, the fundamental educational entitlement outlined can withstand this objection for two important reasons. First, securing basic fundamental functionings, which are essential to participate effectively in society, means giving people those transformational resources that will allow them to choose the kind of life they have reason to value. It therefore means assuring their well-being and expanding their freedoms. Since this is the fundamental variable upon which people's relative positions in social arrangements should be evaluated, this meets the requirements of the approach and the demands of equality. Second, since the basic educational functionings are at the same time fundamental in expanding other and future capabilities, providing people with this subset means securing those enabling conditions upon which to base higher educational as well as other functionings and capabilities. After all, higher educational functionings cannot be achieved without the prior achievement of fundamental enabling conditions, such as literacy and numeracy. However, setting this basic educational entitlement leaves open the important issue of the promotion of higher levels of functionings beyond the basic entitlement outlined, which is a matter that I will analyse in a further section of this chapter.

The second objection concerns how to conceptualize this educational entitlement in relation to disability and special educational needs, and hence while evaluating functionings and capabilities restrictions. More specifically, it concerns how we can think of equality of sets of educational capabilities when certain disabilities may limit functionings and capabilities, sometimes in consistent ways. The next section addresses this issue in more detail.

3. Elements of a Fundamental Educational Entitlement for Students with Disabilities and Special Educational Needs

A capability perspective on educational equality defines it in terms of equal effective opportunities to achieve levels of functionings that are necessary to participate in society. This constitutes a fundamental educational entitlement, and establishes a threshold level of basic capabilities that should be guaranteed to individuals. Students with disabilities and special educational needs are entitled to the achievement of educational functionings established as a matter of justice for all individuals. However, as we have seen in previous chapters, disability and special educational needs imply functionings and capabilities limitations, which may result in difficulties in the achievements of those levels of educational functionings. It follows, therefore, that students with disabilities and special needs should receive educational opportunities and resources necessary to achieve effective levels of functionings in their dominant social framework. This implies the provision of additional opportunities and resources, where necessary, as a matter of justice. Ultimately, equalizing opportunities and securing fundamental educational functionings in the case of children with disabilities and special educational needs means exactly providing those additional opportunities and resources necessary to these children for the achievement of an effective participation in society.

In this sense, therefore, a child with dyslexia is entitled to additional opportunities and resources that will allow her to achieve reading and writing functionings appropriate to participate effectively in her social framework. The aim here is not simply the fairness of the share of resources, but, more appropriately, it is ensuring levels of functionings.

While answering the central question related to educational equality for students with disabilities and special educational needs, i.e. what allocation of resources is just for them, this perspective presents fundamental positive insights, both normatively and for more practice-oriented issues. First, the educational entitlement is set within a normative framework where competing demands of equality for disabled and non-disabled children are evaluated comparatively. In providing the normative basis upon which to reconsider the contentious issue of resource allocation, the capability approach presents a justified answer to long-debated issues. More specifically, in identifying an educational entitlement, it allows considering the additional requirements of resources for children with disabilities and special educational needs as requirements of justice.

Second, determining an educational entitlement that indicates a threshold level of capabilities, necessary to the individual to function effectively in society, helps in avoiding a possible problem related to the resource provision for disabled people, i.e. the problem of infinite demand.[11] This problem arises, for instance, in relation to severe impairments, like multiple cognitive impairments, when compensatory models would imply an infinite allocation of resources in order to get the individual to an even starting point, as compared to other individuals, so that she had a real chance for equality over a lifetime. In setting a threshold level within the basic educational capabilities and in specifying this as the level for effective functioning in society, we avoid the problem of infinite demand in two ways. First, we set an actual limit on how much resources should be distributed, and that limit corresponds to the opportunities and resources necessary to the individual's effective participation. Second, the demands of disability and special educational needs are considered within a framework of equality, which evaluates it in relation to the demands of other individuals. Thus, an infinite allocation of resources to a disabled child that would deplete the others of resources necessary to achieve levels of functionings to participate effectively in society is not possible, since it is contrary to the same principle upon which the distribution takes place in the first instance.

Third, the educational entitlement proposed provides a possible, although provisional, answer to the problem of indexing capabilities, or, more specifically, to the question of what capabilities to foster and promote in relation to the limitations of disability and special educational needs. Recall here that the capability approach faces the question of which capabilities to promote equally among individuals, and hence which capabilities are of egalitarian concern. The proposed entitlement suggests a possible answer by outlining basic educational capabilities essential to function effectively in society, and which should therefore be provided as a matter of justice. However, this answer needs further specification when related to some of the complexities of disability and special educational needs. Consider, for instance, severe and multiple cognitive disabilities. There are situations where teachers and parents of severely cognitive disabled children decide to privilege the promotion of certain capabilities and the achievement of certain functionings, for instance that of establishing positive social relationship, over capabilities and achieved functionings like numeracy ones, for instance. In such cases, therefore, teachers and parents, under external resource constraints and considering the child's individual characteristics, apply mild perfectionist considerations in deciding which capabilities would help the child to flourish in life. On the one hand, the educational entitlement outlined applies exactly this kind of mild perfectionist considerations: it selects a list of capabilities that, once fostered, will allow individuals to function effectively in society, therefore giving them the bases to flourish. In this sense, the capability approach is here very useful, not only because it allows us to focus on those essential freedoms, but also because it provides considerations relating to means-ends, where ends are the expansion of the individual's freedom to choose the life she has reason to value. Perfectionist considerations, of a mild nature, ultimately, are necessary to the project and lead to useful answers.

However, on the other hand, the same considerations constitute also the limit of the approach. More specifically, the selection of basic capabilities as constitutive of the educational entitlement may present problems. Reconsider here the example of the severely cognitive disabled child. Suppose the child's flourishing rests almost entirely on her enjoyment and fruition of music, and hence on functionings like listening to music and singing, and on her swimming and exercising in water. Obviously, the child's well-being is paramount; and hence the promotion of these functionings can be seen as a matter of justice. However, the educational entitlement proposed does not consistently account for these instances, thus presenting a substantial limit (this objection is also addressed further on).

Finally, a further positive insight of this perspective concerns its important practice-oriented implications, which relate primarily to the distribution of resources for the education of children with disabilities and special educational needs. The educational entitlement determines the additional opportunities and resources for these students as a matter of justice, and it furthermore specifies a threshold level for enactment of the distribution. The threshold is set at the level of the individuals' effective functioning in society. I believe that this constitutes an important insight for the design of educational policies, in that it suggests a normative framework upon which to draw more precise funding formulae for inclusive and special education. The latter, moreover, is drawn on a framework that considers the competing demands of disabled and non-disabled students, and hence on a comprehensive perspective on some of the demands of equality in education.

Despite these positive insights, there are, however, two main and consistent limits to this perspective. The first concerns the possible element of 'reductionism' implied in an educational entitlement and in the related selection of basic capabilities. Reconsider here the case of severe cognitive disabilities: in this case supporting the achievement of musical and swimming functionings enhances the well-being of the child. Why should we propose an educational entitlement based on basic capabilities necessary to an effective participation in society, when some impairments restrict functionings in such substantial ways that the actual well-being of the individual is better promoted through securing other functionings? Should we not instead reconsider the full set of educational capabilities and promote it? Moreover, even in its broader understanding entailing alternative ways of functionings, are we not suggesting an idealized and somehow 'normalized' view of what 'effective functioning and participating in society' may mean? This first limit is interrelated with the second one, which concerns the possible discriminatory and oppressive use of any threshold level, however carefully designed, in separating those individuals that achieve the set levels from those who do not. Disabled people's movements have long denounced these discriminatory and stigmatizing perspectives and oppose the idea of threshold levels, however well intentioned they may be.[12] Why not propose the promotion of capabilities and functioning achievements and abandon any idea of threshold levels?

I shall admit at once that I do not have a full defence of the proposed framework against these questions, and that I share many of the perplexities they raise. However, some considerations may clarify the reasons in support of an educational entitlement. First, there are considerations of justice that endorse the proposed entitlement. Questions of justice arise in situations of scarcity of resources, and the just design of social and institutional arrangements implies an evaluation of the distribution of benefits and burdens among individuals. Society, or the design of social and institutional arrangements, cannot equally promote the countless possible capabilities that people may have reasons to value. A selection criterion is needed when considering issues of equality. In the specific case of education, the criterion chosen relates to the possibility to function effectively in society, and the basic educational capabilities selected respond to this requirement. The aim and the criterion meet egalitarian ideals, and seem justified for selecting both the capabilities and the level at which they should be distributed: remember that we are providing people with the transformational resources that will allow them to choose the life they have reasons to value. Moreover, in promoting people's functioning and participation in society, they are provided with the effective freedom for exercising agency and citizenship, which is one of the aims of disabled people's movements and activisms. Second, the entitlement is based on an idea of educational equality as equal opportunities and presents the threshold level as an indication of the proposed achieved functionings in order to set levels of distributions that, for instance, do not incur in the problem of infinite demand. In this sense, the threshold level is not meant to discriminate between people or to evaluate their competence in a range of functionings (as certain understandings of the medical model of disability, for instance). Rather, it establishes a presumptive aim for the distribution to be at the same time equal and effective. While these considerations do not fully respond to the objections raised, I believe they provide useful specifications to attenuate their force.

   The view presented so far, however, leaves open the fundamental aspect of providing and promoting higher levels of educational functionings, which appears important in itself, for the intrinsic value of education, and instrumentally, in light of the complex structures of contemporary post-industrial societies. This last aspect of the framework is addressed in the final section of this chapter.

4. Towards a Principled Framework for a Just Distribution of Educational Resources to Students with Disabilities and Special Educational Needs

Although an effective participation and the possibility of taking part as equals in society do not require individuals to achieve high levels of educational functionings, their promotion is important both in light of the intrinsic value of education and of its instrumental value. For instance, the possibility of interpreting complex literary theories or understanding the scientific underpinnings of the Human Genome Project are not necessary to participate effectively in society. However, their pursuit may enhance the well-being of some, for instance those who love literary works or scientific endeavours, while also proving instrumentally valuable in giving access to better or preferred job opportunities. At the same time, these endeavours may yield positive results for people other than those undertaking them. For instance, some implications of the Human Genome Project may prove helpful in alleviating genetic conditions. It follows, therefore, that considerations about the provision for higher educational functionings are not only important, but necessary too. Our interest in equality requires an analysis of this provision.

Sen clearly states that the capability approach does not constitute a theory of justice, but a normative framework for the assessment of inequalities. The approach, therefore, does not specify the principles upon which to establish a just distribution of resources and these have to be drawn on other theories. In particular, Rawls's seminal work on justice as fairness outlines fundamental principles that can guide the just distribution of resources, while also providing valuable insights for permissible inequalities. Rawls's theory has been addressed in several sections of this book, but it is perhaps worth recalling some of its fundamental elements once more.

Rawls's theory of justice stipulates two fundamental principles. According to the first, the Liberty Principle, each person has the same claim to a fully adequate scheme of equal basic liberties, which include freedom of thought and speech, as well as freedom of conscience. The Second Principle consists instead of two parts. It states, first, that social and economic inequalities are to be attached to offices and positions open to all under fair equality of opportunity. Second, that these inequalities have to be to the benefit of the least advantaged members of society (Rawls, 2001: 42–3), understood as all those with the lowest shares of income and wealth. This second part is known as the 'difference principle' and regulates what inequalities are permissible under conditions of justice. Rawls further specifies the First Principle as prior to the Second, and fair equality of opportunity as prior to the difference principle. It follows, therefore, that inequalities are permissible only against a background where the prior principles are satisfied, and hence against a background where people have equal basic liberties and are provided with fair chances of attaining rewarding positions. While constituting a strictly distributive norm (Rawls, 2001: 61), Rawls inscribes the difference principle within a conception of social co-operation, and specifies it essentially as a principle of reciprocity. He maintains that however great the inequalities in income and wealth may be, and however consistent the differences among people in exerting effort and earning a greater share of output, inequalities must contribute to the benefit of the least advantaged. Furthermore, this contribution must be effective, and hence it requires that to each improvement in the legitimate expectations of the more advantaged must correspond an equal improvement in those of the least advantaged (Rawls, 2001: 64). In this sense, considerations of efficiency are central to the difference principle. Finally, according to Rawls, '[T]his condition brings out that even if it uses the idea of maximising the expectations of the least advantaged, the difference principle is essentially a principle of reciprocity' (Rawls, 2001: 64). In this sense, the difference principle requires that inequalities are to benefit others, as well as ourselves (Rawls, 2001: 64).

How can Rawls's principles of justice help in determining how to distribute opportunities and provide effective access to higher levels of educational functionings? The difference principle appears particularly relevant in the context of determining this distribution, since it limits permissible inequalities within considerations of justice and efficiency. Applied to education, these considerations lead to the distribution of resources and opportunities for higher functionings in ways that allow for inequalities to be used by those with a greater capacity in relation to the design of the educational arrangements. At the same time it requires these inequalities to serve the interests of the least well off. In other words, it seems plausible to argue that beyond the threshold level of fundamental capabilities guaranteed to everyone, those who can obtain the highest functionings in education should receive resources to that aim, providing that the benefits they gain from their education corresponded to an equal long-term prospective improvement and benefits for those least successful. In this sense, for instance, higher levels of functionings achieved by some may provide the rest of us with more advantages than we would have otherwise had, and therefore improve our long-term well-being in considerable ways. Similarly, severely disabled children or children with profound and multiple impairments might benefit from the higher educational functionings achieved by others, and this ultimately justifies applying considerations of efficiency to the distribution of resources for higher educational functionings.

We can now, therefore, attempt to provide a (provisional and tentative) conception of the principled framework for a just distribution of opportunities and effective access to educational functionings for children with disability and special educational needs. This framework consists of two parts. The first stipulates that equal opportunities for fundamental educational functionings be provided at levels necessary to individuals for an effective participation in society. It sets a threshold level of capabilities and states that all should have effective equal opportunities for the achievement of those fundamental educational functionings. From the conception of disabilities and special educational needs as functionings and capabilities limitations, it follows that necessary and legitimate additional resources have to be devoted to children designated as having disabilities and special educational needs. The second part of the framework applies considerations of efficiency to the distribution of opportunities and resources for the effective access and achievement of higher levels of functionings. It states that beyond the threshold level of fundamental functionings, resources should be devoted in ways that allow the higher achievements of some to benefit those achieving at a lower level. While this framework does not provide a theory of educational equality, it nevertheless helps in providing a possible answer to the debated question of what constitutes educational equality for children with disabilities and special educational needs.

Concluding Comments

In this chapter I have provided an initial answer to the question of what constitutes a just educational provision for students with disabilities and special educational needs, and, in particular, what and how much educational resources should be distributed to these students, by outlining an understanding of educational equality in terms of a principled framework for a just distribution of resources.

I have tried to show how the capability approach substantially helps in conceptualizing educational equality by focusing on the fundamental educational capabilities that are essential prerequisites for functioning as an equal and effective participant in society. On this view, educational equality consists in equal effective opportunities and access to basic functionings (people's actual beings and doings). Students with disabilities are entitled to achieve educational functionings established for all. Therefore, they should receive educational opportunities and resources to achieve effective levels of functionings. This is the principled justification for additional resources and sets the measure of the differential amount due to students with disabilities and special educational needs. Finally, beyond the level of educational capabilities identified as a just entitlement, considerations of efficiency, drawn on John Rawls's principles of justice, may be applied to the necessary promotion of higher or more complex educational functionings.

This principled framework provides a partial, but I hope promising, answer to the question of equality in education for students with disabilities and special educational needs. There are, however, several objections that can be raised against its validity, and addressing them is therefore extremely important. That is my task in the next chapter.

Chapter 8

Objections to the Principled Framework for Educational Equality: A Response

The principled framework outlined in the last chapter provides legitimate answers to the complex question of what constitutes a just educational provision for students with disabilities and special educational needs, and, as such, it should offer guidance for the design of educational policies. However, the case for the principled framework, and, in particular, its core idea of a threshold of capability for effective participation in society, is not fully accomplished unless the possible objections to it are addressed. In this chapter, I discuss and offer counterarguments to three of these objections.[1] These critiques question primarily the liberal position underlying the framework, and specifically the ideal of educational equality, either as distributive principle as such, or as expressed in terms of equality of opportunity.

In particular, the first objection disputes the coherence of the notion of equal opportunity in its application to education, and further questions the understanding of equality of educational resources. Given their logical inconsistence, it is claimed, concepts of equal opportunities and educational equality should not guide the design of policies. Rather, resources in education should be distributed on the basis of the best use that students can make of them. As we shall see, this view rests on a questionable account of both equal opportunity and educational resources, and, as such, its rejection of these ideals proves to be ultimately unjustified. Moreover, if extended to the education of students with disabilities and special educational needs this position may lead to the problematic conclusion that these students should receive only a limited education, given their possible 'poor' use of resources.

The second objection argues that educational equality is not only a misplaced ideal, but it has also been used to justify the debatable involvement of the state in the provision of schooling. Although egalitarians claim to support equality – the objection contends – what they really invoke is a kind of sufficiency or adequacy, beyond which the results of any distribution of whatever goods are deemed valuable does not represent a concern of justice. Applied to education, this translates into the view that the state should not be directly responsible for the provision of education, but should only make sure that all children receive an adequate minimum education, with full provision left to parental means. I shall argue that this view seems to misrepresent egalitarian theories, while drawing partial conclusions from their arguments. Moreover, I shall outline the normative difference between promoting a minimum adequate education for all, and arguing, as I do, for equal effective opportunities for fundamental educational capabilities. While the first perspective denies the relevance of equality in education, the second represents a possible and legitimate conception of it.

The third objection maintains instead that distributive ideals of justice, such as the one endorsed in my work, substantially fail to identify and account for the fundamental aspect of equal recognition and parity of participation in society for under-represented groups. This perspective, emerging mainly from feminist theory, presents similarities with positions in disability studies and the much-endorsed 'politics of difference'.[2] I shall argue that while this view rests perhaps on a partial rendering of theories of distributive justice and underestimates substantive differences among them, it also primarily fails to acknowledge the theoretical and normative reach of the capability approach in promoting both issues of distribution and recognition.

The chapter is organized in three sections, each analysing and providing a counter-argument to a single objection. I start by addressing the first critique, the incoherence of educational equality and the correlated idea of an elitist use of resources.

1. Should We Distribute Educational Resources According to Individuals' Ability to Make Use of Them?

In his article 'Does Equality (of Opportunity) Make Sense In Education?' John Wilson (1991) argues against educational equality as equal opportunity for learning and, in particular, against the idea of equality of educational resources.[3] Wilson's argument proceeds in two stages, with the second specifically relevant to the case of educational provision for students with disabilities and special educational needs. Consequently, my analysis addresses, first, the general lines of Wilson's discussion, and, second, its implications for the education of these students. As we shall see, Wilson's position rests on a partial understanding of the principle of equal educational opportunities, and its conclusions prove therefore unjustified. Furthermore, generically arguing, as Wilson seems to do, for the distribution of resources on the basis of people's abilities to use them

violates principles of justice and casts moral doubts on the view of education, and, more broadly, on the kind of society proposed. I start by
analysing Wilson's main position.

According to Wilson, 'some human activities simply do not lend themselves to the context of distributive justice at all' (Wilson, 1991: 27), and
education is certainly one of these. The idea that we can allocate opportunities for learning is, in his view, logically incoherent, since it only makes
sense to say that a person has the opportunity to do X if they have the
power to do X (Wilson, 1991: 28). Thus, Wilson says,

> [To] see this, consider the case where a person is quite unable to do
> X. Given a particular situation on the football field, a person may seem
> to have the opportunity to break through the opposing players and
> score. But he is quite unable to do this: he is . . . [*for instance*] too weak
> . . . He has the opportunity only if he has the power.
>
> (Wilson, 1991: 28)

Wilson maintains that this is specifically the case in education, since
people have different powers and capacities to learn and, consequently,
certain pursuits can be learned by some people, but not by everyone. It
therefore follows that equality of opportunity in education is an incoherent ideal.

However, as Brighouse (2000b: 142) rightly points out, the conclusion of
this argument does not seem to follow from its premise. To say that certain
activities can only be learned by some people and not by others does not
imply that equality of educational opportunity is incoherent. Brighouse's
counter-argument proceeds in two stages. First, he says, we could choose
to teach only those activities that can be learned by everybody, thus
avoiding the alleged incoherence of equality of educational opportunities.
This solution would certainly result in undesirable policies, since it would
not only infringe peoples' liberties, but it would also yield unwanted
consequences in depriving society of the valuable contribution of those
who can learn and produce goods for the benefits of many. Nevertheless,
it would respond to Wilson's objection. Second, Brighouse points out that
the meaning of equality of opportunities in education does not correspond to providing exactly the same opportunities. Rather, it refers to the
provision of equal arrays of chances to learn. In this sense, two students
with different abilities and powers (to use Wilson's terminology) could still
be given equal opportunities to learn, providing these opportunities were
not the same ones (Brighouse, 2000b: 142–3). So, to illustrate this point,
if Lily has good abilities to learn foreign languages and Mark has the

ability to learn to play the cello, Lily and Mark can be given equal opportunities to get their goods, but these opportunities will not be *exactly the
same*. Likewise, if Lily is visually impaired, while Mark is able-bodied, we
can still provide Lily with equal educational opportunities in terms of
Braille resources and appropriate teaching methodologies, for instance.
Consequently, the alleged incoherence of equal educational opportunities
does not seem to be sustained.

There is, however, a second part in Wilson's argument, whose logical
consequence is relevant to the educational provision for children with
disabilities and special educational needs, and should, therefore, be specifically discussed in this context. Wilson argues that even trying to address
the incoherence of equality of educational opportunities through notions
of equality of access, or resources or anything similar, is problematic
(Wilson, 1991: 29). In his view, resources in general, but educational
resources in particular, can only be considered as such if they are taken up
and used to educational purposes. Thus, he argues,

> the notion of an *educational* resource (and this includes access-oppor-
> tunities and anything else we may *prima facie* seem able to distribute
> equally) still contains the concept of uptake. For instance, having a
> computer is only an *educational* resource if it is seen and used for
> learning: that is, if the owner can actually (and will actually) become
> more educated by his possession of it.
>
> (Wilson, 1991: 30)

Consequently, given people's differential abilities and willingness to use
resources and to become educated, Wilson maintains that the idea of educational equality as equal distribution of resources is a logically incoherent
principle and should not inform policies. Further, an appropriate policy
should consist instead in 'first establishing the learning-activities which we
think important, and then ensuring that all individuals who meet the
criteria of selection for those activities are not debarred from pursuing
them' (Wilson, 1991: 30). Thus, given situations of scarcity of resources,
Wilson concludes that educational resources should only be distributed to
those who can make the best use of them. For instance, higher education,
seen as a valuable pursuit, should only be made available to those students
who will demonstrate levels of excellence, since 'not everyone can in fact
make *as good* use of higher education as anyone else' (Wilson, 1991: 29).

There are several problems with this position, but two, in particular, are
worth addressing. First, as Brighouse argues, the concept of resource does
not necessarily require any uptake and, more specifically, the notion of an

educational resource, counting only as such when appropriately used, is rather implausible (Brighouse, 2000b: 143). Brighouse supports his counter-argument by noting, for instance, that the nutritional value of a peanut is not compromised in the case of somebody not eating it, or eating it before feeling sick, or forgetting to eat it and so forth. What is missing in these circumstances is simply making use of the peanut's nutritional value. Similarly, the fact that a monolingual Italian speaker cannot make use of an English dictionary does not compromise the status of the dictionary as an educational resource (Brighouse, 2000: 143–4). Therefore, the notion of an educational resource does not require an uptake of any kind: the educational value of a resource is there, despite the good or bad use that can be made of it. In this sense, Wilson's argument shows theoretical difficulties.

Second, there are problematic implications with Wilson's proposal of distributing resources on the basis of their optimal usage. This is directly relevant to the case of the educational equality I am defending, and it seems therefore important to evaluate Wilson's considerations in relation to the education of students with disabilities and special educational needs. Two elements will guide my analysis: the normative principles of distributive justice, and the moral domain underpinning them. To begin with, let us consider the example of Lily and Mark used above. Suppose that Lily can excellently learn foreign languages, whereas Mark can learn to play the cello, but only at a mediocre level. Should we distribute resources only to Lily, since she can make the best use of them? As Brighouse comments, '[i]t is a harsh theory which yields these results' (2000b: 144). Not only this, but also such a theory misinterprets the normative assumptions of distributive principles, which are 'to distribute goods among persons, not to distribute uses amongst resources' (Brighouse, 2006: 145). But let us extend the analysis to the education of children with disabilities and special educational needs. Why, after all, should we distribute resources according to egalitarian principles, however specified, and provide the minority of children with disabilities with additional resources, when we could actually invest those resources in providing the majority of children with, say, better sports facilities and playgrounds? Here again, the basic assumption that should guide our judgement is not the best use that children can make of the resources, but the possibility of distributing these resources with the aim of giving children equal chances to participate effectively in society, thus ultimately to lead worthwhile lives. This relates to my second consideration, namely the moral domain of justice and equality. Since considerations of distributive justice and equality are underpinned by the equal moral worth of each person, and by the equal consideration they should receive from social and institutional arrangements, it seems that Wilson's focus on resources and their best use overlooks this fundamental concern. On his view, Mark would indeed receive less consideration given his supposed lower talent in using resources and, presumably, children with disabilities and special educational needs would be considered similarly. As I have consistently tried to show in discussions in previous chapters, such an assumption needs clear and detailed arguments, and it is unlikely to be morally justified.

There is, however, an aspect of Wilson's objection that needs further evaluation, since, if distributing resources according to their best use is questionable, under conditions of scarcity of resources the latter have to be used effectively according to precise principles of justice (an aspect that Wilson does not address in his discussion). This is fundamental in the case of educational equality and the correlated distribution of resources for students with disabilities and special educational needs. The distinction that seems more appropriate in this case is between a fundamental level of education and a highly specialized level of higher education, such as, for instance, the Oxbridge education mentioned by Wilson. Hence it appears reasonable to argue for equal opportunities for educational resources, or, as in my framework, for fundamental educational functionings necessary to participate as equals in society, while determining the promotion of further and higher capabilities on the basis of principles of justice, further specified. In this sense, equality in education is meant to provide individuals with the effective transformational resources that will allow them to lead fulfilling lives and choose among valuable options. As we have seen, Wilson's discussion does not contemplate this distinction, but only allows for the generic allocation of resources to those who can best use them, and, therefore, his position proves highly objectionable. And this appears to argue convincingly against supporting the distribution of resources according to their best use.

Ultimately, therefore, educational equality does not appear to be the incoherent ideal claimed by Wilson, but maintains its validity against this first objection. In the next section, I address and argue against the second objection, the case for a minimum adequate education for all, set against my egalitarian view of equal effective opportunities to achieve fundamental educational functionings.

2. Is a Minimum Adequate Education for All Acceptable?

One of the ideas often invoked against egalitarian principles is that justice demands only a notion of sufficiency or adequacy, thus requiring that everyone has enough of whatever goods are distributed.[4] What matters on this view, therefore, is not that people have equal shares of what is valuable, but that they all have enough. And although there may be different and contrasting conceptions of sufficiency, providing that everyone has reached the level agreed as correspondent to it, the subsequent distribution loses importance (Swift, 2001: 121).

James Tooley endorses this perspective and applies it to education. Tooley claims that the egalitarian concern about educational equality is not only misplaced, but has also been wrongly used as the main reason for justifying government intervention in education (Tooley, 2000: 62). He maintains that a closer look at the notion of equity or equality of opportunity reveals that not equality but a minimum adequate education for all is what justice requires (Tooley, 2000: 62). Tooley further argues that empirical evidence suggests that state intervention in education does not achieve more equitable results than private initiatives, and seems even to fail the objective of achieving education for all. On these bases, therefore, he claims that state intervention in providing education is not only unnecessary, but also mainly unjustified (Tooley, 2000: 77). The only role of the state in education should be to ensure that children from very poor backgrounds receive a minimum adequate education. Above the minimum level identified, educational opportunities should not be independent or insulated from family circumstances (Brighouse, 2000b: 146).

Is Tooley's objection to educational equality sustained? Is it really the case that the analysis of the notion of equality of opportunity shows that not equality, but minimum adequacy is what counts? Brighouse argues effectively against Tooley's objection by showing that it is based on an incorrect reading of principles of justice, and by demonstrating that its conclusions on the adequacy of a minimum education are not acceptable. In addressing Tooley's concerns, I shall, first, presents Brighouse's arguments, and, second, proceed to outline the substantive normative differences between endorsing a criterion of adequacy and providing a threshold of educational capabilities. Finally, I shall consider the possible implications of Tooley's position for inclusive and special education.

Tooley addresses his objection primarily to John Rawls's theory of justice and specifically to its principle of fair equality of opportunity. Recall here once more that Rawls's theory is based on two principles, a Liberty Principle, which stipulates that the basic liberties should be equally distributed, and a Second Principle, which regulates the legitimate inequalities among individuals. It is perhaps worth restating here the Second Principle, since Tooley bases his critique upon it. According to the Second Principle,

> Social and economic inequalities are to satisfy two conditions: first they are to be attached to offices and positions open to all under conditions of fair equality of opportunity; and second, they are to be to the greatest benefit of the least-advantaged members of society (the difference principle).

> (Rawls, 2001: 42–3)

Furthermore, Rawls specifies that the First Principle is prior to the Second and that within the Second Principle, fair equality of opportunity is prior to the difference principle. This means that conditions of fair equality of opportunity constrain, but cannot be constrained by, inequalities benefiting the least advantaged members of society (Rawls, 2001: 43).

Although the interpretation of the concept of fair equality of opportunity is complex, as Brighouse notices, Rawls specifies it by broadly stipulating that those with 'the same level of talent and . . . [with] the same willingness to use them, should have the same prospects of success, regardless of their initial place in the social system' (Rawls, cited in Brighouse, 2000b: 147). Brighouse then points out that this understanding of fair equality of opportunity underpins educational equality, since it requires educational opportunities to be provided independently of family circumstances. This is further consistent with Rawls's statement that 'society must also establish, among other things, equal opportunities of education for all regardless of family income' (Rawls, 2001: 44). Thus, educational inequalities due to the higher power expenditures of certain families over others violate equality of opportunities, and are therefore unjustified (Brighouse, 2000: 147). Furthermore, state intervention in education is necessary, among other reasons, exactly in order to enact this principle.

However, Tooley's interpretation of Rawls's theory assumes that fair equality of opportunity is mitigated by the difference principle, i.e. by the idea that inequalities should benefit the least advantaged in society. Further, Tooley maintains that the difference principle is actually unjustified within Rawls's theory and that inequalities should be acceptable not in the strict sense of being only for the benefit of the least advantaged in society, but in the sense of providing a minimum, an adequate level to the least favoured (Brighouse, 2000: 148). Consequently, Tooley maintains that justice requires an adequate minimum education, and that the prin-

ciple of educational equality is indeed misplaced. However, as seen in
Rawls's restatement of his principles of justice, and as Brighouse concludes
in counter-arguing Tooley's interpretation, the latter is based on an incorrect understanding of Rawls's theory. Rawls clearly stipulates that the principle of fair equality of opportunity constrains the possible inequalities
benefiting the least advantaged people in society, and not the opposite.
The upshot of the discussion is that inferring, as Tooley does with regard
to Rawls's theory, that justice requires a minimum adequate education for
all, is theoretically questionable. It follows, therefore, that educational
equality is not the misplaced ideal claimed by Tooley, and its normative
validity is reinstated (Brighouse, 2000b: 149). Consequently, and following
from the previous points, the presumed unjustified intervention of the
state in education proves indeed to be legitimate.

I shall not take this discussion any further here, since what is important
to note is that the principle of educational equality withstands this second
possible objection, and that, contra Tooley, when referring to equality in
education we are not endorsing the notion of sufficiency or adequacy he
advocates. I now turn my analysis to the differences between supporting a
minimum adequate education for all, and suggesting a possible conception of educational equality based on equal effective opportunities for
fundamental functionings. This seems an important step at this stage,
because the framework I suggest theorizes a threshold level of functionings, which can be seen as an adequacy criterion. What, therefore, are the
differences between the two positions?

The first, obvious difference consists in the normative framework within
which the two positions are inscribed. As we have seen, Tooley's perspective of a minimum adequate education for all is not underpinned by a
theory of justice, nor is it concerned primarily with equality. Rather, it
appears more in line with the libertarian critique of egalitarian
approaches, maintaining that egalitarians transfer too much power from
the individual to the state, thus illegitimately limiting liberty. This seems
also consistent with Tooley's insistence on the unnecessary intervention of
the state in education, and his proposal that educational provision should
be left to parental means, rather than being insulated from individuals'
background (Tooley, 2000: 80). This leads to the second main difference
between the two approaches. The minimum adequate education for all
endorsed by Tooley, in denying equality of opportunity and the necessary
separateness of educational opportunities from family endowments and
circumstances, allows for substantial inequalities to be reinforced through
education. Recall here that education is a complex good, which yields not
only an intrinsic but also, and importantly, an instrumental value, in that

it allows for better future opportunities and life prospects. The point of equality of opportunity and its defence within the Rawlsian scheme is exactly to impose constraints to material inequalities, given that the family is excluded from the principles governing the basic structures of society, and to ensure that individuals are not unfairly advantaged or disadvantaged by family circumstances. Tooley's minimum adequate education for all seems, therefore, rather inadequate, since it not only leaves the educational provision under-specified, but also, in connecting the provision of education to family circumstances, de facto legitimates inequality. Conversely, the principled framework for equal educational opportunities to fundamental functionings I suggest, although implying a threshold level of achieved functionings, links the threshold to the effective equal opportunities that should guarantee its achievement, thus actually requiring and safeguarding conditions for equality. Further, the framework I propose specifies the criterion for adequacy, which pertains to the level of fundamental educational functionings to be achieved, thus promoting equality and determining the effective conditions for its enactment.

There is, finally, a further aspect implied by, yet not explicit in, Tooley's objection, namely the possible provision for students with disabilities and special educational needs. Tooley does not specifically consider this aspect, and hence we need to extend his perspective to include it. Presumably, therefore, according to Tooley, children with disabilities should receive a minimum adequate education, provided by the state, if they are extremely poor, or by their parents in all other cases. Beyond that level, their education should be left to parental means, and parents should be allowed to choose among different educational options in a market system. We may, however, question the adequacy of such a provision, as implying at least two fundamental problems. The first relates to specifying what would constitute an adequate education for these students. Would it be the same minimum education for all, or a specific minimum education? But we can bypass this problem and simply suppose that it would be the same education provided to all. However, the question then arises with respect to the possible costs associated with the education of children with disabilities and special educational needs. This cost might be higher than the one for educating non-disabled students, due, for instance, to extended learning time and specific or atypical educational resources needed. Should the family be expected to provide for this? Or should it be expected to do so beyond the minimum adequate education? This position, moreover, seems also objectionable on the basis of recent empirical research which shows the possible negative effects for the education of students with disabilities and special educational needs resulting from the introduction of quasi-market mechanisms in the schooling system.[5] Further problems seem therefore to arise. For instance, how could the element of resource cost-effectiveness be considered in relation to this provision and in order for private institutions to act competitively, as they are supposed to do in a quasi-market structure? These hypothetical scenarios serve the purpose of highlighting the absence of attention and guidance of Tooley's perspective for the educational provision to students with disabilities, and lead us to consider the possible limitations of such a view. Therefore, Tooley's suggestion of a minimum adequate education fails to be convincing under this respect, too.

Ultimately, the ideal of educational equality withstands this second objection, and seems to provide a valid principle upon which to reconsider not only general educational provision, but also an inclusive and special one. In the third and final section of this chapter I address a further objection to the concept of equality as distributive ideal. This is the critique of the lack of attention that theories of distributive justice, including the capability approach, give to equal recognition and parity in participation.

3. Is Capability Equality in Education Unable to Account for Equal Recognition?

Recent perspectives on justice question the egalitarian concern for issues of distribution as the best enactment of the ideal of equality, and propose instead views based on the positive definition and recognition of differences. In particular, the widely endorsed politics of difference maintains that institutional arrangements should provide 'mechanisms for the effective recognition and representation of the distinct voices' of oppressed and marginalized groups in society: ethnic, 'racial' and sexual minorities, women and disabled people (Young, 1990: 184). These perspectives are often juxtaposed with egalitarian theories of social justice promoting equality as a distributive ideal.

Nancy Fraser (1998) challenges this polarization between redistribution and recognition by arguing that it is not only a false antithesis, but also that 'justice today requires *both* redistribution and recognition, since neither alone is sufficient' (Fraser, 1998: 5). Fraser maintains that theories of distributive justice are unable to account for issues of recognition, and conversely, that theories of recognition are unable to accommodate issues of redistribution. In order to overcome what she maintains is a false opposition, Fraser proposes a 'bivalent' conception of justice, which encompasses both concerns, without, she says, reducing either of them to the other. The normative core of her framework is the notion of parity of participation, which 'requires social arrangements that permit all (adult) members of society to interact with one another as peers' (Fraser, 1998: 30). According to Fraser, two conditions are necessary for participatory parity to be accomplished: an objective precondition, which states that material resources should be distributed to ensure individuals' independence and 'voice'; and an intersubjective condition, stipulating that cultural and social arrangements should express equal respect for all and ensure equal opportunity for achieving self-esteem (Fraser, 1998: 31). The main aim of 'bivalent' justice is to avoid unilateral views, and to address the complex nature of inequalities both from 'distributive' and 'recognition' positions.

In this section I engage with Fraser's critique of distributive theories of justice.[6] As I have mentioned above, Fraser maintains that these theories, by concentrating uniquely on economic and material equality, fail to account for the fundamental aspect of the social and cultural recognition of disadvantaged and marginalized groups in society. Furthermore, she holds that the theoretical framework of these theories is unable to account for aspects of recognition. Although Fraser does not refer specifically to a single theory, nor does she explicitly list any of the authors she is addressing, from footnotes and references it can be inferred that her critique is directed to John Rawls, Ronald Dworkin and Amartya Sen (Robeyns, 2003b: 540). As Robeyns notices, it is unfortunate that Fraser does not provide a clear distinction between these otherwise quite different theories, but deals with them comprehensively, thus substantially limiting the validity of her account (Robeyns, 2003b: 540). Nevertheless, if sustained, the suggestion that the critiqued theories, and in particular Sen's one, cannot accommodate issues of recognition would substantially question the conception of educational equality presented in my work. More specifically, it would lead to the undermining of the normative reach of the framework I suggest, and its legitimacy in informing policy aimed at educational equality for students with disabilities and special educational needs. Fraser's critique, moreover, appears fundamentally in line with social model theorists, who have long demanded the valorization of all differences in society, as well as in education. Hence Fraser's assertion is even further enhanced by this convergence with positions expressed by disabled people's movements and proponents of educational perspectives based on the social model of disability.

In what follows I shall try to ascertain whether egalitarian perspectives really fail to accommodate the positive recognition of differences by focusing only on economic and material inequalities. I shall argue that

Fraser's objection is not sustained, and that her claims do not pay sufficient attention to different perspectives within the egalitarian debate, but seem to be 'simply stated without much supporting evidence or argument' (Robeyns, 2003b: 540). In particular, I shall argue that, among distributive theories, the capability approach provides a normative framework that not only includes both redistribution and recognition, but also expands the egalitarian thought with respect to considerations of justice for under-represented groups, which are the concern of the politics of difference.[7] I shall focus particularly on the recognition of disabled people and, in so doing, recall some of the elements of the capability perspective on disability and special educational needs that I present and defend in this book.

The distinctive element that makes the capability approach able to account for justice in terms of redistribution and recognition is its attention to human diversity and its centrality within the approach. Recall here that, as we have seen in Chapters 4 and 5, according to Sen human heterogeneity is not a secondary aspect to be reintroduced *a posteriori* in a given theory of justice, but is among the main concerns of equality. Furthermore, central in Sen's view is people's conversion factors of resources into valued functionings. This encompasses, together with personal differences, also environmental, cultural and social elements. Hence the impact of individual, social, environmental and cultural factors on a person's set of capabilities is fundamental for the evaluation of people's relative positions and their advantages or disadvantages. The centrality of human diversity in the capability approach, and its clear definition, make the approach sensitive to the reconsideration of differences associated with disability, for instance. Moreover, differences are here evaluated in their interaction with social and cultural arrangements, thus leading to a perspective that does not undermine diversity as an individual limitation with respect to given ideas of 'normality'.

There is, furthermore, a second element that restates the possibility of the capability approach of accounting for both dimensions of justice: the attention to the process of democratic decision-making and open public reasoning with respect to the selection of valuable capabilities. Recall here that, according to Sen, democratic processes of choice should be implemented for the selection of people's relevant capabilities, thus requiring the direct participation of those affected by the selection. In this sense, the approach substantially theorizes a space for the individual and collective expression of people's voices, thus providing the normative space for the important aspect of recognition. Furthermore, the approach is also sensitive to 'the cultural and non-material social constraints on choice that influence which option a person will choose from their capability set' (Robeyns, 2003b: 547) and requires critical examination of them, too. As Robeyns states, within the capability approach, 'preference formation, socialization, subtle forms of discrimination and the impact of social and moral norms are not taken for granted or assumed away but analyzed upfront' (Robeyns, 2003b: 547).

To illustrate these aspects, let us recall how the capability approach allows, for instance, the reconsideration of impairment, disability and special educational needs and how this has an impact on both redistribution and recognition. As we have seen, within a capability perspective disability and special educational needs are specific aspects of human diversity emerging from the interaction of individual and social factors. Since they affect people's valuable functionings and capabilities, disability and special educational needs constitute vertical inequalities, and, as such, they have to be addressed as a matter of justice. The capability perspective emphasizes the relational aspect of disability and special educational needs with the design of social and institutional arrangements, thus not locating either of them unilaterally within the individual or society. Furthermore, this perspective is concerned with expanding people's capability sets, and hence their capability to choose valued beings and doings. In this sense, the approach provides a useful framework when we want to address the injustice, both material and of recognition, associated with disability and special educational needs. For instance, in evaluating the capability set of a wheelchair user, the capability perspective considers how the personal characteristics of the individual interact with the design of social and environmental arrangements. It thus legitimates the additional resources and the modifications to the environmental and social design necessary for the person's full participation in society. Furthermore, the approach considers the cultural and non-material social constraints that can hinder the choice and the broadening of the capability sets available to the person. Negative images and forms of discrimination could therefore be seen as compromising elements for the pursuit of individuals' well-being, and, as such, would be appropriately addressed. Finally, the approach requires that the voice of wheelchair users in the selection of their relevant capability be a necessary part of the democratic process of policy-making, thus accounting for, and requiring, their effective participation in society.

Ultimately, the theoretical and normative features of the capability approach confirm, contra Fraser, that the approach can, and indeed does, accommodate issues of distribution and recognition in substantial and legitimate ways, thus counteracting her claims. However, before drawing this discussion to its conclusion, a further aspect needs addressing, although only briefly. This concerns the ways in which both redistribution and recognition inform the principled framework for a just distribution of opportunities for fundamental educational functionings to students with disabilities and special educational needs that I have formulated in my work. Recall that the framework requires equality of effective opportunity for the fundamental educational functionings necessary to participate as equals in society, and draws a threshold level of achieved functionings, beyond which the distribution follows specified principles. Hence, the additional resources to be distributed ensure the just distributive aspect of the framework. Second, the aspect of recognition is encompassed by the choice of the fundamental capabilities and their aim of promoting people's effective participation in society on an equal level. Correlated to these aspects, the kind of education that appears more conducive to these aims seems to be a form of education for autonomy, which, if not in itself a guarantee of equal opportunity for self-esteem, constitutes nevertheless one of its necessary requirements. And these final elements respond to Fraser's concern about the inability of the capability approach to accommodate justice as distribution and recognition.

Concluding Comments

Three main objections to educational equality substantially fail in their intent of arguing against it as a valid and important ideal. Thus, educational equality, in terms of equality of opportunity, is not an incoherent principle and its specification does indeed make sense in education. In this chapter, I have argued against the idea that educational resources should be distributed only to those who can make the best use of them, and proved that such a position misinterprets the aim of distributive justice and overlooks its normative and ethical dimensions. Secondly, I have argued against a notion of a minimum adequate education and shown that it would constitute an inadequate provision, both generally and for students with disabilities and special educational needs in particular. Finally, by demonstrating that the capability approach encompasses justice both in terms of redistribution and recognition, I have reaffirmed the theoretical and normative validity of the framework I am suggesting for justice and equality in education for learners with disabilities and special educational needs. Since the framework withstands these critiques, it appears a valuable groundwork for educational theory and practice. However, further critiques may emerge and require due attention.

Conclusion

I started this book by outlining the importance of educational equality as a fundamental value of social justice, and by claiming that, although difficult to conceptualize, educational equality has a crucial role to play at two interconnected levels: the level of ideal theory, concerned with norms and values, and the level of policy, where these norms and values can be enacted. I have further stated that a precise conception of educational equality requires a normative framework, theoretically and ethically justified, in order to provide guidance for the design of more just educational policies. One of the most complex aspects of a conception of educational equality, I have also noted, consists in adjudicating the just demands of students with disabilities and special educational needs. Furthermore, it is in the educational provision for these students, as we have seen, that inequalities seem to be most pervasive, and where, consequently, a principled framework is urgently needed. My explicit aim in this book has therefore been to articulate such a normative framework, that is, to provide a principled position which could respond to the complex demands of justice and equality in education for children with disabilities and special educational needs. I have outlined this principled position, based on the capability approach, as entailing two main elements: a redefinition of disability and special educational needs in terms of functionings and capability, and a principled framework for capability equality in education. These, in my view, are the two main theoretical contributions of this book.

In particular, redefining impairment and disability within the capability approach implies redefining them in terms of functionings and capabilities. Impairment is a personal characteristic, which may affect certain functionings, and thus become a disability. Consequently, disability is a restriction in functionings. This is the result of the interlocking of personal and circumstantial features. Likewise, special educational needs are restricted functionings resulting from the interrelation between specific characteristics of the learner and the design of the educational system. Since functionings are constitutive of well-being, and capability represents the various combinations of functionings that a person can achieve, a restriction in functionings results in a restriction in the set of functionings available to the person, and hence in a limitation in capabilities. Evaluated within a capability metric, these restrictions in capabilities constitute vertical inequalities, and, as such, they have to be addressed as a matter of justice. This capability perspective on disability and special educational needs advances current debates in disability studies and liberal egalitarianism by providing a relational view, which sees disability and special needs as the result of the interlocking of individual and circumstantial features, thus going beyond problematic unilateral views identifying them either as individual deficits or as social constructs. Further, this perspective positively contributes to the debate about disability within liberal egalitarianism, by suggesting a metric that is sensitive to disability and special educational needs, and that avoids oversimplified responses to them.

This capability perspective underpins the principled framework for justice and equality in education for students with disabilities and special educational needs proposed in this book. On this view, educational equality consists in equal opportunities for functionings necessary to participate effectively and as equals in society. Students with disabilities are entitled to achieve educational functionings established for all. Therefore, they should receive educational opportunities and resources in order to achieve effective levels of functionings. This is the principled justification for additional resources, and sets the measure of the differential amount due to students with disabilities and special educational needs. Finally, beyond the level of educational capabilities identified as a just entitlement, other considerations, drawn on John Rawls's principles of justice, may be applied to the necessary promotion of higher or more complex educational functionings. While this principled framework does not constitute a theory of educational equality, it nevertheless provides a legitimate answer to the complex problem of determining what distribution of resources is just for students with disabilities and special educational needs. Furthermore, the framework provides the groundwork upon which to design educational policies aimed at equality, as well as to evaluate the fairness of current systems.

This latter point leads to the book's third theoretical contribution. In clarifying what educational equality requires in relation to provision for children with disabilities and special educational needs, the framework suggested connects the normative aspect of political philosophy to that of education. Thus, it articulates a common ground where normative principles inform, but are also informed by, the more empirical and

practice-based dimension of educational theory and policy-making. The principled framework outlined is arrived at by applying the standard philosophical methodology of reflective equilibrium to educational problems. Reflective equilibrium, as we have seen, consists in proposing normative principles, testing them against well-founded intuitions, and adjudicating the conflicts between principles and intuitions, when they arise. The result is a precise and defensible normative account that can provide guidance for educational theory and policy. Therefore, a perspective developed in the way presented in this book could help educationalists and policy-makers to articulate their frameworks for actions.

There are, however, numerous tensions in the process of connecting normative positions to educational theory and policy-making. And while the exploration of these tensions is beyond the scope of this work, it is nevertheless worth indicating at least two of them. First, tensions may arise between some of the 'non-instrumental aspects of philosophical exploration' and the more technical and practical task of policy-making (McLaughlin, 2000: 451). In this sense, the elucidation of the meaning of educational equality for children with disabilities and special educational needs may not result in a straightforward process of decision-making with respect to policy. Second, tensions can arise in relation to the constructive critique offered by philosophical arguments, for instance those I applied to the current policies in inclusive and special education, and the more 'decisional' aspect involved in drawing feasible policies. Again, the relation between philosophical argumentation and practical realization is not a straightforward and linear one. However, despite these possible tensions, a clear definition of principles plays the significant role of providing guidance for the design and reform of social institutions, and the judgement of whether a policy is good or bad (Brighouse, 2001: 1). Ultimately, it is not the task of philosophical enquiry to decide what policy reforms and policy-making will enact specific principles and achieve valuable outcomes, but to outline compelling arguments for these principles and outcomes, and to elucidate their possible interpretations. This, in my view, is the precise and defensible role for the perspective that I have developed in this study.

The philosophical method of reflective equilibrium has indeed informed from the start of the book my analysis of current perspectives and policies in inclusive and special education, as well as current models and understandings within disability studies, as these underpin educational positions. It has also been used to address some of the main arguments in liberal egalitarianism, particularly in relation to their evaluations of disability. Thus, a philosophical method of enquiry has guided my analysis of perspectives, drawn on different disciplines, which have a bearing on the question of educational equality for children with disabilities and special educational needs. Undoubtedly, however, this process will have disappointed some readers. Educationalists, for instance, and in particular those specifically interested in inclusive and special education, will have found the suggested principled framework limited because of its abstract nature, or its lack of explicit policy proposals. Further, they will have found the lack of a specific argument for, or indeed against, inclusive education problematic. The framework I suggest leaves open the question of providing a conception of inclusive education. Strictly related to the level of provision suggested, this issue is important not only for policy and practice in education, but also for any theory of justice for learners with disabilities and special educational needs. This is specifically the case in countries like the UK, where provision entails both inclusive and special schools, and where the debate on inclusion for students with disabilities and special educational needs is certainly contentious. However, from the start of the book I have indicated that my aim has been to provide not a set of policy indications, but a principled position for educational equality that could inform such policy, while restating the validity of the ideal of equality for theory, policy and practice in education. This is one of the possible legitimate roles of philosophical enquiry, as noted above. Further, while acknowledging the crucial importance of issues of inclusion and inclusive education, I believe that the discussion about disability and special educational needs should not be uniquely focused on the location of schooling, whether mainstream or special. In my view, a principled framework for educational equality can provide a compelling starting point for debating and considering the main questions of inclusive education. This, however, in no way undermines the fundamental discussion about inclusive schooling and its relevance for students with disabilities and special educational needs.

But philosophers, too, will have been critical of parts of this project. For instance, they may find it problematic that the book does not engage the broader issue of positioning educational equality in a theory of justice, and even that the framework developed does not constitute a full theory of educational equality, thus not engaging in detail with the task of what kind of argument is the one for equality in education. Moreover, some may think that further analysis should have been devoted to the implications of proposing an adequacy criterion in the form of a threshold level of fundamental capabilities in education. While restating that some of these issues were not parts of my initial goal and would have taken the analysis to different domains, I nevertheless do acknowledge their relevance and the fact that they might inform future projects.

All things considered, however, I believe that the argument developed in this book makes a significant contribution to current philosophical and educational debates on equality in several ways. First, it contributes an understanding of equality in education in terms of a principled position, drawn on liberal theories. While this may appear uncontroversial to many philosophers, the absence of such a framework both from current policies and perspectives in education, as we have seen, makes the case for elucidating principles and restating their importance quite crucial. The principled position suggested in this book, rather than displacing more critical accounts of what actually takes place in education policy and theory, as some educationalists may think, provides exactly the groundwork for setting priorities and guiding educational policy and theory towards equality. Second, the principled framework for capability equality in education provides an understanding of educational equality in terms of a threshold of functionings that should be ensured to all children, thus setting a precise and justified account of what is owed to each child. While the idea of a threshold level in educational equality is not novel, I believe that my formulation in terms of achieved functionings, and thus corresponding capabilities to be provided, is a step forward towards formulating educational policies that could, if not completely eliminate inequalities, at least considerably lessen them. Finally, and crucially, the framework specifies what we owe, through the design of educational institutions, to some of the most vulnerable children in our educational systems, that is, children with disabilities and special educational needs. It thus provides a justified answer to long-debated and quite complex educational problems. This answer, moreover, entails a unified and coherent framework, which sees the interplay of redefining disability and special educational needs in terms of capability limitations, and of determining the terms of a just educational provision as capability equality. Of course, further research and more work is needed in order to provide operative indications from the framework suggested.

In conclusion, I believe that the argument I have developed in this book provides a significant understanding of educational equality for students with disabilities and special educational needs, and a clear framework for trying to overcome persistent inequalities with more just educational policies. I would like to suggest that the principled framework for capability equality in education should be implemented in the design of education policies, if these are to respond to the fundamental aim of contributing to the creation of a society where each individual participates as an equal among others. This, I believe, is what we owe to students with disabilities and special educational needs, and we certainly owe it as a matter of justice.

Notes

Introduction

1 The literature on the labelling use of categories in education is extremely wide and mainly developed by sociologists of education. See, for instance, Barton, 1993 and 2003; Corbett, 1996; Daniels, 2006; Keil et al, 2006; Riddell, 1996; Tomlinson, 1982. For a more philosophical position, see Wilson, 2000. This aspect of the debate is discussed in Chapters 1, 2 and 3, where I also provide more precise references.

Chapter 1

1 The United Kingdom consists of four separate but interconnected countries: England, Wales, Northern Ireland and Scotland. While England and Wales share almost the same educational policy, Northern Ireland and Scotland have distinct arrangements. However, the National Assembly for Wales – rather than the newly formed Department for Children, Schools and Families (DCSF) – directs Welsh education.

2 Geoff Lindsay has addressed the controversial aspect of the argument for efficiency and efficacy in relation to inclusive education, and has outlined how the Statement asserts the effectiveness of inclusion in the absence of clear empirical evidence (Lindsay, 2003). See also Lindsay, 2007 for a discussion of the limits of a perspective based on rights.

3 This Act has been superseded since by the 1993 Education Act, the 1996 Education Act and the 2001 Special Educational Needs and Disability Act (Marsh, 2003: 14).

4 Local Authorities (LAs), or until recently Local Education Authorities (LEAs), in England are governmental institutions at local level and provide services to the schools under their responsibility.

5 These considerations draw substantially on Norwich 2002 and 1996.

6 See, among others, Barton, 1993; Evans and Lunt, 1994; and Rouse and Florian, 1997; see also Marsh, 2003 for a detailed study of the funding of inclusive education and for discussions on the effects of the 1988 ERA.

7 In response to the CSEF survey, only half of the states were able to provide data with a 'high degree of confidence'. However, in the absence of other sources, the data collected in the survey have been used in several studies (Wolman and Parrish, 1996: 215) and are considered here as valid and reliable, although not complete.

8 These perspectives will be analysed in Chapter 3, following my philosophical critique of the social model of disability in Chapter 2.

9 These considerations are based on the work of scholars in the UK who support

a view of 'full inclusion', which does not require the identification of difference, or specific additional provision. The work of other UK and US scholars
supporting the social model of disability does not entirely endorse this
reading. These scholars debate how best to respond to impairment.

Chapter 2
1 Accredited impairments refer to the definition used in the medical and
  indeed the social models of disability, which will be addressed in the course of
  the discussion.
2 The model has various and important internal articulations. These include
  positions in the UK that emphasize primarily the social causes and the ideological construction of disability, and positions in the USA that endorse a more
  relational view of impairment, disability and the design of social arrangements. See, for instance, Anita Silvers, 1998: 74–6.
3 World Health Organization (1980), *The International Classification of Impairments, Disability and Handicaps* (ICIDH). Geneva: World Health Organization;
  see also World Health Organization (1997), *The International Classification of
  Impairments, Activities and Participation* (ICIDH-2). Geneva: World Health
  Organization. More recently the WHO has issued the *International Classification of Functioning, Disability and Health* (ICFDH), which revises the assumptions of the previous classifications to include elements pertaining to the social
  and circumstantial domain of disability. In particular, the new classification
  shifts the focus from the causes to the 'impact' of disability, and concentrates
  on classes of functionings in certain contexts. This will be referred to in
  relation to the Capability Approach in Chapter 4.
4 Oliver has recently reasserted this position and urged the disability movement
  to engage in the enactment of the social model in policy and practice, rather
  than debating it for what is has never aimed to be, i.e. a theory of disablement.
  See Oliver, 2004, pp.24 and 30–31.
5 As I mentioned in the introduction, Rawls theorizes justice as fairness as specifying the principles of justice required in a fair system of co-operation among
  citizens viewed as free and equal persons, and as fully co-operating members
  of society over a complete lifetime (Rawls, 2001: 176). Rawls intentionally
  excluded the position of disabled people from his account, maintaining that
  their case could be addressed at a later stage. This exclusion has recently been
  the subject of analyses and critiques. Attempts have been made to extend the
  Rawlsian framework in order to accommodate the distinct demands of disability (among others, see, for instance, Eva Feder Kittay, 2003; and Harry
  Brighouse, 2001). On the other hand, critiques have been raised in relation to
  the contractarian nature of Rawls's account, which, as a paradigm of successful bargaining among similar individuals, is seen as de facto excluding
  disabled people (see, for instance, Nussbaum, 2006a). See also Silvers and
  Francis (2005) for an interesting discussion of the position of disabled people
  in contract theories. Notwithstanding these important elements, and while
  acknowledging the limitations of Rawls's theory in relation to considerations
  of disability, Buchanan's position is important in alerting us to the possibilities
  of inclusion inherent in the Rawlsian framework.
6 It is important to note here the difference between an understanding of dis-

ability as entirely socially caused and constructed, presented by Oliver and endorsed by the disability movement in the UK, and the more interactive nature of the relation between impairment and disability informing some versions of the social model in the American debate. As Silvers notices in relation to the latter, 'The model explains the isolation of people with disabilities not as the unavoidable outcome of impairment but rather as the correctable product of how such individuals interact with stigmatizing social values and debilitating social arrangements . . . None of this is to deny that, in the main, disablement correlates with anomalous, non-ideal, or troubling biological conditions' (Silvers, 1998: 76). These considerations highlight the heterogeneity of positions within the social model perspective, and especially the difference between the debate in Britain and in the USA.

7 I am very grateful to Mary Mahowald for her insightful comments on these issues presented at the 2006 American Philosophical Association (APA) Pacific Division invited 'Symposium on Disability and Disadvantage'. Mahowald, M. (2006), 'Comments on L. Terzi's Paper'. Manuscript in the author's possession.

Chapter 3

1 See Ainscow, 1999: 183.
2 The debate on IQ (Intelligence Quotient) is used here only for the purpose of illustrating the non-normative status associated to psychological notions.
3 See Young, I. M. (1990), *Justice and the Politics of Difference*, Princeton, NJ: Princeton University Press. This aspect will be addressed more thoroughly in Chapter 8, where I respond to possible objections to distributive theories of justice and to the idea of educational equality I defend.
4 See, for instance, Dworkin, 2000; Brighouse, 2000 and 2001.
5 For a more extensive discussion of misunderstandings of liberalism in education theory, see Brighouse, H. and Swift, A., 2003: 355–73.

Chapter 4

1 Ingrid Robeyns highlights the importance of these dimensions of human diversity in Sen's approach. See Robeyns, I. (2003), 'Is Nancy Fraser's critique of theories of distributive justice justified?'. *Constellations*, 10, 4, 538–53 at pp.544–5.
2 I address below the relationship between disability and disadvantage in Sen's view.
3 I owe this observation to discussions with Harry Brighouse.
4 I owe this insight to discussions with Eamonn Callan.
5 Furthermore, Nussbaum's version of the capabilities approach in relation to justice for mentally impaired citizens suggests interesting insights towards the development of a full normative theory encompassing the demands of disabled people. I leave the discussion of these insights and their potential or limitations to a further occasion.
6 See Chapter 2, Note 3.
7 Anita Silvers challenges the view that the interests of disabled and those of non-disabled people are necessarily competing. She maintains that a sound project of inclusion would encompass an understanding of disability in terms

of atypical modes of functioning (which does not imply lowered levels of functionings or compromised levels of productivity), and should consider the
interest of disabled and non-disabled people as parallel rather than contrasting. See Silvers, 2003. See also Chapter 2 above.

8 I am grateful to Dan Brock, Leslie Francis and Kimberley Brownlee for raising
this point and making me think harder on its implications for the perspective
suggested.

9 See above, pp. 91 and 101.

10 See Brighouse, 2004: 71–2.

11 I am grateful to David Archard for this formulation of the problem and for
challenging an earlier, and much less critical, version of my analysis.

Chapter 5

1 In the example provided here, dyslexia is understood as emerging from neurological conditions that affect reading and writing functionings. However, it
is important to notice that the debate on the precise nature of dyslexia is controversial, entailing positions that relate it to specific impairments, and others
that deny this relationship altogether. For an interesting analysis of pedagogi-
cal issues about dyslexia, see, for instance, Read, G. (2005), 'Dyslexia', in
A. Lewis and B. Norwich (eds), *Special Teaching for Special Children?: Pedagogies
of Inclusion*. Maidenhead: Open University Press.

2 Indeed this perspective could envisage, for more practice-oriented means, the
reference to the WHO *International Classification of Functioning, Disability and
Health* (WHO, 2001), providing that the important theoretical and ethical
insights of the capability approach were not sidelined. This Classification has
been presented in more detail in Chapters 2 and 4.

3 For an interesting analysis of the development of ideas concerning the nature
of autistic spectrum disorders, and the complex dimensions of skills and disabilities these involve, see Wing, L. (2007). For a challenging perspective from
a parent's voice, see Moore, C. (2007).

4 See D. Murray and W. Lawson (2007) for an interesting analysis of the use of
IT in the education of students within the autistic spectrum disorders, and for
related considerations about the different impact of autism on children's functionings when the educational system is designed in specific ways. In this case,
the interaction with technological tools, i.e. computers, is presented as a very
helpful device in developing children's social functionings. As the authors
note, computers

> can put them [*children with autism*] on an equal footing with their peers,
> allowing them to process and respond to communications in their own
> time with minimal pragmatic, expressive, or auditory issues getting in the
> way. It gives them a chance to make a favourable impression on their peers
> and to win their respect . . . Further, computers may be the *only* way to com-
> municate effectively with those who find speech unmanageable. Learning
> IT can open a way to explore other areas of the curriculum in a supportive
> environment. E-learning can be a route towards the acquisition of all sorts
> of qualifications.
>
> (Murray and Lawson, 2007: 153–4)

5 The role of education as foundational to the expansion of freedoms is explored in Chapter 7.
6 See in particular the Introduction and, Chapters 6 and 7. For an interesting and extensive discussion of Pogge's critique, see Berges, S. (2007), and Unter-halter and Brighouse (2007). My position draws on the latter contribution.
7 See Rawls, J. (2001), *Justice as Fairness: A Restatement*. Cambridge, MA: Harvard University Press, and specifically p.58.
8 This example is introduced and discussed in Chapter 2 in relation to the social model of disability. It is subsequently recalled in several passages in order to illustrate the possible restrictions in functionings which cannot at present be successfully addressed by changes in the design of institutional and social arrangements.
9 Robeyns (2003) argues that the capability approach positively includes both issues of equal distribution of resources, and issues of equal recognition. Thus, she maintains that the approach is theoretically richer and wider than other perspectives in distributive justice, which focus more exclusively on distribu-tional aspects. See Robeyns, I. (2003a), 'Is Nancy Fraser's critique of theories of distributive justice justified?'. *Constellations*, 10, 4, 538–53.
10 I address this aspect also in relation to the possible objections to the capabil-ity perspective in Chapter 8.
11 I am referring here to technical and environmental designs as they are now.

Chapter 6

1 See for instance Nagel, 1979: 107; Dworkin, 2000: 1–2, 11–12; and Sen, 1992: 17.
2 The intrinsic value of equality is a complex aspect of the debate, and has been addressed by several authors. While some maintain that equality is good in itself and there are no more arguments to be provided in support of this view, others find this answer unsatisfactory, and thus see it as 'begging the question'. For a more detailed discussion see, among others, Nagel, 1979, and Sen, 1992.
3 See Dworkin, 2000 and specifically Chapters 1 and 2. This general distinction, although not exhaustive of all possible positions, is the main framework used in egalitarian debates. See also Clayton, M. and Williams, A. (1999) and, more recently, Kaufman, A. (2006), pp.1–14.
4 It is perhaps important to notice here that the formulation of equality of resources thus provided should not be understood as a kind of equality of outcome. Rather, as we shall see further on, one of the more prominent views of equality of resources envisages a distributive mechanism in the form of an insurance market, or a fair lottery for the initial sharing of resources.
5 The discussion about the overall merits of the primary goods approach over the capability approach or vice versa is ongoing and not conclusive. See, among others, Clayton and Williams, 1999; Pogge, 2004; Robeyns, 2004; Unterhalter and Brighouse, 2007. This debate has been addressed also in Section 2.2 of Chapter 5.
6 The important focus on functionings as crucial in adjudicating the relative merits of the capability approach over the primary goods one is well discussed by Sandrine Berges in her article 'Why the Capability Approach is Justified',

Journal of Applied Philosophy, 2007, 24, 1, pp.18–19. See also Chapter 5 and note 4 above.

7   As Richard Arneson notices, 'Dworkin's account of equality of resources is complex, but without entering into its details I can observe that Dworkin is discussing a version of what I call "equal opportunity for resources".' Arneson, 1989: 93 note 12.

8   See Anderson, 1999, pp.303 and 309, for an interesting discussion of the insurance market device in relation to deficits in internal assets.

9   See Clayton and Williams, 1999: 448–53 for an extensive discussion of this point.

10 In his critique of welfare egalitarianism, Ronald Dworkin has shown how both expensive and cheap tastes fundamentally compromise an account of egalitarian justice based on welfare. See Dworkin, 2000, and in particular Chapter 2, pp.65–119.

11 These concepts have been more extensively presented and discussed in Chapters 4 and 5.

Chapter 7

1   The liberal ideal of educational equality in terms of equality of opportunity, which, albeit in a minimal understanding of it, is at the core of contemporary liberal democracies, is contested by sociological perspectives in education, which tend to see this approach as 'displacing' more socially just analyses. However, even if the discussion of sociological views of educational equality is beyond the scope of this research, it is perhaps important to notice that these views usually lack a principled position on educational equality, which is the topic of this monograph. The value and merits of a liberal normative perspective on educational equality are discussed more extensively in the Introduction to this volume.

2   See Brighouse, 2000: 134–5.

3   For an extensive discussion of education in the capability approach, see, for instance, Robeyns, I., 2006; Saito, M., 2003; Walker, M. and Unterhalter, E. (eds) 2007; and Walker, M., 2006. The capability approach to education is a growing and evolving area of study, and numerous theoretical and empirical researches are in process. An overview of the topics and the studies produced is available on the website of the *Human Development and Capability Approach*, at www.capabilityappraoch.org.

4   This view, which will be outlined in more detail later on, draws on Elizabeth Anderson's influential article 'What is the point of equality?' in *Ethics*, 109, (2), 287–37. Anderson develops the idea that what matters is securing the ability of all to participate effectively in a democratic society. Amy Gutmann, in *Democratic Education* (1987), argues for a view of educational equality as equal educational opportunities aimed at ensuring that children can participate effectively in the democratic process. My position draws on these ideas.

5   I have explored the understanding of education as a basic capability in Terzi, L. (2007b), 'The Capability to be Educated' in M. Walker and E. Unterhalter (eds), *Amartya Sen's Capability Approach and Social Justice in Education*. New York: Palgrave Macmillan, pp.25–43. This section draws consistently on that contribution.

6 This allows for people's deliberate choice to refrain from meeting certain basic needs in order to pursue other aims, providing that the relevant capabilities of meeting basic needs are still retained. As Alkire illustrates,

> For example a hunger striker or a Brahmin may regularly refrain from eating, because they personally value the religious discipline or the exercise of justice-seeking agency, but the side-effects of pursuing these is that they will not be well nourished . . . while the Brahmin's 'functioning' of being well-fed would indeed be blighted by fasting, her *life* might be regal and radiant.
>
> (2002: 171)

Thus, what Alkire brings to the fore is the fundamental element of choice, constitutive of and explicit in the concept of capability, and its relation to the pursuit of people's valuable ends and objectives, and hence of their well-being. Both are fundamental dimensions that the capability approach explicitly provides with respect to accounts based on basic human needs.

7 See Brighouse, 2000; Robeyns, 2006; Saito, 2003; Unterhalter and Brighouse, 2007; Swift, 2003; and Walker and Unterhalter, 2007.

8 Interesting insights on these enabling functionings can be drawn on the concept of 'serving competencies' developed by Charles Bailey (1984) in his analysis of the aims and content of liberal education. Bailey suggests that a considerable part of education should of necessity be based on promoting certain functional capacities, or serving competencies, which allow the achievement of subsequent more complex objectives (1984: 111). This concept presents important similarities with that of basic educational functionings, which are fundamental in themselves and in promoting other ones. I owe this insight to professor Terry McLaughlin.

9 I have extensively discussed the implications of this choice of functionings and capabilities in Terzi, L. (2007b), 'The Capability to be Educated', in Walker, M. and Unterhalter, E. (eds), *Amartya Sen's Capability Approach and Social Justice in Education*. New York: Palgrave Macmillan, as well as compared and contrasted it with Nussbaum's selection of Central Human Capabilities.

10 I am considering here only some insights from the vast and complex literature on autonomy-promoting and autonomy-facilitating education, constitutive of the debate on liberal education. I am not therefore addressing any implication related either to this distinction, or to the arguments in support of autonomy in education. For a deeper analysis of these issues, see, among others, Archard, 2002; Brighouse, 2000b and 2006; Callan, 1997, 1998 and 2002; Gutmann, 1987; Levinson, 1999; and Saito, 2003.

11 For an extensive discussion of the problem of infinite demand, see Veatch, 1986: 159; and Gutmann, 1987: 136–44.

12 For an interesting and well-argued critique of establishing threshold levels in relation to disability, and the related possible discrimination and oppression, see for instance Silvers, A. and Francis, L. (2005), 'Justice Through Trust: Disability and the "Outlier Problem" in Social Contract Theory', *Ethics*, 116, (1), 54, and Wasserman, D. (2006), 'Disability, capability and thresholds for dis-

tributive justice', in Kaufman, A. (ed.), *Capabilities Equality: Basic Issues and Problems.* New York and London: Routledge, pp.214–34.

Chapter 8

1 The discussion of the first two objections draws mainly on Brighouse, 2000, Chapter 7, pp.141–62, while the third is based on Robeyns, 2003b.

2 The politics of difference, briefly touched upon in Chapter 3, has been mainly proposed and defended by Iris M. Young (1990).

3 As noted above, Wilson's argument has been fully addressed by Brighouse (2000b) and my account of its general framework draws consistently on that contribution.

4 For instance, Brighouse refers to the work of Harry Frankfurt (1987), *The Importance of What We Care About*, in his discussion of Tooley's objection to educational equality (2000b: 146). Similarly, Joseph Raz has questioned the concept of equality and presented instead a notion of diminishing principles, which asserts that the reason for giving someone a good depends on the degree to which they need the good. Although different, notions of sufficiency and diminishing principles act on the same premise that equality as such does not matter for justice. For further discussions of these issues, see Raz, 1986; Sen, 1992, and Swift, 2001: 121–2.

5 See Chapter 1 for a more detailed discussion of this problem.

6 This aspect of my critique draws on Robeyns, 2003b, 'Is Nancy Fraser's Critique of Theories of Distributive Justice Justified?', in *Constellation*, 10 (4), 538–53. See also Chapter 5 of this book for a discussion of issues of positive recognition of differences relating to disability and special educational needs in the capability perspective suggested. The literature on questions around distribution and recognition is broad and articulated. See, for instance, N. Fraser and A. Honneth (2003), *Redistribution and Recognition: A Political-Philosophical Exchange.*

7 In what follows I shall concentrate only on Sen's approach, while leaving the analysis of Rawls's and Dworkin's positions to further investigations.

Bibliography

Abberley, P. (1987), 'The Concept of Oppression and the Development of a Social Theory of Disability'. *Disability, Handicap & Society*, 2 (1), 5–19.

Ainscow, M. (ed.) (1991), *Effective Schools for All*. London: Fulton.

Ainscow, M. (1999), *Understanding the Development of Inclusive Schools*. London: Falmer Press.

Ainscow, M. and Muncey, J. (1989), *Meeting Individual Needs*. London: Fulton.

Albrecht, G. L., Seelman, K. D. and Bury, M. (eds) (2001), *Handbook of Disability Studies*. London: Sage Publications.

Alderson, P. and Goodey, C. (2003), 'Autism in special and inclusive schools: "there has to be a point to their being there"'. In M. Nind, K. Sheehy and K. Simmons (eds), *Inclusive Education: Learners and Learning Contexts*. London: David Fulton.

Alkire, S. (2002), *Valuing Freedoms: Sen's Capability Approach and Poverty Reduction*. Oxford: Oxford University Press.

Alkire, S. (2006), 'Public Debate and Value Construction in Sen's Approach'. In Kaufman, A. (ed.), *Capabilities Equality: Basic Issues and Problems*. New York and London: Routledge.

Anderson, E. S. (1999), 'What is The Point of Equality?' *Ethics*, 109 (2), 287–337.

Archard, D. (2002), 'Children, Multiculturalism and Education'. In Archard, D. and Macleod, C. (eds) (2002), *The Moral and Political Status of Children*. Oxford: Oxford University Press.

Armstrong. D. (2005), 'Reinventing "Inclusion": New Labour and the Cultural Politics of Special Education'. *Oxford Review of Education*, 31, (1), 135–51.

Armstrong, D., Armstrong, F. and Barton, L. (2000), 'Introduction'. In Armstrong, F., Armstrong, D. and Barton, L. (eds), *Inclusive Education: Policy, Contexts and Comparative Perspectives*. London: David Fulton.

Armstrong, F. (1998), 'Curricula, "Management" and Special Inclusive Education'. In Clough, P. (ed.), *Managing Inclusive Education: From Policy to Experience*. London: Paul Chapman Publishing.

Armstrong, F., Armstrong, D. and Barton, L. (eds) (2000), *Inclusive Education: Policy, Contexts and Comparative Perspectives*. London: David Fulton.

Armstrong, F. and Barton, L. (1999), *Disability, Human Rights and Education: Cross-cultural Perspectives*. Buckingham: Open University Press.

Armstrong, F. and Barton, L. (2007) 'Policy, Experience and Change and the Challenge of Inclusive Education: The Case of England'. In Barton, L. and Armstrong, F. (eds), *Policy, Experience and Change: Cross-Cultural Reflections on Inclusive Education*. Dordrecht: Springer.

Arneson, R. (1989), 'Equality and Equal Opportunity for Welfare'. *Philosophical Studies*, 93 (1), 77–93.

Arneson, R. (2000), 'Luck, Egalitarianism and Prioritarianism'. *Ethics*, 110 (2), 339–49.

Audit Commission (2002), *Special Educational Needs: A Mainstream Issue*. London: Audit Commission Publications.

Bailey, C. (1984), *Beyond the Present and the Particular: A Theory of Liberal Education*. London: Routledge and Kegan Paul.

Barnes, C. (1990), *Cabbage Syndrome: The Social Construction of Dependence*. Lewes: Falmer Press.

Barnes, C. and Mercer, G. (eds) (1996), *Exploring the Divide: Illness and Disability*. Leeds: The Disability Press, University of Leeds.

Barnes, C., Mercer, G. and Shakespeare, T. (eds) (1999), *Exploring Disability: A Sociological Introduction*. Cambridge: Polity Press.

Barnes, C., Oliver, M. and Barton, L. (2002), *Disability Studies Today*. Cambridge: Polity Press in association with Blackwell Publishers.

Barton, L. (1993), 'Labels, Market and Inclusive Education'. In J. Visser and G. Upton (eds), *Special Education in Britain after Warnock*. London: David Fulton.

Barton, L. (1996), *Disability and Society: Emerging Issues and Insights*. Harlow, Essex: Longman.

Barton, L. (1998), 'Markets, Managerialism and Inclusive Education'. In Clough, P. (ed.), *Managing Inclusive Education: From Policy to Experience*. London: Paul Chapman Publishing.

Barton, L. (2001), *Disability, Politics and the Struggle for Change*. London: David Fulton.

Barton, L. (2003), *Inclusive Education and Teacher Education: A Basis for Hope or a Discourse of Delusion*. London: Institute of Education.

Barton, L. and Armstrong, F. (1999), *Difference and Difficulty: Insights, Issues and Dilemmas*. Sheffield: University of Sheffield.

Barton, L. and Oliver, M. (1997), *Disability Studies: Past, Present and Future*. Leeds: The Disability Press.

Berges, S. (2007), 'Why the Capability Approach is Justified'. *Journal of Applied Philosophy*, 24 (1), 16–25.

Bickenbach, J. E., Chatterji, S., Badley, E. M. and Ustun, T. B. (1999), 'Models of Disablement, Universalism and the International Classificiation of Impairments, Disabilities and Handicaps'. *Social Science and Medicine*, 48, 1173–87.

Booth, T. (1995), 'Mapping Inclusion and Exclusion: Concepts for All?' In C. Clark, A. Dyson and A. Millward (eds), *Towards Inclusive Schools?* London: Fulton.

Booth, T. (1999), 'Viewing Inclusion from a Distance: Gaining Perspective from Comparative Study'. *Support for Learning*, 14 (4), 164–9.

Bowers, T. and Parrish, T. (2000) 'Funding of Special Education in the United States and England and Wales'. In M. McLaughlin and M. Rouse (eds), *Special Education and School Reform in the United States and Britain*. London: Routledge.

Brett, J. (2002), 'The Experience of Disability from the Perspective of Parents of Children with Profound Impairment: Is It Time for an Alternative Model of Disability?' *Disability & Society*, 17 (7), 826–43.

Brighouse, H. (2000), *Education Equality and the New Selective Schooling*. Southend on Sea: Philosophy of Education Society of Great Britain.

Brighouse, H. (2000a), *A Level Playing Field: The Reform of Private Schools*. London: The Fabian Society.

Brighouse, H. (2000b), *School Choice and Social Justice*. Oxford: Oxford University Press.

Brighouse, H. (2001), 'Can Justice as Fairness Accommodate the Disabled?' *Social Theory and Practice*, 27 (4), 537–60.

Brighouse, H. (2002), *Egalitarian Liberalism and Justice in Education*. London: Institute of Education.

Brighouse, H. (2004), *Justice*. Cambridge: Polity Press.

Brighouse, H. (2006), *On Education*. London: Routledge.

Brighouse, H. and Swift, A. (2003) 'Defending Liberalism in Education Theory'. *Journal of Education Policy*, 18 (4), 335–73.

Buchanan, A. (1990), 'Justice as Reciprocity Versus Subject-centered Justice'. *Philosophy and Public Affairs*, 19 (3), 227–52.

Buchanan, A., Brock, D. W., Daniels, N. and Wikler, D. (eds) (2000), *From Choice to Chance: Genetics and Justice*. Cambridge: Cambridge University Press.

Bury, M. (1996), 'Defining and Researching Disability: Challenges and Responses'. In C. Barnes and G. Mercer (eds), *Exploring the Divide*. Leeds: The Disability Press.

Bury, M. (2000), 'A Comment on the ICIDH2'. *Disability & Society*, 15 (7), 1073–7.

Callan, E. (1997), *Creating Citizens: Political Education and Liberal Democracy*. Oxford: Clarendon Press.

Callan, E. (1998), *Autonomy and Schooling*. Kingston and Montreal: McGill-Queen's University Press.

Callan, E. (2002), 'Autonomy, Child-Rearing, and Good Lives'. In D. Archard and C. M. Macleod (eds), *The Moral and Political Status of Children* (pp.118–41). Oxford: Oxford University Press.

Campbell, C. (ed.) (2002), *Developing Inclusive Schooling: Perspectives, Policies and Practices*. London: Institute of Education.

Clark, C., Dyson, A. and Millward, A. (eds) (1998), *Theorising Special Education*. London: Routledge Falmer.

Clark, C., Dyson, A. and Millward, A. (eds) (1995), *Towards Inclusive Schools?* London: David Fulton Publishers.

Clayton, M. and Williams, A. (1999), 'Egalitarian Justice and Interpersonal Comparison'. *European Journal of Political Research*, 35, 445–64.

Clough, P. (ed.) (1998), *Managing Inclusive Education: From Policy to Experience*. London: Paul Chapman Publishing.

Clough, P. and Barton, L. (1995), *Making Difficulties: Research and the Construction of Special Educational Needs*. London: Paul Chapman.

Clough, P. and Corbett, J. (eds) (2000), *Theories of Inclusive Education: A Student's Guide*. London: Paul Chapman.

Cole, B. (2005), '"Good faith and effort?" Perspectives on educational inclusion'. *Disability and Society*, 20, (3), 331–44.

Corbett, J. (1996), *Bad Mouthing: The Language of Special Needs*. London: Falmer Press.

Corbett, J. and Slee, R. (2000), 'An International Conversation on Inclusive Education'. In Armstrong, F., Armstrong, D. and Barton, L. (2000) (eds), *Inclusive Education: Policy, Contexts and Comparative Perspectives*. London: David Fulton.

Corker, M. (1999), 'Differences, Conflations and Foundations: The Limits to "Accurate" Theoretical Representation of Disabled People's Experience?' *Disability & Society*, 14 (5), 627–42.

Corker, M. and French, S. (eds) (1999), *Disability Discourse*. Buckingham: Open University Press.

Crocker, D. (1995), 'Functionings and Capabilities: The Foundations of Sen's and Nussbaum's Development Ethics'. In M. C. Nussbaum and J. Clover (eds), *Women, Culture and Development: A Study of Human Capabilities*. Oxford: Clarendon Press.

Crocker, D. (2006) 'Sen and Deliberative Democracy'. In Kaufman, A. (ed.), *Capabilities Equality: Basic Issues and Problems*. New York and London: Routledge.

Daniels, H. (2006), 'The Dangers of Corruption in Special Needs Education'. *British Journal of Special Education*, 33 (1), 4–8.

Daniels, N. (2003), 'Democratic Equality: Rawls's Complex Egalitarianism'. In S. Freeman (ed.), *The Cambridge Companion to Rawls* (pp.241–76). Cambridge: Cambridge University Press.

Department for Education and Science (1978), *Special Educational Needs: Report of the Committee of Enquiry into the Education of Handicapped Children and Young People* (The Warnock Report). London: HMSO.

Department for Education (1994), *Code of Practice on the Identification and Assessment of Special Educational Needs*. London: DfE.

Department for Education and Employment (1997), *Excellence for All Children: Meeting Special Educational Needs*. London: DfEE.

Department for Education and Employment (1998), *Fair Funding: Improving Delegation to Schools*. London: DfEE.

Department for Education and Skills (2001a), *Special Educational Needs Code of Practice (revised)*. London: DfES.

Department for Education and Skills (2001b), *The Distribution of Resources to Support Inclusion*. London: DfES.

Department for Education and Skills (2003), *Every Child Matters*. London: HMSO.

Department for Education and Skills (2004), *Removing Barriers to Achievement: the Government's Strategy for SEN*. London: DfES.

Disability Rights Commission (2002a) *Code of Practice for Schools – Disability and Discrimination Act 1995*. London: Disability Rights Commission.

Disability Rights Commission (2002b), *Code of Practice Post 16 – Special Educational Needs and Disability Act 2001*. London: Disability Rights Commission.

Drèze, J. and Sen, A. (2002), *India: Development and Participation*. New Delhi: Oxford University Press.

Dworkin, R. (2000), *Sovereign Virtue: The Theory and Practice of Equality*. Cambridge, MA: Harvard University Press.

Dyson, A. (2001), 'Special Needs in the Twenty-first Century: Where We've Been and Where We're Going'. *British Journal of Special Education*, 28 (1), 24–9.

Dyson, A. and Millward, A. (2000), *Schools and Special Needs: Issues of Innovations and Inclusion*. London: Paul Chapman Publishing.

Dyson, A., Millward, A., Crowther, D., Elliott, J. and Hall, I. (eds) (2002), *Decision-Making and Provision within the Framework of the SEN Code of Practice*. London: Department for Education and Skills.

Equalities Review (2007), *Fairness and Freedom: The Final Report of the Equalities Review*. London: Equalities Review.

Evans, J. (2007), 'Forms of Provision and Models of Service Delivery'. In Florian, L. (ed.) *The SAGE Handbook of Special Education*. London: SAGE.

Evans, J., Castle, F. and Cullen, M. A. (2000), *Exploring Funding Mechanisms and Students' Outcomes with Reference to Special Educational Needs*. Slough: National Foundation for Educational Research.

Evans, J., Castle, F. and Cullen, M. A. (2001), Fair Funding? LEA Policies and Methods for Funding Additional and Special Needs and Schools' Responses. Slough: National Foundation for Educational Research.

Evans, J. and Lunt, I. (1994), *Markets, Competition and Vulnerability: Some Effects of Recent Legislation on Children with Special Educational Needs*. London: Tufnell Press.

Evans, P. (2001), 'Equity Indicators Based on the Provision of Supplemental Resources for Disabled and Disadvantaged Students'. In W. Hutmacher, D. Cochrane and N. Bottani (eds), *In Pursuit of Equity in Education: Using International Indicators to Compare Equity Policies* (pp.253–66). Dordrecht: Kluwer Academic.

Farrell, P. (2001), 'Special Education in the Last Twenty Years: Have Things Really Got Better?' *British Journal of Special Education*, 28 (1), 3–9.

Finkelstein, V. (1980), *Attitudes and Disabled People: Issues for Discussion*. New York: World Rehabilitiation Fund.

Florian, L. and Pullin, D. (2000), 'Defining Difference: A Comparative Perspective on Legal and Policy Issues in Education Reform and Special Educational Needs'. In M. McLaughlin and M. Rouse (eds), *Special Education and School Reform in the United States and Britain* (pp.11–37). London: Routledge.

Frankfurt, H. G. (1987), *The Importance of What We Care About: Philosophical Essays*. Cambridge: Cambridge University Press.

Fraser, N. (1998), 'Social Justice in the Age of Identity Politics: Redistribution, Recognition and Participation'. In G. B. Peterseon (ed.), *The Tanner Lectures On Human Values: XIX* (pp.1–67). Salt Lake City: University of Utah Press.

Fraser, N., and Honneth, H. (2003), *Redistribution or Recognition: A Political-Philosophical Exchange*. London: Verso.

Freeman, S. (ed.) (2003), *The Cambridge Companion to Rawls*. Cambridge: Cambridge University Press.

French, S. (1993), 'Disability, Impairment or Something in Between?' In J. Swain, V. Finkelstein, S. French and M. Oliver (eds), *Disabling Barriers, Enabling Environments* (pp.17–25). Buckingham: Open University Press.

Frith, U. (2003), *Autism: Exploring the Enigma*. Oxford: Blackwell.

Great Britain – Elizabeth II (2001), *Special Educational Needs and Disability Act 2001*. London: HMSO.

Gregory, S. (2005), 'Deafness'. In Lewis, A. and Norwich, B. (eds), *Special Teaching for Special Children? Pedagogies for Inclusion*. Maidenhead: Open University Press.

Gutmann, A. (1987), *Democratic Education*. Princeton: Princeton University Press.

Hegarty, S. (2001), 'Inclusive Education – A Case to Answer'. *Journal of Moral Education*, 30 (3), 243–9.

Hutmacher, W., Cochrane, D. and Bottani, N. (eds) (2001), *In Pursuit of Equity Indicators in Education: Using International Indicators to Compare Equity Policies*. Dordrecht: Kluwer Academic.

Jarvis, J. (2007), '"Jig-sawing it Together": Reflections on Deaf Pupils'. In Cigman, R. (ed.), *Included or Excluded? The Challenge of the Mainstream for Some SEN Children*. London: Routledge.

Kaufman, A. (2006) 'Introduction'. In Kaufman, A., (ed.), *Capabilities Equality: Basic Issues and Problems*. New York and London: Routledge.

Keil, S., Miller, O. and Cobb, R. (2006), 'Special Educational Needs and Disability'. *British Journal of Special Education*, 33, (4), 168–72.

Kittay, E. F. (1999), *Love's Labor: Essays on Women, Equality, and Dependency*. New York: Routledge.

Kittay, E. F. (2001), 'A Feminist Public Ethic of Care Meets the New Communitarian Family'. *Ethics*, 111 (3), 523–47.

Kittay, E. F. (2003), 'A Response to Martha Nussbaum's Tanner Lecture on Justice for Mentally Disabled Citizens'. Unpublished manuscript.

Ladenson, R. (2003), 'Inclusion and Justice in Special Education: The Case of Beth B'. In Curren, R. (ed.), *A Companion to the Philosophy of Education*. Oxford: Blackwells Publishing.

Lee, T. (1996), *The Search for Equity: The Funding of Additional Educational Needs Under LMS*. Aldershot: Avebury.

Levinson, M. (1999), *The Demands of Liberal Education*. Oxford: Oxford University Press.

Lindsay, G. (2003), 'Inclusive Education: A Critical Perspective'. *British Journal of Special Education*, 30 (1), 3–12.

Lindsay, G. (2007), 'Rights, Efficacy and Inclusive Education'. In Cigman, R. (ed.) *Included or Excluded? The Challenge of the Mainstream for Some SEN Children*. London: Routledge.

Lipsky, D. K. and Gartner, A. (1996), 'Equity Requires Inclusion: The Future for All Students with Disabilities'. In C. Christensen and F. Rizvi (eds), *Disability and the Dilemmas of Education and Justice* (pp.145–55). Buckingham: Open University Press.

Lipsky, D. K. and Gartner, A. (1997), *Inclusion and School Reform: Transforming America's Classroom*. Washington: Paul Brookes Publishing.

Lipsky, D. K. and Gartner, A. (1999), 'Inclusive Education: A Requirement of a Democratic Society'. In H. Daniels and P. Garner (eds), *World Yearbook of Education 1999: Inclusive Education* (pp.12–23). London: Kogan Page.

Lunt, I. (2002), 'The Challenge of Inclusive Schooling for Pupils with Special Educational Needs'. In C. Campbell (ed.), *Developing Inclusive Schooling: Perspectives, Policies and Practices*. London: Institute of Education.

Lunt, I. and Evans, J. (1994), *Allocating Resources for Special Educational Needs*. Stafford: NASEN.

Lunt, I. and Norwich, B. (1999), *Can Effective Schools Be Inclusive Schools?* London: Institute of Education.

MacKay, G. (2002), 'The Disappearance of Disability? Thoughts on a Changing Culture'. *British Journal of Special Education*, 29 (4), 159–63.

Mahowald, M. (2006) 'APA-Commentary'. (Portland: American Philosophical Association, Pacific Division: Workshop on 'Disability and Disadvantage', March 2006). Manuscript in the author's possession.

Marsh, A. J. (1998), 'Resourcing Inclusive Education: The Real Economics'. In P. Clough (ed.), *Managing Inclusive Education*. London: Chapman.

Marsh, A. J. (2003), *Funding Inclusive Education: The Economic Realities*. Aldershot: Ashgate Publishing.

McLaughlin, M. and Rouse, M. (eds) (2000), *Special Education and School Reform in the United States and Britain*. London: Routledge.

McLaughlin, T. (2000), 'Philosophy and Educational Policy: Possibilities, Tensions and Tasks'. *Journal of Educational Policy*, 15 (4), 441–57.

Meijer, C., Soriano, V. and Watkins, A. (2003), 'Special Needs Education in Europe: Inclusive Policies and Practices'. In C. Meijer, V. Soriano and A. Watkins (eds), *Special Needs Education in Europe, Thematic Publication* (pp.7–18). Denmark: European Agency for Development in Special Needs Education.

Miliband, D. (2004), 'Personalised Learning: Building a New Relationship with Schools'. Speech delivered at the North of England Education Conference, Belfast, 8 January 2004. Available at http://www.dfes.gov.uk/speeches.

Mitchell, D. (ed.) (2004), *Special Educational Needs and Inclusive Education.* London: Routledge Falmer.

Moore, C. (2007), 'Speaking as a Parent: Thoughts about Educational Inclusion for Autistic Children'. In Cigman, R. (ed.), *Included or Excluded? The Challenge of the Mainstream for Some SEN Children.* London: Routledge.

Morris, J. (1991), *Pride Against Prejudice: Transforming Attitudes to Disability.* London: The Women's Press.

Murray, D. and Lawson, W. (2007), 'Inclusion through Technology for Autistic Children'. In Cigman, R. (ed.), *Included or Excluded? The Challenge of the Mainstream for Some SEN Children.* London: Routledge.

Nagel, T. (1979), *Mortal Questions.* Cambridge: Cambridge University Press.

Nagel, T. (2002), *Concealment and Exposure and Other Essays.* Oxford: Oxford University Press.

Norwich, B. (1993), 'Has "Special Educational Needs" Outlived its Usefulness?' In J. Visser and G. Upton (eds), *Special Education in Britain after Warnock.* London: David Fulton.

Norwich, B. (1996), *Special Needs Education, Inclusive Education or Just Education for All?* London: Institute of Education.

Norwich, B. (1999), 'The Connotation of Special Education Labels for Professionals in the Field'. *British Journal of Special Education*, 26 (4), 179–83.

Norwich, B. (ed.) (2001), *The Equity Dilemma: Allocating Resources for Special Educational Needs.* Tamworth: NASEN.

Norwich, B. (2002), 'Education, Inclusion and Individual Differences'. *British Journal of Educational Studies*, 50 (4), 482–502.

Norwich, B. (2007), 'Dilemmas of Inclusion and the Future of Education'. In Cigman, R. (ed.), *Included or Excluded? The Challenge of the Mainstream for some SEN Children.* London: Routledge.

Nussbaum, M. C. (1997), *Cultivating Humanity: A Classic Defence of Reform in Liberal Education.* Cambridge, MA: Harvard University Press.

Nussbaum, M. C. (2000), *Women and Human Development: The Capabilities Approach.* Cambridge: Cambridge University Press.

Nussbaum, M. C. (2002), 'Education for Citizenship in an Era of Global Connection'. *Studies in Philosophy and Education*, 21 (4–5), 289–303.

Nussbaum, M. C. (2004) 'Women's Education: A Global Challenge'. *Sign: Journal of Women and Culture in Society*, 29, (2), 325–55.

Nussbaum, M. C. (2006a), *Frontiers of Justice: Disability, Nationality, Species Membership.* The Tanner Lectures on Human Values. Cambridge, MA, and London, England: The Belknap Press of Harvard University Press.

Nussbaum, M. C. (2006b), 'Capabilities as Fundamental Entitlements: Sen and Social Justice'. In Kaufman, A. (ed.), *Capabilities Equality: Basic Issues and Problems.* New York and London: Routledge.

Nussbaum, M. C. and Glover, J., (1995), *Women, Culture and Development: A Study of Human Capabilities.* Oxford: Clarendon.

Nussbaum, M. C. and Sen, A., (1993), *The Quality of Life: A Study Prepared for the World Institute for Development Economics Research (WIDER) of the United Nations University.* Oxford: Clarendon Press.

OECD (1995), *Integrating Students with Special Needs into Mainstream Schools.* Paris: OECD.

OECD (1997), *Implementing Inclusive Education.* Paris: OECD.

OECD (1999), *Inclusive Education at Work: Students with Disabilities in Mainstream Schools.* Paris: OECD.

OECD (2000), *Special Education Needs: Statistics and Indicators.* Paris: OECD.

OECD (2004), *Equity in Education: Students with Disabilities, Learning Difficulties and Disadvantages: Statistics and Indicators.* Paris: OECD.

OECD (2005), *Students with Disabilities, Learning Difficulties and Disadvantages: Statistics and Indicators.* Paris: OECD.

OECD (2007), *Special Educational Needs: Statistics and Indicators.* Paris: OECD.

OFSTED (1999), *The SEN Code Of Practice: Three Years On.* London: HMSO.

Oliver, M. (1988), 'The Social and Political Context of Educational Policy: The Case of Special Needs'. In Barton, L. (ed.), *The Politics of Special Educational Needs.* Lewes: Falmer Press.

Oliver, M. (1990), *The Politics of Disablement.* London: Macmillan.

Oliver, M. (1993), 'Re-defining Disability: A Challenge to Research'. In J. Swain, V. Finkelstein, S. French and M. Oliver (eds), *Disabling Barriers – Enabling Environments* (pp.61–8). Buckingham: Open University Press.

Oliver, M. (1996), *Understanding Disability: From Theory to Practice.* Basingstoke: Palgrave.

Oliver, M. (2004), 'The Social Model in Action: If I Had a Hammer'. In C. Barnes and G. Mercer (eds), *Implementing the Social Model of Disability: Theory and Research.* Leeds: The Disability Press.

Oliver, M. and Barnes, C. (1993), 'Discrimination, Disability and Welfare: From Needs to Rights'. In J. Swain, V. Finkelstein, S. French and M. Oliver (eds), *Disabling Barriers – Enabling Environments.* Buckingham: Open University Press.

Oliver, M. and Barnes, C. (1998), *Disabled People and Social Policy: From Exclusion to Inclusion.* London: Longman.

Parrish, T. (2000), 'Restructuring Special Education Funding in New York to Promote the Objective of High Learning Standards for All Students'. *Economics of Education Review,* 19, 431–45.

Parrish, T., Chambers, J. G. and Guarino, C. M. (eds) (1998), *Funding Special Education.* Thousands Oaks: Corwin Press.

Parrish, T. and Wolman, J. (1998), 'Trends and New Development in Special Education Funding: What the States Report'. In T. Parrish, J. G. Chambers and C. M. Guarino (eds), *Funding Special Education.* Thousand Oaks: Corwin Press.

Parrish, T. and Wolman, J. (2004), 'How is Special Education Funded? Issues and Implications for School Administrators' in *NASSP Bulletin,* 88, 57: 68.

Perry, J., Macken, E. and Israel, D. (1999), 'Prolegomena to A Theory of Disability, Inability and Handicap'. In L. Moss, J. Ginzburg and M. De Rijke (eds), *Logic, Language and Computation.* Stanford: CSLI Publications.

Perry, J., Macken, E., Scott, N. and McKinley, S. (1996), 'Disability, Inability and

Cyberspace'. In B. Friedman (ed.), *Designing Computers for People: Human Values and the Design of Computer Technology.* Stanford: CSLI Publications.

Pijl, S. J. and Meijer, C. (1994), *New Perspectives in Special Education: A Six-Country Study of Integration.* London: Routledge.

Pijl, S. J., Meijer, C. and Hegarty, S. (eds) (1997), *Inclusive Education: A Global Agenda.* London: Routledge.

Pogge, T. (2004), 'Can The Capability Approach Be Justified?' *Philosophical Topics,* 30, 167–228.

Rawls, J. (1971), *A Theory of Justice.* Oxford: Oxford University Press.

Rawls, J. (1980) 'Kantian Constructivism in Moral Theory: The Dewey Lectures 1980'. *Journal of Philosophy,* 77, 515–72.

Rawls, J. (1982), 'Social Unity and Primary Goods'. In Sen, A. and Williams, B. (eds), *Utilitarianism and Beyond* (pp.159–85). Cambridge: Cambridge University Press.

Rawls, J. (2001), *Justice as Fairness: A Restatement.* Cambridge, MA: Harvard University Press.

Raz, J. (1986), *The Morality of Freedom.* Oxford: Oxford University Press.

Read, G. (2005), 'Dyslexia'. In Lewis, A. and Norwich, B. (eds), *Special Teaching for Special Children? Pedagogies for Inclusion?* Maidenhead: Open University Press.

Rèe, J. (1999), *I See a Voice: A Philosophical History.* London: Flamingo.

Riddell, S. (1996), 'Theorising Special Educational Needs'. In L. Barton (ed.), *Disability and Society: Emerging Issues and Insights.* London: Longman.

Riddell, S. (2002), *Special Educational Needs.* Edinburgh: Dunedin Academic Press.

Rioux, M. H. (2002), 'Disability, Citizenship and Rights in a Changing World'. In M. Oliver, C. Barnes and L. Barton (eds), *Disability Studies Today.* Cambridge: Polity Press.

Robeyns, I. (2001), 'Understanding Sen's Capability Approach'. Available online at: www.ingridrobeyns.nl – consulted July 2006.

Robeyns, I. (2003a), 'Sen's Capability Approach and Gender Inequalities: Selecting Relevant Capabilities', *Feminist Economics,* 9 (2–3), 61–92.

Robeyns, I. (2003b), 'Is Nancy Fraser's Critique of Theories of Distributive Justice Justified?' *Constellations,* 10 (4), 538–53.

Robeyns, I. (2004), 'Justice as Fairness and the Capability Approach'. Paper presented at the Fourth International Conference on the Capability Approach, Pavia, Italy, September 2004.

Robeyns, I. (2006) 'Three Models of Education: Rights, Capabilities and Human Capital'. *Theory and Research in Education.* 4 (1), 69–84.

Rothstein, L. (1999), 'School Choice and Students with Disabilities'. In S. D. Sugarman and F. R. Kemerer (eds), *School Choice and Social Controversy.* Washington: Brooking Institution Press.

Rouse, M. and Florian, L. (1997), 'Inclusive Education in the Market-Place'. *International Journal of Inclusive Education,* 1 (4), 323–36.

Rouse, M. and McLaughlin, M. (2007), 'Changing Perspectives of Special Education in the Evolving Context of Educational Reform'. In Florian, L. (ed.), *The SAGE Handbook of Special Education.* London: SAGE.

Saito, M. (2003), 'Amartya Sen's Capability Approach to Education: A Critical Exploration'. *Journal of Philosophy of Education,* 37 (1), 17–33.

Scanlon, T. M. (1991), 'The Moral Basis of Interpersonal Comparison'. In Elster, J. and Roemer, J. (eds), *Interpersonal Comparisons of Well-Being.* Cambridge: Cambridge University Press.

Seaton, N. (1999), *Fair Funding or Fiscal Fudge: Continuing Chaos in School Funding.* London: Centre for Policy Studies.

Sen, A. (1980), *Equality of What? The Tanner Lectures on Human Values.* McMurrin, S. (ed). Salt Lake City: University of Utah Press.

Sen, A. (1984), *Resources, Values and Development.* Cambridge, MA: Harvard University Press.

Sen, A. (1992), *Inequality Reexamined.* Oxford: Clarendon Press.

Sen, A. (1999), *Development as Freedom.* Oxford: Oxford University Press.

Sen, A. (2001), *Other People.* London: The British Academy.

Sen, A. (2002), 'Response to Commentaries'. *Studies in International Comparative Development,* 27, (2), 78–86.

Sen, A. (2004), 'Capabilities, Lists and Public Reason: Continuing the Conversation'. *Feminist Economics,* 10, (3), 77–80.

Sen, A., Muellbauer, J., Kanbur, R., Hart, K. and Williams, B. (1985), *The Standard of Living.* Cambridge: Cambridge University Press.

Sen, A. and Williams, B. (1982), *Utilitarianism and Beyond.* Cambridge: Cambridge University Press.

Shakespeare, T. (1997), 'Cultural Representation of Disabled People: Dustbins of Disavowal?' In L. Barton and M. Oliver (eds), *Disability Studies: Past, Present and Future.* Leeds: Disability Press.

Silvers, A., (1998), 'Formal Justice'. In Silvers, A., Wasserman, D. and Mahowald, M. B. (eds), *Disability, Difference, Discrimination: Perspectives on Justice in Bioethics and Public Policy.* Oxford: Rowman & Littlefield Publishers.

Silvers, A., (2003) 'On the Possibility and Desirability of Constructing a Neutral Conception of Disability'. *Theoretical Medicine,* 24, 471–87.

Silvers, A. and Francis, L. (2005), 'Justice through Trust: Disability and the "Outlier Problem" in Social Contract Theory'. *Ethics,* 116 (1), 40–76.

Silvers, A., Wasserman, D. and Mahowald, M. B. (1998), *Disability, Difference, Discrimination: Perspectives on Justice in Bioethics and Public Policy.* Oxford: Rowman & Littlefield Publishers.

Sparrow, R. (2005) 'Defending Deaf Culture: The Case of Cochlear Implants'. *The Journal of Political Philosophy,* 13, (2) 135–52.

Stone, D. (1985), *The Disabled State.* London: Macmillan.

Sugarman, S. D. and Kemerer, F. R. (eds) (1999), *School Choice and Social Controversy: Politics, Policy, and Law.* Washington: Brookings Institution Press.

Swift, A. (2001), *Political Philosophy: A Beginners' Guide for Students and Politicians.* Cambridge: Polity Press.

Swift, A. (2003), *How Not to Be a Hypocrite: School Choice for the Morally Perplexed Parents.* London: Routledge.

Terzi, L. (2007a), 'Beyond the Dilemma of Difference: The Capability Approach to Disability and Special Educational Needs'. In Cigman, R. (ed.), *Included or Excluded? The Challenge of the Mainstream for Some SEN Children.* London: Routledge.

Terzi, L. (2007b), 'The Capability to be Educated'. In Walker, M. and Unterhalter, E. (eds), *Amartyn Sens' Capability Approach and Social Justice in Education.* New York and London: Palgrave Macmillan.

Thomas, C. (1999), *Female Forms: Experiencing and Understanding Disability.* Buckingham, Philadelphia: Open University Press.

Thomas, C. (2002), 'Disability Theory: Key Ideas, Issues and Thinkers'. In C. Barnes, M. Oliver and L. Barton (eds), *Disability Studies Today.* Cambridge: Polity Press.

Thomas, G. and Loxley, A. (2001), *Deconstructing Special Education and Constructing Inclusion*. Buckingham: Open University Press.

Tomlinson, S. (1982), *A Sociology of Special Education*. London: Routledge and Kegan Paul.

Tooley, J. (2000), *Reclaiming Education*. London: Cassell.

UN (1982), *World Program of Action Concerning Disabled Persons*, Resolution 37/52 (Official Records of the General Assembly Supplement No.51 ed., Vol. A/37/51).

UN (1990), *World Conference on Education for All*. New York: UN Report.

UN (1993), *Standard Rules on the Equalizations of Opportunities for Persons with Disabilities*. New York: UN Report.

UN (2006), *Convention on the Rights of Persons with Disabilities*. http://www.un.org/esa/socdev/enable/rights.

UNESCO (1994), *The Salamanca Statement and Framework for Action on Special Needs Education*. Paris: UNESCO.

Unterhalter, E. and Brighouse, H. (2007), 'Distribution of What for Social Justice in Education? The Case of Education for All by 2015?'. In Walker, M. and Unterhalter, E. (eds), *Amartya Sen's Capability Approach and Social Justice in Education*. New York: Palgrave Macmillan.

UPIAS (1976), *Fundamental Principles of Disability*. London: Union of The Physically Impaired Against Segregation.

US House of Representatives (1975), Education for All Handicapped Children Act, (94th Congress, 1st Session, Report No. 94-332). US Senate. Pub. L. 94-142.

US Congress (1990), *The Americans with Disabilities Act* (ADA), US Public Law 10.

US Senate (1991), *The Individuals with Disabilities Education Act* (IDEA). US Senate. Pub. L. 101-476.

US Senate (1997), *The Individuals with Disabilities Education Act* (IDEA). US Senate. PL 105-117.

US Senate (2001) *No Child Left Behind Act* (NCLB). PL 107-110.

US Senate (2004), *Individuals with Disabilities Education Improvement Act 2004*. PL 108-446.

Veatch, R. M. (1986), *The Foundations of Justice: Why the Retarded and the Rest of Us Have Claims to Equality*. Oxford: Oxford University Press.

Vincent, C., Evans, J., Lunt, I. and Young, P. (1994), 'The Market Forces? The Effects of Local Management of Schools on Special Educational Needs Provision'. *British Educational Research Journal*, 20 (3), 261–77.

Visser, J. and Upton, G. (eds) (1993), *Special Education in Britain after Warnock*. London: David Fulton.

Walker, M. (2006), *Higher Education Pedagogies: A Capabilities Approach*. Maidenhead: Open University Press.

Walker, M. and Unterhalter, E. (2007) 'The Capability Approach: Its Potential for Work in Education'. In Walker, M. and Unterhalter, E. (eds), *Amartya Sen's Capability Approach and Social Justice in Education*. New York: Palgrave Macmillan.

Warnock, M. (1978), *The Concept of Educational Need*. Swansea: The University College of Swansea, The Publications Office.

Warnock, M. (1978), *Meeting Special Educational Needs*. London: Department of Education and Science.

Warnock, M. (1978), *Special Educational Needs*. London: Department of Education and Science.

Warnock, M. (2005), *Special Educational Needs: A New Look.* Philosophy of Education Society of Great Britain: IMPACT Series No.11.

Wasserman, D. (1998), 'Distributive Justice'. In A. Silvers, D. Wasserman and M. B. Mahowald (eds), *Disability, Difference, Discrimination: Perspectives on Justice in Bioethics and Public Policy* (pp.147–207). Oxford: Rowman & Littlefield Publishers.

Wasserman, D. (2006), 'Disability, Capability and Thresholds for Distributive Justice'. In Kaufman, A. (ed.), *Capabilities Equality: Basic Issues and Problems.* New York and London: Routledge.

Wendell, S. (1996), *The Rejected Body: Feminist Philosophical Reflections on Disability.* London: Routledge.

White, S. (2006), *Equality.* Cambridge: Polity Press.

WHO (1980), *International Classification of Impairment, Disability and Handicap.* Geneva: World Health Organization.

WHO (1997), *International Classification of Impairments, Activities and Participation.* Geneva: World Health Organization.

WHO (2001), *International Classification of Functioning, Disability and Health.* Geneva: World Health Organization.

Williams, A. (2002), 'Dworkin on Capability'. *Ethics,* (113), 23–39.

Williams, B. (1985), 'The Standard of Living: Interests and Capabilities'. in Sen, A. and Williams, B. (eds), *The Standard of Living.* Cambridge: Cambridge University Press.

Wilson, J. (1991), 'Does Equality (of Opportunity) Make Sense in Education?' *Journal of Philosophy of Education,* 25 (1), 27–31.

Wilson, J. (2000), '"Learning Difficulties", "Disability" and "Special Needs": Some Problems of Partisan Conceptualisation'. *Disability & Society,* 15 (5), 817–24.

Wing. L. (2007), 'Children with Autistic Spectrum Disorders'. In Cigman, R. (ed.), *Included or Excluded? The Challenge of the Mainstream for some SEN Children.* London: Routledge.

Wolman, J. A. and Parrish, T. B. (1996), *Escalating Special Education Costs: Reality or Myth?.* The CSEF Resource. Palo Alto, CA: American Institute for Research, Centre for Special Education Finance.

Wolff, J. (2007), 'Disability Among Equals'. Paper presented at the Workshop on 'Disability and Disadvantage', Manchester Centre of Political Theory, 22–24 May 2007.

Wolff, J. and De-Shalit, A. (2007), *Disadvantage.* Oxford: Oxford University Press.

Young, I. M. (1990), *Justice and the Politics of Difference.* Princeton, NJ: Princeton University Press.

Index